Prison Rules:
A Working Guide

The Millennium edition,
fully revised and updated

Nancy Loucks

PRISON
REFORM
TRUST

The work of the Prison Reform Trust is aimed at creating a just humane and effective penal system. We do this by inquiring into the workings of the system; informing prisoners, staff and the wider public; and by influencing Parliament, Government and officials towards reform.

This edition first published in 2000 by the Prison Reform Trust, 15 Northburgh Street, London EC1V 0JR.

© 2000 Prison Reform Trust

ISBN: 0 946209 46 4

Cover photos by James Stenson.

Nancy Loucks is currently based in Scotland where she works as an independent researcher in criminology and prison policy. She is an Honorary Fellow of the Department of Social Work, University of Edinburgh.

PRISON RULES:
A WORKING GUIDE

The Millennium edition, fully revised and updated

ACKNOWLEDGEMENTS

No work such as this is ever done alone. My special thanks go to Stephen Shaw and all the staff at the Prison Reform Trust, without whom the production of this volume would not have been possible. Peter Quinn at Prison Service Headquarters has been particularly generous, as usual. Thanks also to Brian Peddie and the rest of the Legal Policy Unit in the Scottish Prison Service, as well as to Ed Wozniak and Jim Carnie in Research Branch. I am also indebted to Hamish Arnott at the Prisoners' Advice Service in London, and to Kieran McEvoy at the Institute of Criminology in Belfast. Final thanks as always for the continuous patience and support from my husband Niall.

Nancy Loucks   December 1999

FOREWORD TO THE MILLENNIUM EDITION

This Millennium edition marks the fourth time the Prison Reform Trust has issued a new version of the book *Prison Rules: A Working Guide*. The book is one of PRT's initiatives of which we are most proud and which has proved most successful. In detailing and explaining prison regulations, prison law, and prison administration, *Prison Rules: A Working Guide* has been recognised as an invaluable aid to prison and probation staff, members of Boards of Visitors, lawyers, and all students of penal policy. It has also proved a unique self-help guide for prisoners, their friends and relatives.

As will be apparent to those in possession of earlier editions, the text has been comprehensively revised to take account of changes both in Prison Service policy and in the climate within which that policy is interpreted in jails up and down the country. I have in mind the shift in policy from Woolf's justice model in the early '90s to the 'prison works' ethos of Michael Howard; the creation of the office of Prisons Ombudsman; the fall-out from the highly publicised escapes from HMPs Parkhurst and Whitemoor and the consequent emphasis on security in the Woodcock and Learmont reports; and most recently the redrafting of the Prison Rules 1964, and impending implementation of the Human Rights Act 1998. All have sweeping implications for the interpretation and application of the Prison Rules.

The Prison Reform Trust is greatly indebted to Nancy Loucks, editor of the third edition, for returning to the fray some seven years later. Nancy has shown extraordinary diligence and commitment to the project, and this new edition is worthy testament to her skills as a criminal justice researcher. Thanks too to Nicola Padfield for her continuing contribution to the process.

PRT also gratefully acknowledges the generous support of the Trustees of the Robert Gavron Charitable Trust in helping meet the costs of this publication.

Juliet Lyon
Director, Prison Reform Trust   February 2000

INTRODUCTION

At long last, after 35 years the Prison Rules in England and Wales have been redrafted rather than simply amended. This is not to say that, with a few notable exceptions, the new Rules differ substantially from the previous version, nor has the Prison Act 1952 been re-written. However, the Prison Rules 1999 are a welcome change from the piecemeal approach to amendments seen since the last consolidation in 1964 and criticised by the Prior Committee in 1985, the Chief Inspector of Prisons in 1990, and Lord Justice Woolf in 1991.

Notable changes to the Rules include the deletion of references to prisoners under a sentence of death (previously rules 72-76), and the reference to special accommodation (rule 25), which allowed unconvicted prisoners to pay for specially fitted accommodation, complete with private furniture, utensils, and valet - a positively comical 'allowance'. Rule 29 on Education (now r 32) has been revised to provide for the possibility of distance learning.

Most welcome is the abolition of what was previously rule 47(21), a disciplinary rule which penalised behaviour which "in any way offends against good order and discipline". Repeated calls for its abolition came from sources such as Justice (1983), Quinn (1995), and from the Prison Reform Trust (Loucks 1995)).

Additions to the Rules are also evident, such as the new rules on visitors and on bringing drugs in through visits. However, the language of the Rules remains inappropriate, such as its reference to disciplinary punishments as 'awards' and its use of masculine pronouns throughout.

According to Livingstone and Owen, "Prison is an extensively rule-bound institution where the prison authorities can almost always point to a rule at some level of the hierarchy as the basis for any action that they take" (1999: 16.07). The Prison Rules lie at the heart of prison policies, and an examination of the Rules is relevant because of what they reveal about the day-to-day administration of prisons. In the gradual shift towards increased harmonisation with European policies, an examination of how the Rules in England and Wales compare with European guidance is perhaps even more relevant now than in the past.

The current edition of this book comes when the European Convention on Human Rights is soon to be incorporated into domestic law. It also comes at a time when the format of guidance regarding the administration of prisons is in a state of transition, with the gradual shift from Circular Instructions and Standing Orders to Prison Service Instructions and Orders. The next section of this book explains the status of the Rules themselves and describes the documents which influence the Prison Rules (Standing Orders, Circular Instructions, Prison Service Instructions and Orders, and the European Prison Rules). It also touches on the development of prisoners' litigation domestically and before the European Court of Human Rights, and traces the movement for minimum standards.

The layout of this book has changed from previous editions. First, while it still compares the Prison Rules for England and Wales to the European Rules, it does this only within the context of the commentary; the European Rules themselves are listed at Annex A. Second, the emphasis of the Guide is primarily on the Rules as they apply to adult convicted prisoners in England and Wales. As in past editions, the Guide acknowledges that

Prison Rules and legislation in Scotland and in Northern Ireland are separate from those in England and Wales. Northern Ireland in fact has its own excellent guide to prisoners' rights and law (Committee on the Administration of Justice 1998). Further, the Prison Service has redrafted the Rules for Young Offender Institutions, as it has the current Prison Rules, and may create a separate set of Rules specifically for remand prisoners.

But as in earlier editions, the main section of this book sets out each of the Prison Rules, followed by a commentary on each section. The commentary compares the Rules in England and Wales with the European Rules and, where appropriate, cites reports, articles, and periodicals, case law, Standing Orders and Circular Instructions, Prison Service Instructions and Orders, and reports of HM Inspectorate of Prisons, the Prison Service, and of the Prison Ombudsman.

The code of minimum standards called for in the original version of this book in 1985 has yet to be realised (see 'Basis and Status of the Prison Rules' below), although the Prison Service has made significant steps in other areas such as the provision of information to prisoners.

Information to prisoners and staff

During research for the earlier editions of this book, it became apparent that many staff were unclear about specific rules and varied widely in the interpretation and enforcement of the rules which they did know. A large number of both staff and prisoners interviewed commented that improvements in initial and ongoing training could remedy these inconsistencies. HM Chief Inspector reported the same situation in his 1991 Annual Report:

> "Some prisoners also complain to us that there is a lack of consistency of treatment even within different parts of the same establishment. Some believe, as do many staff, that there is no one co-ordinating the work of the establishment as a whole. We are convinced that in a number of establishments the quality of communication between managers and uniformed staff, and sometimes between the different ranks of uniformed staff, has deteriorated ... Junior officers in particular feel isolated. They are expected to make decisions on the basis of the information that is available to them ... Many officers have little contact with their counterparts in other groups within the same establishment and cannot readily check whether they are dealing with particular matters in the same way ... We believe that there is ... a need to provide staff with more training, including refresher training, in interpersonal skills" (para. 3.98).

He further commented on the limited access to other legal advice in prisons: "Access to advice about legal aid, appeals and bail is a major concern to most prisoners. We found that establishments had sufficient trained officers to provide such advice, but the quality, nature and accessibility of this service varied widely" (1991: 3.14).

The Woolf Report emphasised that the Prison Service must make:

> "...a substantial change in the manner in which most prisoners are treated [in order to reduce re-offending]. This in turn requires a substantial contribution from prison officers. They will only be able to make such a contribution if they are properly trained. For this reason, and because it could also improve the present state of morale in the

Prison Service, we recommend that more attention be paid by the Prison Service to training. A greater commitment to training would also help to show that the Prison Service cares about its staff" (paras. 13.107-13.108).

Prisoners may also have problems with access to prison libraries, as the Chief Inspector has noted: "Opening hours are often restricted to times when not all inmates can attend and are often further affected by non-availability of staff" (1991: 3.52). The Education, Science and Arts Committee of the House of Commons has expressed its concern at the limited availability of library facilities in prisons:

> "If education tends to be seen as being of low priority, libraries suffer even more from the same attitude: in emergencies or periods where prison officers are short staffed, the officer(s) responsible for escorting inmates to the library tend(s) to be the first to be diverted elsewhere ... Limited opening hours may mean that not all prisoners have access to the library, and that access may be infrequent and brief, with no time to browse or use reference books. Many libraries are run with flair and imagination, offering information, displays and support for learning activities. It is a matter of regret and concern if such facilities are not being fully used" (1991: 52).

Probation officers at Wormwood Scrubs Prison reported in their evidence to the Woolf Inquiry that: "Prisoners feel cut off from all sources of information. Often, they neither know what is going on in the prison nor what is going on at home. Of course, they hear rumours and official announcements about the wider world and the prison ... But often the official pronouncements are either delayed or contradictory or nonsensical ... It would not seem unreasonable to suggest that prisoners should receive at least weekly bulletins from the authorities about policy changes in the wings where they live, if those policy changes will make any real difference to their daily routines" (para. 14.280). Woolf recognised the importance of improving communications with prisoners, saying that "If prisoners have a greater understanding of what is happening to them in prison and why, they are less likely to be aggrieved and become disaffected. This should, in turn, improve relations between staff and prisoners" (para. 14.275). He believed access to information was especially important regarding administrative decisions which materially or adversely affect prisoners and recommended that prisoners be told the reasons behind such decisions. The government accepted this recommendation in the 1991 White Paper *Custody, Care and Justice*.

Standing Order 7B directs prison establishments to obtain and display the Prison Rules, the European Prison Rules, documents relating to parole, advice on petitioning the European Court of Human Rights, the Prison Discipline Manual, and so on, although the Inspectorate's reports have indicated that these documents are not always available in all prisons as the Standing Order requires, nor do prisoners always realise they are available.

On reception, prisoners should be provided with the *Prisoners' Information Book*, compiled by the Prison Reform Trust in conjunction with the Prison Service, rather than with the Prison Rules themselves. Locally produced publications may supplement the *Prisoners' Information Book*, but should not replace it. Circular Instruction 32/1991 requires officers to ensure that prisoners receive a copy of the Book, and Standing Order 1A makes the governor responsible for ensuring that the information is explained to them if necessary (SO 1A: 50; see also commentary to r 10).

Legislation and case law have also improved prisoners' access to information. The Access to Health Records Act 1990 gave prisoners the right of access to their health records. The Court of Appeal in *Wilson* (1992) gave prisoners access to reports against them so they can adequately represent themselves at parole hearings. The Court of Appeal in *Walsh* (1992) allowed discretionary lifers to know the length of their tariff and, particularly importantly, the House of Lords in *Doody* (1994) entitled mandatory lifers to know the length of their tariff, the reason for its length, and whether the Home Secretary increased the period which the court recommended.

The Citizen's Charter (1991) states that "It is especially important in prisons that no one is denied information to which they are entitled about decisions affecting their lives and well-being. We are therefore introducing a number of measures to ensure that prisoners receive clear and basic information from the start of their time in custody about decisions affecting them and preparations for their release." Mr. Joe Pilling, then Director General of the Prison Service, confirmed this stance in June 1992, saying that prisoners have the right to demand information about their entitlements, answers to reasonable questions, and honest apologies for mistakes and injustices (*Independent,* 12 June 1992).

Gaps in the Prison Rules

The Prison Rules in England and Wales have a number of significant gaps. For example, both the Prison Service Key Performance Indicators and Operating Standards (see below) refer to the amount of structured activities available, and the Operating Standards refer to the amount of time prisoners spend out of their cells. Neither of these issues are mentioned in the Prison Rules. The Rules also make no mention of discharge or discharge grants, sentence planning, personal officer schemes, or the impact of custody on rights such as voting and marriage. Probably the most significant omissions are sentence calculation and parole, although they were in fact once part of the Rules.

Briefly, the Operating Standards recommend a minimum of 12 hours daily out of cells, subject to security, control and discipline (Op. Std. U2), and 42 hours per week of structured activities (U1). Prisoners should have the opportunity for association when they are unlocked but not in structured activities (N21), and the opportunity for cell hobbies when they are locked in their cells (U22).

Sentence planning is designed to help longer-term prisoners plan their time in custody, including what goals they intend to achieve. All adult prisoners sentenced to a year or more and all Young Offenders serving at least four weeks should have a sentence plan.

Sentenced prisoners, including those unlawfully at large or on temporary release are legally debarred from voting (Representation of the People Act 1983). However unconvicted, convicted unsentenced, and civil prisoners age 18 or over are entitled to vote, as are people imprisoned for contempt of court or in default of another sentence (e.g. fine default or people in breach of probation or Community Service Orders). These people must have registered to vote before they entered custody (PSI 68/1997, with additional instructions in PSI 19/1997). Operating Standards Q32-33 state that prisoners should be allowed to marry while in custody.

Sentence calculation and parole are probably the most complex areas of prison administration. The Prison Service publishes a manual on sentence calculation as well as one entitled *Parole, Early Release and Recall* (PSI 15/1998), both of which should be available to prisoners. This account therefore only summarises the most basic aspects of both.

Prison Service Order 6000 covers parole arrangements for determinate sentence prisoners. Prisoners sentenced after 1 October 1992 fall under the provisions of the Criminal Justice Act 1991 (as amended). Prisoners sentenced to under a year in custody are automatically released at the half-way point of their sentence. Those sentenced from one year to less than four years are also released at the half-way point, but are then supervised up to the three-quarter point (Automatic Conditional Release). Finally, prisoners sentenced to four years or more are subject to Discretionary Conditional Release. This means they become eligible for parole half-way through their sentence, are released by the two-thirds point (the Non-Parole Date) at the latest, and remain under supervision to the three-quarters point of their original sentence. Prisoners sentenced prior to 1 October 1992 are eligible for parole after serving a third of their sentence, then are released unconditionally at the two-thirds point or Earliest Date of Release.

Days added for disciplinary punishments (unless remitted) put back a prisoner's automatic release or parole eligibility date, the Non-Parole Date, and the licence expiry date, as do days lost on appeal. Time spent in custody on remand counts towards the Parole Eligibility Date, but it does not reduce the period of compulsory supervision after release. In fact, all applicable time from a person's arrival at a police station after arrest is credited as time served (IG 20/1996). Time which young people spend on remand in local authority accommodation, even if this is not secure accommodation, as long as liberty was restricted, counts towards their sentence, though time out on bail, home leave, and so on does not count (IG 51/1995).

Each prison is responsible for compiling a prisoner's parole dossier. This must include the prisoner's application, details of the offence and sentence, the record of previous convictions, sentence plan details and reviews, reports from probation officers and prison medical officers, and the prison's parole assessment. The prison is also responsible for issuing licences and for arranging release dates for parolees.

Useful guides on all aspects of imprisonment are *The Prisons Handbook* (Leech 1999) and *Prison Law* (Livingstone and Owen 1999).

Prison administrators and staff must continually balance the constraints of security and control with safeguards over the exercise of discretionary power. The Prison Rules and related guidance are designed to help them do this. A proper understanding of and access to these tools for prisoners, staff, and managers is therefore an essential part of maintaining that balance in the daily life of prisons. The next section explains the basis and status of the Prison Rules in England and Wales, while the final section comments in detail about each of the Rules in turn.

BASIS AND STATUS OF THE PRISON RULES

(1) The Prison Rules and guidance for their use

To the observer, regulations governing the minutiae of prison life often represent an impenetrable bureaucracy. In order to uncover management policy, one has to unravel layers of rules upon rules. Lawyers can have just as much difficulty unravelling the legal rights of prisoners: the law is unclear, and judges often disagree in their interpretation of it. All that can be said with certainty is that prisoner litigation has forced upon the courts a growing, if reluctant, recognition of prisoners' rights.

The Act of Parliament which specifies the legal rules applying in prisons is the **Prison Act 1952**. S. 47(1) of the Prison Act 1952 states that the Secretary of State "may make rules for the regulation and management of prisons ... and for the classification, treatment, employment, discipline and control of persons required to be detained therein." The **Prison Rules 1999** (S.I. 1999, No. 728) are made under the authority of this Act. The **Young Offender Institution Rules 1999** (S.I. 1999, No. 962, as amended) are very similar to the Prison Rules.

The Prison Rules leave a great deal of discretion to the prison authorities, so the Prison Service issues many other documents for guidance on the use of these Rules. Following recommendation 60 in the Woodcock Report (1994) which called for the simplification and consolidation of such guidance, this comes in the form of Prison Service Orders and Instructions. **Prison Service Orders** (PSOs) are permanent directions which replace the current mixture of Standing Orders, Circular Instructions, Instructions to Governors, and manuals containing mandatory requirements. PSOs take precedence over other mandatory items and should be the first point of reference. Prisoners generally have access to these through prison libraries, and the Orders are publicly available unless "given a protective marking" (PSO 0001). Those with a protective marking "may be disclosed in limited circumstances where this is considered to be in the public interest for example in the course of legal proceedings" (*ibid.*). In such cases, the Prison Service will advise and must be consulted. **Prison Service Instructions** (PSIs), on the other hand, are short-term directions which include a mandatory element, roughly similar to the previous Circular Instructions. Finally, **Information and practice documents** are non-mandatory guides to advise and inform prison staff, as are Staff and Personnel information sheets.

Prison Service Orders and Instructions have not yet replaced all relevant Standing Orders, Circular Instructions, and so on, which will remain in force until the PSOs replace them. **Standing Orders** indicate how discretion is to be exercised, with a view to promoting consistency. **Circular Instructions** (CIs) amend Standing Orders (SOs) and provide further detail which in the past were eventually absorbed into the Standing Orders. The fact that all of these modes of guidance are still in use is very confusing. The guidance should be clearer once Prison Service Orders and Instructions have replaced all remaining Standing Orders, Circular Instructions, and Instructions and Advice to Governors (IGs and AGs) still in force.

The Prison Service **Manual on Security** also informs governors about the interpretation of the Prison Rules. This document is unavailable for public use. A letter from the then Director General of the Prison Service, Derek Lewis, to governors following the publication of the Woodcock Report in December 1994 stated that "... the Manual [on Security] is the definitive set of rules on security matters - it is not discretionary." Even this mandatory set of rules for prison governors is, however, not legally binding in a court of law.

It is worth noting that prison officers, as civil servants, are subject to the Official Secrets Act in what they say about their work. However, under the Official Secrets Act 1989 the disclosure of information relating to prisons will only be an offence in so far as it facilitates the commission of a crime.

(2) The legal status of the Prison Rules

The Prison Rules were not designed to be legally enforceable, and the courts have not allowed prisoners to sue for breach of a statutory duty. This is confusing in light of the fact that the Rules are a Statutory Instrument, and therefore that they "have statutory force and should not be ignored" (Prison Ombudsman 1998).

Successive Governments have treated the Standing Orders which inform the Rules as "management instructions issued for official purposes" (384 HL Debate 27 June 1977, col. 994) rather than as legally binding documents. It is puzzling therefore that Prison Service Order 0001 states that the word 'mandatory' in PSOs and Instructions "implies that some legal liability, disciplinary punishment or managerial disapproval may follow if the order is not carried out", as is the case with terms such as 'must', 'will', and 'are required to'. Livingstone and Owen comment that, "Despite their greater formality, Prison Service Orders and Instructions enjoy no greater legal status than the previous system of Standing Orders and Circular Instructions. In other words they have no legal status whatsoever despite the fact that they contain massive detail relevant to the conduct of daily life in prison" (1999: 1.39). Prison Service Orders and Instructions are never debated by Parliament.

The courts have reflected this approach. For example, in *Arbon v Anderson* (1943) Lord Goddard stated: "It would be fatal to all discipline in prisons if governors and wardens had to perform their duties always with the fear of an action before their eyes if they in any way deviated from the rules." In *Becker v Home Office* (1972), Lord Denning M.R. expressed the same view: "If the courts were to entertain actions by disgruntled prisoners, the governor's life would be made intolerable. The discipline of the prison would be undermined. The Prison Rules are regulatory directions only. Even if they are not observed, they do not give rise to a cause of action." Again, in *Williams v Home Office (No. 2)* (1981), where the Home Office pleaded the Prison Rules as part of its amended defence, the judge emphasised that reliance on the Rules was unnecessary, because a breach of the Rules could not be relevant to the question whether the defendant could justify in law the detention of the plaintiff.

The legal status of the Prison Rules was discussed in *Raymond v Honey* (1982), but the point was unresolved. More recently, the House of Lords' discussion of the subject has been even more ambiguous. In *R v Deputy Governor of Parkhurst Prison ex p Hague, Weldon v Home Office* (1991), Lord Jauncey expressly accepted a Home Office submission that the rule-making power in s. 47 of the Prison Act did not authorise the creation of any private law rights to prisoners and thus any rule which expressly sought to do so would be *ultra vires* (beyond its authorised powers). Lord Bridge disagreed, stating that the powers conferred by s. 47 with its express reference to the creation of rules for the treatment of prisoners was broad enough to cover the enactment of rules providing a cause of action for breach of statutory duty. Thus Lord Bridge left open the possibility of an amendment of the rules to give prisoners the right to sue for breach of statutory duty without the need for fresh primary legislation.

Interestingly, the Prison Officers' Training Manual, in describing the responsibilities of prison officers concerning the use of force under Prison Rule 44(1) states: "These rules are statutory rules and accordingly have the force of law." It may be that as prisoners continue to argue the point in court, the legal force of the Prison Rules will eventually be established.

(3) Prisoners' rights

The fact that the courts have not yet allowed a prisoner to sue for breach of a statutory duty does not mean that prisoners are without rights. The ordinary law of the land, both civil and criminal, applies in prisons, even if it is difficult to enforce.

(i) Civil Law

According to Lord Wilberforce in *Raymond v Honey* (1982), "Under English law, a convicted prisoner, in spite of his imprisonment, retains all civil rights which are not taken away expressly or by implication." A prisoner has no contractual relationship with the prison authorities (although the Woolf Report suggests, as discussed later, that all prisoners should have a "compact" or "contract setting out the prisoner's expectations and responsibilities in the prison in which he or she is held"), and so must rely on the law of tort. However, the courts remain reluctant to recognise these rights in individual cases.

(a) Negligence

To succeed in an action for negligence, a prisoner must prove that the prison authorities were in breach of their duty of care. If the prison management, without legal authority, inflicts injury on a prisoner which would be actionable if inflicted by one individual on another, the injured prisoner may bring a claim in negligence against the authority as if it were any other private defendant. Thus, in *D'Arcy v Prison Commissioners* (1956) a prisoner received £190 damages for injuries caused by other prisoners; in *Ferguson v Home Office* (1977) Caulfield J. awarded a prisoner £15,500 for injuries caused by a circular saw which he had used with inadequate training; and more recently in *H v Home Office* (1992) a prisoner was awarded £50 for the negligence of the prison authorities in revealing to other prisoners the fact that the prisoner had previous convictions for sex offences which resulted in his being assaulted in his cell.

However, the courts have been unwilling to impose too onerous a burden on the authorities, stressing the problem of staff resources and administrative convenience. It remains extremely difficult for a prisoner to prove that the authorities have acted unreasonably. In *Egerton v Home Office*

(1978), a prisoner formerly segregated for his own protection was beaten up by other prisoners. The court held that though the officer supervising the group in which the attack took place should have been told the prisoner's history, staff were not in breach of the duty of care since the spontaneous attack could not have been anticipated. In *Knight v Home Office* (1990), Pill J held that the prison authorities were not liable in that particular case for the suicide of a prisoner, stressing that the standard of care is lower in a prison than in a hospital.

More recently, the Court of Appeal held in *H v Home Office* (1992) that a prisoner could sue in negligence in respect of "intolerable conditions", but the problem of proving that the conditions are "intolerable" remains. In that case, the prisoner sought damages for being held in solitary confinement for his own protection due to the authorities' negligence in revealing his previous conviction for sex offences. The Court held that since removal from association is expressly authorised in the Prison Rules, segregation could not itself constitute intolerable conditions. In *Olotu v Home Office and Crown Prosecution Service* (1997), the plaintiff was detained longer than the time limit allowed for the case but unsuccessfully sought damages for unlawful detention prior to trial. The Court held that the only private law remedy in this case was against the solicitor for negligence.

(b) Trespass to the person/False imprisonment

Trespass to the person includes the torts of assault, battery, and false imprisonment. The courts continue to be reluctant to allow prisoners to sue in the tort of false imprisonment, but it may be that this is another area where prisoner litigation is beginning to have some effect in changing prison policy.

Until recently, claims of false imprisonment clearly failed. In *Williams v Home Office (No. 2)* (1981), the Court of Appeal stressed that the tort of false imprisonment goes to the fact, not the quality of detention. (See commentary to r 45 for a further discussion of this case.) Another example of the courts' reluctance to recognise this tort is *Freeman v Home Office (No. 2)* (1984), where a prisoner claimed that a prison doctor had given him drugs for the purpose of control rather than treatment. The Court of Appeal dismissed the appeal and refused to award him damages for trespass to the person (see commentary to rr 20-21 Medical attendance.).

However, it appears that this tort may be arguable in some circumstances. Ackner LJ suggested in *Middleweek v Chief Constable of the Merseyside Police (Note)* (1990) that "a person lawfully detained in a prison cell would ... cease to be so lawfully detained if the conditions in that cell were such as to be seriously prejudicial to his health if he continued to occupy it, for example, because it became and remained seriously flooded, or contained a fractured gas pipe allowing gas to escape into the cell." However, the European Court held that keeping a prisoner overnight in a cell which contained the smell of stale urine and faeces (*8025/78 v UK*) or three weeks in a cell infested with cockroaches (*Reed v UK*) did not violate Article 3 of the Convention.

The Court of Appeal in both *R v Deputy Governor of Parkhurst Prison, ex parte Hague* (1990) and in *Weldon v Home Office* (1990) was clearly of the opinion that a prisoner was entitled to bring a claim for false imprisonment in respect of both the "residual liberty" and the "intolerable conditions" argument. Ralph Gibson LJ in *Weldon* suggested that bad faith might be an additional ingredient: "that the defendant had continued the confinement of the prisoner in intolerable circumstances with knowledge that the circumstances were intolerable," but the other judges appeared not to agree. Taylor LJ pointed out in *Hague* that to require proof of bad faith would be to alter the tort of false imprisonment, and in effect create a new tort special to prisons and prisoners. The House of Lords overruled the Court of Appeal in both these decisions, holding that a prisoner has no residual liberty, the deprivation of which can give rise to an action for false imprisonment, whatever the conditions of imprisonment, arresting what appeared to be a hopeful development in the case law in this area. Those arguing for greater private law rights for prisoners could seek to develop the 'common sense' approach of the two differently constituted Courts of Appeal in these cases.

The torts of assault and battery are rarely used today, and damages are generally very difficult to get in prison cases. One exception to this was a case in which the Clerkenwell Magistrates' Court awarded £12,000 in exemplary damages to a prisoner who had been assaulted by prison officers (reported in the *Guardian* 25 July 1996).

(c) Misfeasance in Public Office

The courts continue to suggest that one avenue open to the aggrieved prisoner is to sue for misfeasance in public office. Since the plaintiff is required to prove malice, or the conscious abuse of power by someone for whose acts the Home Office was in the circumstances liable, it is very difficult to succeed under this head. For example, in the case of *Racz v Home Office* (1992), the court decided that the Home Office could not be held responsible for the actions of prison officers, and therefore the prisoner could not sue for misfeasance in public office.

(ii) Criminal law

Criminal proceedings may be brought against both prisoners and prison officers. Thus, if anyone is deliberately killed in prison, the offender is likely to be prosecuted for murder or manslaughter. Crimes of violence in English law are laid down in the Offences against the Persons Act 1861, and there is a considerable overlap between these and the disciplinary offences described in Rule 51 of the Prison Rules. The prison authorities take the decision whether to call in the police with a view to court proceedings.

(iii) Judicial review

A prisoner may challenge the legality of any action taken by the authorities in pursuit of a statutory power or duty by way of a public law claim for judicial review. The distinction between public and private law is important for two main reasons: first, because the procedure for judicial review entails a time limit of three months (s. 31 of the Supreme Court Act 1981), and secondly, because the procedure for judicial review is governed not by the traditional writ or originating summons, but by a procedure specified by Order 53 of the Rules of the Supreme Court.

Judicial review has been an important vehicle for promoting prisoners' rights: "where any person or body exercises a power conferred by statute which affects the rights or legal expectations of citizens and is of a kind which the law requires to be exercised in accordance with the rules of natural justice, the court has power to review the exercise of that power" (*Leech* 1988). In *Hague and Weldon* (1991) Lord Bridge went so far as to say that: "the availability of judicial review as a means of questioning the legality of action purportedly taken in pursuance of the Prison Rules is a beneficial and necessary jurisdiction which cannot properly be circumscribed by considerations of policy or expediency in relation to prison administration."

None of this guarantees success on the prisoner's part. In *McAvoy* (1984), the court reviewed the legality of the transfer of a remand prisoner from Brixton to Winchester Prison. Whilst Webster J was clear that the transfer decision was reviewable, overriding security reasons led him to refuse to quash the decision. Again in *Hickling and JH (a minor)* (1986), the Court of Appeal rejected an application for judicial review of a governor's decision to remove a mother and baby from a mother and baby unit because of the mother's disruptive behaviour, which resulted in the baby being taken into care. The case of *Thynne, Wilson and Gunnell* (1991) determined that although the domestic courts have allowed progressively more access to the courts for judicial review, judicial review is inadequate to meet the requirements of Article 5(4) of the Convention for parole cases. In other types of cases, the Commission has considered judicial review to be an effective remedy, such as for transfers and segregation (see *Hague*).

However, as Owen (1991) pointed out, "the history of the *Hague* appeal (which only went to the House of Lords on the issue of private law remedies) demonstrates the benefits of judicial review to prisoners and confirms that so far as the jurisdiction is concerned there are no longer any 'no-go' areas in prison law" (see r 45 Removal from association for a discussion of this case). Further, the Court of Appeal in *Leech (No. 2)* (1994) and confirmed by Lord Browne-Wilkinson in *Pierson* (1997) extended the approach of the court generally to acts which interfere with a person's legal rights or basic principles of UK law (see commentary to rr 34-35 Communications generally).

Judicial review is one domestic remedy which does not need to be exhausted before a case can be declared admissible to the European Courts, as long as an application for judicial review would have a "reasonable likelihood of success" (*Kavanagh v UK* 1992). Implementation of the Human Rights Act 1998 will, however, increase the difficulty for plaintiffs to plead that domestic judicial proceedings do not constitute an adequate remedy. Many legal challenges pursued through judicial review may, following its introduction, be advanced by claiming a breach of the Human Rights Act.

(4) The European Court of Human Rights and the Human Rights Act 1998

The European Convention on Human Rights came into force on 3 September 1953, and all members of the Council of Europe are now parties to it. Under the Convention, two specially created bodies share the task of protecting human rights, the Commission and the Court of Human Rights, in addition to the Committee of Ministers, the decision-making body of the Council of Europe. The Convention is composed of statements of the rights and freedoms which the member states "shall secure to everyone within their jurisdiction" (Article 2), and of provisions establishing the jurisdiction of the European Commission and Court of Human Rights "to ensure the observance of the engagements undertaken" by the contracting parties (Article 19). The Commission hears inter-state cases as well as applications from individuals or groups of individuals.

The European Convention on Human Rights contains many articles relevant to prison life, in particular articles 2-12. These are that no one should be subjected to torture or inhuman or degrading treatment or punishment (art. 3); that forced labour is prohibited (with the exception of work done in the ordinary course of detention) (art. 4); that everyone has the right to: life (art. 2), liberty and security of person (art. 5), a fair trial (art. 6), privacy (art. 8), freedom of thought, conscience, and religion (art. 9), freedom of expression (art. 10), freedom of association (art. 11), and the right to marry (art. 12); and that people should not be punished for something which was not a crime at the time of its commission (art. 7).

Although the UK has only just incorporated the Convention into domestic law, the right of individual petition has been recognised since 1965. Such applications are only possible after all domestic remedies have been exhausted, and within six months of any final domestic decision. Now that the Convention is part of domestic law, fewer British cases may reach Strasbourg since its own courts can remedy such cases. The Prisoners' Advice Service and INQUEST are preparing a booklet (expected in 1999) which should explain the implications of the Human Rights Act in the British courts.

Under the Human Rights Act, all primary and subordinate legislation must as far as possible be interpreted and given effect in a way that is compatible with the European Convention. Where questions arise, the courts must take into account judgements, decisions, declarations, and opinions from the European Commission and Court, and by the Committee of Ministers of the Council of Europe, though these decisions are not to be treated as binding (Kaufmann 1998).

The Human Rights Act prohibits any public authority to act in a way which is incompatible with the European Convention, unless primary legislation is in itself incompatible. The Act does not affect the validity, continuing operation, or enforcement of primary legislation which is incompatible: in such cases, the courts may only make a 'declaration of incompatibility', with no effect on the status of the legislation or on the rights of the parties involved. The Government then has the discretion whether to introduce new legislation or to amend the conflicting legislation.

According to Kaufmann, "... the [Human Rights] Act is likely to have its greatest impact in the area of the exercise of administrative discretion ... [Added] to the three traditional grounds of judicial review (illegality, irrationality and procedural impropriety) is a fourth: incompatibility with the [European Court of Human Rights]" (1998: 6).

Even after adoption of the Human Rights Act, prisoners retain the right to apply to the European Courts once they have exhausted all domestic remedies (although see 'Judicial Review' above). Applicants may be legally represented and may obtain legal aid from the Council of Europe. Prisoners have always been one of the major groups to use the system. Applications to the Commission (from all sources) now exceed 12,000 a year, with over 4,000 registered by the Commission Secretariat for examination (Livingstone and Owen 1999). The increasing numbers mean even greater delays for successful applicants to have their cases heard.

The European Commission on Human Rights admits only a small

percentage of the applications it receives. Between 1955 and 1991, the Commission admitted 1,038 (5.4 per cent) of the 19,216 individual applications received (Ashman 1992). This proportion has gradually increased: in 1990, roughly 7 per cent of applications were declared admissible, but between 1 December 1997 and 23 January 1998, the Commission declared 186 (18.6 per cent) of the 1,001 applications it examined admissible (Council of Europe 1998).

As of November 1998, the European Court of Human Rights alone deals with both admissibility and merits of cases. The Commission will continue to sit until October 1999 to deal with cases referred before November 1998, otherwise the European Court handles all applications.

Sir James Fawcett, former President of the European Commission of Human Rights, highlighted "the most trenchant criticism" of the Commission and Court apparatus, namely the long delays before decisions are reached. He cited *Campbell and Fell* as an example: the incident which inspired the case took place in September 1976, the applications were introduced to the Commission in March 1977, the Commission's report was adopted in May 1982, and the Court's judgement was published in June 1984 (Fawcett 1985: 76). The European Court of Human Rights is therefore currently not a realistic or practical means of remedying individual grievances for the majority of prisoners. Except for longer-term prisoners and especially those with life sentences, the Court's decisions have value only as a precedent for other prisoners and rarely benefit the individual applicant.

The Commission has never held that prison conditions amount to a violation of Article 3 (which forbids torture or inhuman or degrading treatment or punishment), despite the fact that many prison regimes do not comply with the standards in the European Prison Rules (Ashman 1992).

(5) European Prison Rules

In 1973, the Council of Europe adopted Standard Minimum Rules for the Treatment of Prisoners (ESMRs) based on a 1955 UN Resolution. The European Prison Rules replaced these in 1987. The European Rules do not constitute a Convention: they are not binding in law either internationally or in national systems, but are intended to serve as guidelines for the organs of the Convention and national administrations and courts. The Council of Europe recommends that "governments of member states be guided in their internal legislation and practice by the principles set out in the text of the European Prison Rules ... with a view to their progressive implementation" (Recommendation of the Committee of Ministers to Member States of the European Prison Rules).

The full European Rules are contained in four parts. The first sets out the Rules themselves (see Annex A); the second is an explanatory memorandum with a commentary on each rule; the third details the historical background to the Rules; and the fourth is a concordance of the European Prison Rules and the ESMRs. The details thus provided are intended to enhance understanding and improve the level of implementation. They place new emphasis on "community contacts, the roles and status of staff, modern management techniques, regime planning, rising accommodation standards and the pressures of changing operational circumstances" (Neale 1985: 3). The Committee on Co-operation in Penal Affairs reported to the European Committee on Crime Problems in 1986, and the revised European

Prison Rules were place before the Council of Europe and adopted in February 1987.

The main section of this book shows that the Prison Rules in England and Wales often fail to meet the minimum standards in the European Prison Rules. The tendency is for countries to treat the European Rules as aspirational rather than as basic standards of decency for prisons. Vagg and Dünkel comment that "... it is important to remember that although UN documents [such as the European Rules] provide an important frame of reference for policy and indeed for research, in general they only promulgate *minimum* standards. One recurring theme in the literature on criminal justice is that minimum standards come, over time, to be treated as 'approved specifications' or even 'desirable goals'. Many governments appear to take the view that meeting minimum standards is a guarantee of *adequate* provision, or even that once minimum standards are met, further improvements constitute an unjustifiable use of resources. This is not our view. 'Minimum' so far as we are concerned means 'minimally adequate', not 'appropriate', 'desirable', or 'optimum'" (1994: 947, emphasis in original).

(6) The movement for minimum standards

For the past twenty years a demand for more specific, enforceable standards has come from a broad alliance of interests. These have included the May Committee in 1979, the Chief Inspector of Prisons and Boards of Visitors in 1982, the House of Commons Education, Science and Arts Committee, the Governors Branch of the Society of Civil and Public Servants and the Association of Members of Boards of Visitors in 1983, the National Association for the Care and Resettlement of Offenders (NACRO) in 1984, the National Association of Probation Officers in 1985, Boards of Visitors, the Association of Members of Boards of Visitors (AMBoV), and the Trade Union Congress in 1986, the House of Commons Home Affairs Select Committee in 1987, the 1988 Green Paper "Private Sector Involvement in the Remand System" (a report by Deloitte, Haskins, and Sells), and a report by Silvia Casale and Joyce Plotnikoff on behalf of NACRO in 1989, followed by a report from the Prison Reform Trust by the same authors in 1990. In January 1990, and again that October, the Education, Science and Arts Committee of the House of Commons recommended a code of minimum standards in line with those in the NACRO publications. The Committee promoted the formation of a Prison Regimes Act to protect the entitlements of prisoners and to allow for the centralised monitoring of these rights (1991).

Finally in February 1991, Lord Justice Woolf published a report on his inquiry into the prison disturbances of April 1990 and again emphasised the need for legally enforceable standards. He stated:

> "In order to achieve justice within prisons there must be required standards of conditions and regime within prisons. After proper consultation, the Home Secretary should establish a series of national Accredited Standards applicable to all prisons. It would then be the responsibility of every prison establishment to reach at least that standard. Area Managers ... would be responsible for ensuring that, over a period of time, each prison in their area fulfil all the national Accredited Standards. The Area Manager would certify when a prison

had reached a required standard. When it had fulfilled all the standards, it would be granted Accreditation Status by the Home Secretary, on the recommendation of HM Chief Inspector of Prisons. For the time being, the national standards would have to be aspirational. Once they are achieved, that would be the time to consider whether it was necessary to make them legally enforceable. We would, however, expect that at that stage they would be incorporated in the Prison Rules and so would be legally enforceable by judicial review" (1991: paras. 1.186-1.187).

Despite the apparent consensus on the need for minimum standards, Government's response has been inconsistent. On 17 December 1982, in reply to a question in the House of Commons, the Home Office reiterated its intent to publish a draft code in 1983. No such code appeared, and the question was repeated in the House of Lords on 13 December 1983. The Home Office then indicated its intention to proceed in the context of building standards for new establishments. This change of heart was confirmed on 12 April 1984 when the Home Office stated that, apart from the new building standards, it did not intend to publish anything further in the form of a code.

The Prison Department (as it was then) issued "Current Recommended Standards for the Design of New Prison Establishments" in July 1984. However these were guidelines only and were never incorporated into a Statutory Instrument. Support for a code of minimum standards continued from virtually every sector of penological thinking and from the three Opposition political parties. The House of Commons Home Affairs Committee argued in its report, *State and Use of Prisons*, that "on balance, and in spite of overcrowding, we believe that enforceable minimum standards and the abolition of Crown immunity should be given a chance to show whether they have a helpful contribution to make". Both proposals were rejected in the Government's reply to the Select Committee published in December 1987.

The Government eventually published standards for the design of new prisons in the Prison Design Briefing System in 1989. The Operating Contract of Wolds Remand Prison as well as for other private sector prisons cites very specific standards comparable to those in the 1984 NACRO Code, but failed to extend such standards to prisons outside the private sector. Where targets have been set for public sector prisons through Key Performance Indicators (KPIs; see below), these may require less than the standards set for private sector establishments. One example of this is that the private sector must provide at least 30 hours of purposeful activity for prisoners per week, compared to the 22.5 hours set in KPI 5 (HMCIP 1999). The Chief Inspector commented in his 1998 Annual Report that "there are no incentives to perform better than required, which drive up performance, in either Private or Public Sectors, which I believe should be considered, in line with the given objective of improving effectiveness ... But at least Private Sector prisons, and HMP Manchester [the tender for which was won by the Prison Service], have the advantage of being told precisely what is expected of them, for which they are then resourced, which provides a much more exact explanation of the cost of imprisonment in those prisons than is possible elsewhere" (1999: 25).

Custody, Care and Justice, the White Paper published in September 1991, finally acknowledged the benefits of a code of standards for the Prison

Service and agreed to set such targets. The White Paper did not state when or how the Government would set these standards, but said only that "the Government will consider whether a system of certificates of accreditation is the best way of signifying when the standards have been met", as proposed in the Woolf Report, and that the enforceability of standards and their incorporation into the Prison Rules "should be considered when the standards can be met consistently in all establishments" (paras. 6.20 and 6.21).

Despite what seemed to be another non-committal response to the recommendations for minimum standards, the Prison Service set up a Code of Standards Steering Group to put the proposals from the Woolf Report into effect, after consultation with several "interested parties". The Steering Group set a provisional timetable for a Published Code of Standards to appear in December 1993 after several months of consultation and trial periods in various establishments. The Prison Service Operating Standards eventually appeared in 1994, but again the standards are aspirational rather than enforceable. The introduction to the Standards states that "..standards are not intended to be legally enforceable. The Government has however made clear its intention that it will consider the issue of enforceability, once standards are met more consistently across the Prison Service. The standards represent the level of service which prisons must aim to meet over time, in terms of our service to the public and our treatment of prisoners."

At present, s. 14 of the Prison Act 1952 is the only statutory provision which requires the Home Secretary to satisfy himself regarding adequate size of cells, lighting, heating, ventilation, fittings, etc. through a system of certification by an inspector. The Act provides no independent means of certification, however, and if cells fail to comply with certificates due to overcrowding, the Home Secretary only has to alter the criteria for certification.

One implication of the Prison Service's shift to agency status in 1993 was that it began to set published goals as part of its Corporate and Business Plans. The Home Secretary also sets targets in the form of Key Performance Indicators (KPIs), which measure specific aspects of a prison's performance. These include numbers of escapes, assaults, results of random drug tests, amount of time spent unlocked and in purposeful activity, and so on. The usefulness of KPIs as measures of performance has recently come under scrutiny. The Prison Service Review (1997) recommended that KPIs be reviewed as a measure of effectiveness with a view to the quality of service delivery and overall goals of the Prison Service, rather than simple quantitative measures. The Chief Inspector of Prisons noted the same concern about KPIs in his most recent Annual Report: "KPIs are exactly what they imply: indicators of quantitative measures of performance against laid down targets, nothing more than that. The current list of KPIs do not inform Ministers or the public on the details of treatment and conditions of individual types of prisoners, and the evidence of performance that they give is not wholly relevant as a result" (1999: 23).

Of interest is the Prison Service's move toward Service Delivery Agreements (SDAs), due to start on a trial basis in April 1999 with 15 sites participating by April 2000. This is an extension of Service Level Agreements and links a prison's resources to 'key outputs' it is expected to deliver in return and establishes "clear personal accountability for delivery" (Home Office 1999b). SDAs do not create legally enforceable standards, but they do create financial incentives for prisons to meet specified targets. They should also be "useful tools for achieving consistency of delivery" (HMCIP 1999: 25). Similarly, the Youth Justice Board (YJB), created under the 1998 Crime and Disorder Act, has the role of commissioning, purchasing, and monitoring standards for all people under the age of 18 in the Criminal Justice System, including those in custody. If the Prison Service fails to meet the standards imposed by the YJB, the YJB may refuse to purchase its services.

The Government has given little indication as to when or if minimum standards will be incorporated into the Prison Rules, only that: "The necessary revisions or additions to the Prison Rules will be made as they are required" (*Custody, Care and Justice* 1991: 10.5). Morgan argued that "by far the most superior arrangement would be to move speedily to the adoption of standards which could be made the subject of a new Prison Act and Rules" (1992: 21-22), instead of leaving such standards as part of the legally unenforceable Prison Service Orders and Instructions, Circular Instructions, and Standing Orders.

Nancy Loucks and Nicky Padfield

PRISON RULES: A WORKING GUIDE

STATUTORY INSTRUMENTS
1999 No. 728

PRISONS
The Prison Rules 1999

© Crown Copyright 1999

PART I - INTERPRETATION

GENERAL

PART II - PRISONERS

GENERAL

WOMEN PRISONERS

RELIGION

MEDICAL ATTENTION

PHYSICAL WELFARE AND WORK

EDUCATION AND LIBRARY

COMMUNICATIONS

REMOVAL, SEARCH, RECORD AND PROPERTY

SPECIAL CONTROL, SUPERVISION, RESTRAINT AND DRUG TESTING

OFFENCES AGAINST DISCIPLINE

51. Offences against discipline
52. Defences to rule 51(9)
53. Disciplinary charges
54. Rights of prisoners charged
55. Governor's punishments
56. Forfeiture of remission to be treated as an award of additional days
57. Offences committed by young persons
58. Cellular confinement
59. Prospective award of additional days
60. Suspended punishments
61. Remission and mitigation of punishments and quashing of findings of guilt

PART III - OFFICERS OF PRISONS

62. General duty of officers
63. Gratuities forbidden
64. Search of officers
65. Transactions with prisoners
66. Contact with former prisoners
67. Communications to the press
68. Code of discipline
69. Emergencies

PART IV - PERSONS HAVING ACCESS TO A PRISON

70. Prohibited articles
71. Control of persons and vehicles
72. Viewing of prisons
73. Visitors

PART V - BOARDS OF VISITORS

74. Disqualification for membership
75. Board of visitors
76. Proceedings of boards
77. General duties of boards
78. Particular duties
79. Members visiting prisons
80. Annual report

PART VI - SUPPLEMENTAL

81. Delegation by governor
82. Contracted out prisons
83. Contracted out parts of prisons
84. Contracted out functions at directly managed prisons
85. Revocations and savings

PART I

INTERPRETATION

GENERAL

Citation and commencement

1.   *These Rules may be cited as the Prison Rules 1999 and shall come into force on 1st April 1999.*

Interpretation

2.   *(1) In these Rules, where the context so admits, the expression -*

"controlled drug" means any drug which is a controlled drug for the purposes of the Misuse of Drugs Act 1971[2];

"convicted prisoner" means, subject to the provisions of rule 7(3), a prisoner who has been convicted or found guilty of an offence or committed or attached for contempt of court or for failing to do or abstain from doing anything required to be done or left undone, and the expression "unconvicted prisoner" shall be construed accordingly;

"governor" includes an officer for the time being in charge of a prison;

"legal adviser" means, in relation to a prisoner, his counsel or solicitor, and includes a clerk acting on behalf of his solicitor;

"officer" means an officer of a prison and, for the purposes of rule 40(2), includes a prisoner custody officer who is authorised to perform escort functions in accordance with section 89 of the Criminal Justice Act 1991[3];

"prison minister" means, in relation to a prison, a minister appointed to that prison under section 10 of the Prison Act 1952;

"short-term prisoner" and "long-term prisoner" have the meanings assigned to them by section 33(5) of the Criminal Justice Act 1991, as extended by sections 43(1) and 45(1) of that Act.

   (2) In these Rules -
      (a) a reference to an award of additional days means additional days awarded under these Rules by virtue of section 42 of the Criminal Justice Act 1991;
      (b) a reference to the Church of England includes a reference to the Church in Wales; and
      (c) a reference to a numbered rule is, unless otherwise stated, a reference to the rule of that number in these Rules and a reference in a rule to a numbered paragraph is, unless otherwise stated, a reference to the paragraph of that number in that rule.

PART II

PRISONERS

GENERAL

Purpose of prison training and treatment

3.   *The purpose of the training and treatment of convicted prisoners shall be to encourage and assist them to lead a good and useful life.*

The whole of this publication could easily have been devoted to the purpose of prison. This section therefore merely summarises the debate.

The Prison Service issued its Statement of Purpose in 1988. It is on display in all Prison Service buildings and states: "Her Majesty's Prison Service serves the public by keeping in custody those committed by the courts. Our duty is to look after them with humanity and to help them lead law-abiding and useful lives in custody and after release." The Government still shows no inclination to incorporate this Statement of Purpose into the Prison Rules, and references to Rule 3 in official statements are few and far between. The Prison Service Review at the end of 1997 repeated calls for the Prison Service to have clear Visions, Goals, and Values, and that Key Performance Indicators should be reviewed to be more closely linked with these.

The Prison Service now seems to have a plethora of Visions, Aims Objectives, Values, and Principles. Besides the Statement of Purpose for the Prison Service issued previously, the Home Secretary issued a separate Statement of Purpose for the Home Office, of which the Prison Service is an Executive Agency. This Purpose is: "To build a safe, just, and tolerant society in which the rights and responsibilities of individuals, families, and communities are properly balanced, and the protection and security of the public are maintained." The Home Secretary set seven Aims to achieve the Statement of Purpose. Aim 4 specifically relates to the work of the Prison and Probation Services, namely "Effective execution of the sentences of the courts so as to reduce re-offending and protect the public." The Director General of the Prison Service announced these Aims, Objectives, and Principles for the Prison Service in February 1999 (*Performance Standards Programme* 1999).

Vivien Stern, then director of NACRO, stated that "...prisons are not there for prison staff and prison management. They have a wider social duty, if not to improve the people that are sent to them, at least to minimise the damage that enforced removal from the community into what a prisoner called 'a further education college of crime' can do. It is in the community's interest that the prison system should be just, open and accountable" (1989: 224). The 1991 White Paper, *Custody, Care and Justice*, stated that the role of the Prison Service "must be consistent with international human rights obligations" and "ensure that prisoners are treated with justice, humanity, dignity and respect" (paras. 1.2 and 1.3). It claims that the current Statement of Purpose incorporates these values, although "is not, by itself, a full or sufficient statement of the Prison Service's role in respect of unconvicted prisoners" (para. 7.5).

The Prison Service issued a separate Statement of Purpose for unconvicted prisoners, which states: "Unconvicted prisoners are presumed to be innocent. Subject to the duty to hold them and deliver them to court securely and to the need to maintain order in establishments they will be treated accordingly and, in particular, will be allowed all reasonable facilities to seek release on bail; preserve their accommodation and employment; prepare for trial; maintain contact with relatives and friends; pursue legitimate business and social interests; [and] obtain help with personal problems. They will receive health care appropriate to their needs. They will have opportunities for education, religious observance, exercise and recreation and, where possible, for training and work." The new Prison Service Aims, Objectives, and Principles make no specific reference to unconvicted prisoners, nor do they mention anything about the principle of physical separation of convicted and unconvicted prisoners, as European Rule 11.3 requires (see also r 7 Classification of prisoners).

Rules 3 and 6(3) together are very similar to European Prison Rule 3, although European Prison Rule 66 amplifies how the purpose of imprisonment may be achieved. The European Rules develop at some length the penal philosophy involved, particularly in European Rules 64 and 65 which have no equivalent in the Prison Rules. The Prison Rules also contain no equivalent to European Rules 1 and 2 prohibiting discrimination of any kind, providing for respect for religious beliefs, mandating that "Deprivation of liberty shall be effected in material and moral conditions which ensure respect for human dignity", and ensuring that these principles govern reception arrangements for prisoners. However, the Prison Service issued a highly detailed Race Relations Manual in 1991, which must be available in all prison libraries and has been translated into ten other languages (CI 13/1991), plus a public policy statement on race relations which "must be posted in prominent places where prisoners can see and read [it]," as well as in visitors' waiting areas (Race Relations Manual, pp. 9-10). The policy statement expands the statement in Circular Instruction 56/1983, which said: "The Prison Department is committed absolutely to a policy of racial equality and to the elimination of discrimination in all aspects of the work of the Prison Service. It is opposed also to any display of racial prejudice, either by work or conduct, by any member of this service in his dealings with any other person." The full statement is attached at Annex B.

The Prison Officers' Training Manual acknowledges that official attitudes to r 3 have changed. "The increasing emphasis on reformation over the first half of the twentieth century found expression in the placing of the treatment objective as [r 3]... From the mid-60's, however, the confidence in the treatment objective of prisons has now appeared to wane." The May Report (1979) proposed that r 3 (then known as rule 1) be rewritten so as to replace the treatment model with the concept of positive custody. Prison Service Operating Standards state that prisons should provide and encourage prisoners' participation in programmes which address offending behaviour, behaviour and addiction problems, coping with custody, and behaviour on release (U19). At present, the Prison Rules only allude to this in Rules 3, 4, and 5.

Despite any objectives stated in r 3, the emphasis following the highly publicised escapes from HMPs Whitemoor and Parkhurst in 1994 and 1995 was on security. This was particularly clear in the reports of the Woodcock and Learmont Inquiries following the escapes, but continued a priority in later reports such as that of the Home Affairs Committee in 1997, which described security as the "primary purpose" of the Prison Service (1997: viii). The Chief Inspector of Prisons noted in his 1998 Annual Report that the priorities of the Prison Service seem however to be shifting from security to both security and regimes: "...the fact that so much [money] has been given specifically for improving regimes, sends a very clear message that their provision now enjoys equal status with security" (1999: 2-3).

In its early reports the Inspectorate used r 3 as a general measure in examining the quality of prison regimes. In recent years, however, few if any references have been made to the Rule.

Circular Instruction 40/1988 defined several "regime aims" for Young Offender Institutions. According to the Instruction, such Institutions should "prepare the offender for resettlement in the community. The regimes should build on existing experience in youth custody centres and detention centres, co-ordinating and developing for all offenders positive regime activities designed to promote self-discipline and a sense of responsibility. The personal development of the offender will be achieved through purposeful activity and positive relationships" (CI 40/1988:3). Circular Instruction 40/1988 identified several ways to achieve these objectives, such as through improved personal relationships, a code of behaviour, sentence planning, activities and physical education, pre-release courses, through-care, and so on. However, the Chief Inspector of Prisons commented that, "In very few [of the Young Offender Institutions inspected] did we feel that the stated policy was being achieved or even attempted ... Circular Instruction 40/88 was published with a view to retaining the best of the borstal system and to place it in a contemporary setting. It is an inspirational document. Our experience shows that its spirit has been diluted by a series of initiatives aimed at structures and organisation" (1991: 6.26 and 6.53).

In an important speech in 1992 entitled "Relationships in the Prison Service", the then Director General of the Prison Service, Joe Pilling, said that the work of the Service should be characterised by respect for the prisoner, fairness, individuality, care, and openness (address to the Institute for the Study and Treatment of Delinquency, 11 June 1992). Identifying himself with the conclusion of the Woolf Report that good order in prisons depends on maintaining a balance between the needs of security, control, and justice, Mr. Pilling said:

> "We have a duty not to exacerbate the harmful effects of depriving people of their liberty. Prisoners should be treated according to the same standards we expect of each other. In other words, their basic human dignity and worth must be respected ... The values I have described are values to be adopted at every level of the Service. They apply both to those who make policy and those who implement it; to those in contact with prisoners and to those who manage and support them. They are a template against which all our work as a Service must be judged ... [T]here is renewed optimism about the chances of our making a real difference to the prospects of at least some prisoners leading a law-abiding life after release. The blanket optimism of thirty years ago and more will not come back but we now see that the reaction against that was too extreme ... We are moving from 'nothing works' to 'what works' and 'how to make it work better'."

Outside contacts

4. *(1) Special attention shall be paid to the maintenance of such relationships between a prisoner and his family as are desirable in the best interests of both. (2) A prisoner shall be encouraged and assisted to establish and maintain such relations with persons and agencies outside prison as may, in the opinion of the governor, best promote the interests of his family and his own social rehabilitation.*

The 1999 edition of the Prison Rules moved this rule and the next (After care) to the front of the Rules from their previous position as rules 31 and 32. The wording of the rules themselves has not changed, but the symbolic value of placing them at the front implies an increase in their priority to the Prison Service. To some extent this may be in response to one of the three main recommendations in the 1997 Prison Service Review, which was for a "new focus on the delivery of effective regimes and preparation for release" (1997: 3). The Prison-Probation Review also emphasised the need for increased co-operation between the Prison and Probation Services (Home Office 1998a).

In his 1991 Annual Report, the then Chief Inspector of Prisons commended the community activities and links available for prisoners at many establishments and encouraged the expansion of such projects. "The opportunity for inmates to experience trust and respect and to regain some self esteem are crucial parts of training in personal development. Community activities afford such opportunities to individuals and to groups of inmates in a variety of ways" (para. 3.57). The Association of Metropolitan Authorities, in a memorandum to the Education, Science and Arts Committee, also encouraged links between the prison education service and the outside community. "Wherever possible, prisoners should be encouraged to participate in education outside prisons and members of the outside community should be involved widely in provision within prisons. Social education should include more practical elements, so as to help inmates manage their daily lives within the prison, with a view to facilitating their return to society" (1991: 58).

While this Rule makes no reference to reparation, the Prison Service Operating Standards suggest that prisoners should be encouraged to make reparation through community work and activities (U20). The Operating Standards also state that prisoners should be offered advice and assistance on safeguarding any outside employment and accommodation while they are in custody (O7 and X3-5).

After a crackdown on home leaves and outside work placements in the mid-1990s, many prisoners are once again able to work in the community. The Chief Inspector of Prisons stated that "Current figures suggest that 90 per cent of those leaving prison will be unemployed, at least initially. As a job is one of the three factors that evidence suggests to be most influential in persuading an individual away from a life of crime, preparing him or her for what is most likely to lead to employment must be a key weapon in the fight on re-offending" (1999: 12). The introduction of Home Detention Curfew in 1999 following the 1998 Crime and Disorder Act may also increase the value of r 4 in practice. The Curfew is intended to replace the final period of custody for prisoners aged 18 or over sentenced to at least three months and less than four years. Prison Service Order 6700 sets out the details of eligibility.

(See r 5 After care, r 8 Privileges, r 35 Letters and visits, and r 38 Legal advisers.)

After care

5. *From the beginning of a prisoner's sentence, consideration shall be given, in consultation with the appropriate after-care organisation, to the prisoner's future and the assistance to be given him on and after his release.*

The Prison Rules lack any of the detail provided in European Rules 87, 88, and 89.

Under the Criminal Justice Act 1991, the Probation Service supervises all young offenders and all adult offenders sentenced to one year or more on their release from custody (CI 17/1992). Such supervision is intended to continue the work undertaken during the prisoner's time in custody and pursue or create such links outside, e.g. "training or education courses, by continuing to address particular aspects of offending behaviour, or by building on links established with help agencies in the community" (CI 17/1992 Guidance Notes, para. 2.7).

In its 1986 thematic review, *The Preparation of Prisoners for Release*, the Prison Inspectorate argued that home leave should be used more frequently, that there should be greater access to telephones and visits to contact potential employers, and that prisoners should more systematically be transferred to the prison closest to their discharge address for the period prior to release (1986: 5.21-5.30). Haines (1990) agreed with the need to concentrate on family ties and social links outside prison, saying that "one of the most consistent findings to come out of the British research is that socially isolated prisoners seem to experience more difficulties on their release from prison, and tend to have higher reconviction rates" (1990: 35). The White Paper *Custody, Care and Justice* (1991) accepted the recommendations in the Woolf Report to increase prisoners' contact with the outside community through increased opportunities for home leave, visits, and telephone calls. Throughcare based on prisoners' identified individual needs has been incorporated into the Prison Service Operating Standards (P2; P4 - 8). This includes an onus on establishments to identify prisoners who need help finding accommodation and to offer them advice, assistance, and facilities to obtain suitable accommodation prior to their release (X3). (See also commentary to r 9 Temporary release and r 35 Letters and visits.)

Circular Instruction 12/1991 encouraged prison staff and probation officers to take a more active role in the identification and throughcare of drug misusers. According to the Instruction, such efforts may range from linking the prisoner with "suitable community-based agencies" to "taking or initiating all possible action to find work, training or activity for the discharged prisoner. Similarly a seconded probation officer should make referrals to the community based agencies specialising in helping drug misusers wherever appropriate."

The sentence plans proposed in the Woolf Report and accepted in *Custody, Care and Justice* were intended to make more constructive use of the time spent in prison and to establish links with after-care services. At present, however, sentence plans focus almost entirely on longer term prisoners. Goodman (1986/7) criticised after-care services in England, stating that they are poorly resourced and without clear goals or aims. In addition, the Home Office had given it a low priority in past statements such as in its 'Statement of National Objectives and Priorities' (Haines 1990).

(See also rr 20-21 Medical attendance and r 32 Education.)

Maintenance of order and discipline

6.   *(1) Order and discipline shall be maintained with firmness, but with no more restriction than is required for safe custody and well ordered community life. (2) In the control of prisoners, officers shall seek to influence them through their own example and leadership, and to enlist their willing co-operation. (3) At all times the treatment of prisoners shall be such as to encourage their self- respect and a sense of personal responsibility, but a prisoner shall not be employed in any disciplinary capacity.*

Like r 6, the principle in the Prison Service Operating Standards states that "Prisoners should be treated fairly, with justice, humanity, and respect as individuals whilst in prison custody" (Op. Std. A1). This Standard was designed to reflect the Prison Service Statement of Purpose, which requires that prisoners are treated as individuals. Although these guidelines and r 6 itself stress self-respect, "the Rules go on to regulate or authorise restriction of nearly every element of human existence - the very antithesis of self-respect and personal responsibility" (Marin 1983:72).

Recent research on staff-prisoner relations emphasised that "Staff matter, more than they realise. They embody a prison's regime, and they possess significant distributive power" (Liebling and Price 1999: ii). Referring to r 6, the Prior Report stated: "We cannot over-emphasise the importance we attach to the formation of good relationships between staff and prisoners" (1985: 2.20). European Prison Rule 66(d) notes that communication between prisoners and staff should be facilitated. The 1991 White Paper *Custody, Care and Justice* acknowledged these principles, saying "The quality of the relationship between prisoners and staff is the key to a stable prison system" (para. 1.29).

The Prison Service is considering ways of improving such relations, such as a less militaristic style of uniform (as proposed in the Woolf Report), and has accepted - but not implemented - such proposals as having staff wear badges showing their name and rank or job title (1991: paras. 4.19 and 4.20). Circular Instruction 34/1991 introduces a presumption *against* the wearing of hats and caps as part of the normal uniform since "the wearing of uniform headgear during normal day-to-day duties, particularly when indoors, does not help to foster the development of effective and co-operative relationships between staff and inmates, or between uniformed and non-uniformed staff." Staff at privately-managed prisons often wear civilian-style uniforms such as a jacket and trousers.

HM Chief Inspector of Prisons stated in his 1991 Annual Report, "As change is achieved more by influence than authority, [officers] must learn not to rely on their uniform; we see no need for staff in young offender establishments to wear uniforms" (para. 6.50). The most recent Annual Report continued this theme: "The difference in approach between new and old cultures is best summed up by the word 'attitude', described at HMP Wolds as being the little thing that means so much, both to prisoners and each other. The dominant theme in this is human engagement, a phrase that will, I hope, become much more widely used as a determinant for how staff/prisoner relations should be conducted" (1999: 26).

Rule 6(3) and European Prison Rule 34.1 both prohibit the employment of a prisoner in a disciplinary capacity.

In *Williams No. 2* (1981) Tudor Evans J considered alleged breaches of the Prison Rules, including r 6, in relation to the plaintiff's imprisonment. Williams contended that:

(a) para. 14 of Circular Instruction 35/1974, on setting up control units ("The regime in the unit is not directed towards providing 'treatment'; there is no expectation that it will cure prisoners of wanting to stir up trouble; only demonstrate to them that it does not pay to do so") was in violation of the 'training and treatment' requirement of r 3;

(b) the regime in the control unit constituted a breach of r 6(1) [then r 2], because r 45 [then r 43], providing in effect for cellular confinement, should be read with r 6(1) in mind;

(c) because the staff in the control unit were instructed to be cold and unresponsive, this resulted in breaches of r 6(2) and (3), which provide that prison staff shall influence prisoners by good example, encourage self-respect and a sense of responsibility, and should enlist the prisoners' willing co-operation;

(d) there were breaches of r 7(3) [then r 3], which provides that a prisoner shall not be deprived unduly of the society of persons, and of r 31 [then r 28], which provides that arrangements should be made to allow prisoners to work, where possible, outside cells and in association with one another. The plaintiff submitted that these two rules confer a right to association breached by the regime of the control unit.

The judge found that these breaches were not substantiated, that instructions to the prison staff in the control unit to avoid confrontations with prisoners were not contrary to the Prison Rules, and that the deprivation of the society of other persons was not excessive. For further discussion of this case, see rr 26 and 45.

Classification of prisoners

7.   *(1) Prisoners shall be classified, in accordance with any directions of the Secretary of State, having regard to their age, temperament and record and with a view to maintaining good order and facilitating training and, in the case of convicted prisoners, of furthering the purpose of their training and treatment as provided by rule 3.*

(2) Unconvicted prisoners:

   (a) shall be kept out of contact with convicted prisoners as far as the governor considers it can reasonably be done, unless and to the extent that they have consented to share residential accommodation or participate in any activity with convicted prisoners; and

   (b) shall under no circumstances be required to share a cell with a convicted prisoner.

(3) Prisoners committed or attached for contempt of court, or for failing to do or abstain from doing anything required to be done or left undone:

   (a) shall be treated as a separate class for the purposes of this rule;

   (b) notwithstanding anything in this rule, may be permitted to associate with any other class of prisoners if they are willing to do so; and

   (c) shall have the same privileges as an unconvicted prisoner under rules 20(5), 23(1) and 35(1).

(4) Nothing in this rule shall require a prisoner to be deprived unduly of the society of other persons.

Rule 7 does not provide for individual prisoner planning, whether or not regarded as treatment. Nothing in the rule allows for prisoners' involvement in their own individual treatment programmes or encourages prisoners to assume responsibility "in certain sectors of the institution's activity" (European Rule 62.2). European Rule 11.3 provides that "in principle" untried prisoners shall not be put in contact with convicted prisoners against their will, whereas r 7(2) provides for this only "as far as this can reasonably be done".

Although it mentions age as a factor to be taken into consideration, r 7(1) does not provide for special treatment of young prisoners on remand or after conviction as European Prison Rule 11.4 does. The European Rule states that they are to be "detained under conditions which as far as possible protect them from harmful influences and which take into account the needs peculiar to their age". Article 10(3) of the Civil and Political Rights Covenant, which the UK has ratified, specifies that: "Juvenile offenders shall be segregated from adults and accorded treatment appropriate to their age and legal status." The Chief Inspector of Prisons noted in his thematic review on Young Offenders (1997a) that age mixing was still taking place, in breach of the UN Convention on the Rights of the Child. He recommended the abolition of Prison Service custody for people under the age of 18. A similar proposal by the Chief Inspectors of Prisons and Social Work Services in Scotland (1998) was accepted by the Scottish Office in relation to female offenders under age 18, but the Home Office has yet to make such a commitment. Indeed, it is now assumed that the Prison Service will be a principal provider of places to the Youth Justice Board, established under the Crime and Disorder Act (1998) with responsibility for setting, purchasing, and monitoring standards for the treatment and conditions of all people under the age of 18 who enter the criminal justice system. "The Prison Service now realises that, unless it delivers standards imposed on it by the YJB, its services will not be purchased" (HMCIP 1999: 13). The *Flood* judgement (1998) declared that young offenders under the age of 18 must only be allocated to establishments (or parts of establishments) designated as Young Offender Institutions.

Every prison for adult males falls into one of two basic categories: local prisons and training prisons. Every prisoner is first received into custody at a local prison. Most allocation decisions are taken locally, but decisions on certain prisoners are taken centrally by the Prison Service. Prisoners are classified into four security categories as a matter of administrative practice and not by any statutory requirement.

About 15 per cent of the prison population is awaiting categorisation at any one time, though Operating Standard C1 states that security categorisation should be made within seven days of sentence. The commentary to the Standard emphasises that prisoners should be considered for the lowest security category first, and only moved to a higher category if unsuitable. The Standards also state that sentenced prisoners should be allocated and transferred to the allocated establishment within 28 days (Op. Std. C3), and that this security category and allocation should be reviewed at least annually (C4).

A higher proportion of prisoners have been placed in higher categories of security since the Woodcock and Learmont Inquiries in 1994 and 1995. Learmont emphasised that "categorisation is fundamental to security. It is the key to ensuring the safe custody of prisoners and work on its improvement must be given proper priority" (1995: 5.8). Category 'A' prisoners, or those whose escape would be "highly dangerous to the public, police or security of the state", make up about 2.2 per cent of prisoners (more than double the proportion in 1991). Category 'B' prisoners (those for whom "escape must be made difficult") make up approximately 19 per cent. Category 'C' prisoners (66.4 per cent, compared to 48 per cent in 1991) are those who "cannot be trusted in open conditions but do not have the ability or resources to make a determined escape attempt". Finally, category 'D' prisoners (12.4 percent, compared to 17 per cent in 1991) can be "trusted" in an open prison. Unsentenced prisoners are assumed to be in category 'B' unless provisionally placed in Category 'A' (AMBoV Handbook 1991 and Prison Service Headquarters 1999; these figures do not include female offenders, young offenders, remands, or convicted unsentenced prisoners). *Custody , Care and Justice* signalled the introduction of a formal system of categorisation for remand prisoners (para. 5.22), though this has not yet been put into place.

European Rule 12(b) provides for prisoner classification, "to facilitate their treatment and social resettlement taking into account the management and security requirements"; European Rules 13 and 68 provide for individualisation of treatment and separate units or institutions determined by the nature of the treatment to be provided. Rule 7 does not mention the relation between prisoner classification and different types of establishment. There are wide geographical variations in the categorisation of prisoners, dependent not on the threat to the public or an objective assessment of individual needs but on the availability of accommodation of different security classifications. For example, speaking of the four Prison Department Regions (now twelve areas and a directorate of high security establishments), Professor Rod Morgan wrote: "Midland Region places the highest proportion of prisoners in Category D because it has the most open places to fill: correspondingly, its parsimonious use of Category B reflects its relative shortage of higher security places. The same pattern emerges in all four regions ... There is no suggestion that this variation in regional categorisation decisions has had adverse security repercussions" (Morgan 1980: 35). HM Chief Inspector of Prisons indicated that this practice still occurs: "... in theory no-one should be allowed to move through the system - Category A to B to C to D - unless they have qualified to do so by completing required parts of their sentence plan at each level. However this sensible procedure has been severely disrupted by the effects of overcrowding, the Prison Service having to operate at over capacity the whole time and ensure that every available bed-space is occupied" (1999: 9).

Neither the Prison Rules nor the European Prison Rules provide for a prisoner to be heard on the question of reviewing his classification, and this issue does not fall within the scope of the European Convention (*Brady v UK* 1979). Since the decision in *Hague and Weldon* (1991), administrative decisions such as categorisation procedures are subject to judicial review. Further, the Divisional Court ruled in *Duggan* (1994) that the duty of prior disclosure of the gist of facts or opinions relevant to a proposed allocation of a prisoner to category A was necessary for procedural fairness. The Court also ruled that reasons must be given for any decision to keep a prisoner as category A. However, "... the Prison Service is not obliged to disclose any material which might imperil prison security or the safety of informers" (Livingstone and Owen 1999: 4.15). Allocation as category A upon first reception can be made without these procedural safeguards.

The Court of Appeal in *ex p McAvoy* (1998) maintained that disclosure of the reports themselves was not necessary for procedural fairness, and that the willingness of the review team to consider the individual circumstances of a case regarding whether additional material should be made available was a sufficient safeguard. As yet, the ruling in *Peries* (1997) prevents the safeguards in *Duggan* (1994) (with the exception of the obligation to give reasons for decisions) from being applied in decisions on other security categories. Jowitt J declared this on the grounds that placement in other security categories did not have the same implications as placement in category A. "It follows that unless and until *Peries* is overturned prisoners who are re-categorised within Categories B - D are significantly worse off than prisoners allocated to category A in terms of the requirements of fairness imposed on the Prison Service" (Livingstone and Owen 1999: 4.09).

The High Court in *Purcell* (1998) ruled that convictions which are 'spent' under the Rehabilitation of Offenders Act 1974 may still be taken into account for a prisoner's security classification since the Category A Committee and Review Team each qualify as a 'judicial authority' under the terms of the Act.

Privileges

8.   *(1) There shall be established at every prison systems of privileges approved by the Secretary of State and appropriate to the classes of prisoners there, which shall include arrangements under which money earned by prisoners in prison may be spent by them within the prison.*

   (2) Systems of privileges approved under paragraph (1) may include arrangements under which prisoners may be allowed time outside their cells and in association with one another, in excess of the minimum time which, subject to the other provisions of these Rules apart from this rule, is otherwise allowed to prisoners at the prison for this purpose.

   (3) Systems of privileges approved under paragraph (1) may include arrangements under which privileges may be granted to prisoners only in so far as they have met, and for so long as they continue to meet, specified standards in their behaviour and their performance in work or other activities.

   (4) Systems of privileges which include arrangements of the kind referred to in paragraph (3) shall include procedures to be followed in determining whether or not any of the privileges concerned shall be granted, or shall continue to be granted, to a prisoner; such procedures shall include a requirement that the prisoner be given reasons for any decision adverse to him together with a statement of the means by which he may appeal against it.

   (5) Nothing in this rule shall be taken to confer on a prisoner any entitlement to any privilege or to affect any provision in these Rules other than this rule as a result of which any privilege may be forfeited or otherwise lost or a prisoner deprived of association with other prisoners.

The European Prison Rules deal with privileges in a limited manner, providing prisoners with the means of keeping informed through books, papers, radio or TV "or by any similar means as authorised or controlled by the administration" (European Rule 45), and with the ability of untried prisoners to obtain at their own expense books, papers, writing materials "and other means of occupation as are compatible with the interests of the administration of justice and the security and good order of the institution" (European Rule 97). No guidance is given on reasons for the suspension of privileges in the European Prison Rules or in r 8.

Standing Order 4 states that a 'facility' (still referred to as 'privileges' in practice) includes the retention, acquisition, and use of personal possessions (including smoking materials), use of the prison shop, expenditure of private cash, engaging in cell activities and hobbies, entering public competitions, wearing of own clothes or footwear, and taking part in activities in association (SO 4: 3). Which privileges are available depends on the availability of resources and on management requirements, so therefore may differ even in different parts of the same establishment. A privilege may be forfeited as a punishment for an offence against discipline or may be withdrawn as specified in the Order, but not otherwise.

The Order divides privileges into two groups: those which are available to all prisoners, and those which are at the discretion of the governor. The first category covers facilities to make purchases, newspapers, periodicals and books, personal radios, tobacco, general notebooks and drawing books, and public competitions. The Order takes account of the finding of the European Commission of Human Rights in *Tejendrasingh v UK* (1983) that the Home Office was in breach of the European Convention of Human Rights. The case involved access to notebooks and newspapers while the applicant was subject to disciplinary punishments. Now "A prisoner is entitled to be issued with a general notebook (in addition to notebooks issued by Education Officers) and a drawing book ... [these] will be withdrawn if they are misused in any way likely to affect the security, good order or discipline of the establishment, or if they contain material likely to jeopardise national security or encourage the commission of crime. Where a book is withdrawn a note of the reasons should be made in the prisoner's record and the prisoner informed ...Where a personal newspaper has been withdrawn or withheld from a prisoner, either as part of a punishment for an offence against prison discipline or for any other reason [as set out in the Order], arrangements will be made, e.g. through the availability of newspapers provided at public expense, to ensure that the prisoner is not normally deprived of access to newspapers altogether" (SO 4: 30, 36, and 43).

The second category deals with personal possessions, cell activities, and association. The Order notes that "Prisoners shall be allowed to have sufficient property in possession to lead as normal and individual an existence as possible within the constraints of the prison environment and the limitations under this and other standing orders" (SO 4: 7). Limitations on a prisoner's property through volumetric control place the biggest restraints on these quantities in practice (see discussion in r 43 Prisoners' property). Prisoners may, at their own risk, make mail order purchases through companies which belong to the Mail Order Protection Scheme, though these items must remain the property of the prisoner who purchased them and may not be given, lent, or sold to another prisoner without the governor's permission. Prisoners may not purchase services (such as a barber or hairdresser) or personal tuition, and governors may not arrange for such services to be provided commercially except for recorded language courses or distance learning facilities approved by the Education Officer. Governors may make additions to the published list of the items that prisoners may retain in their possession, subject to the approval of the area manager. The governor may restrict the display of material which he or she believes is likely to cause offence to others "by reason of its indecent, violent or racist content" (SO 4: 37).

The privilege of association with other prisoners is stated to include dining, recreation, and entertainment; work, religious services, and education classes do not count as association under Standing Order 4. Where opportunities for association are limited, convicted and unconvicted prisoners under age 21 will have priority over adults in the same establishment. Prisoners may be excluded or removed from all association or from a specified group activity only in their own interests or for the maintenance of good order and discipline, if they are refractory or violent, to restrain the prisoner pending the governor's initial hearing of a disciplinary charge, or as a result of a punishment given at an adjudication. A governor grade must take any decision to cancel a period of association on all occasions. "Where, exceptionally, the governor decides not to allow a prisoner one or more of the facilities in the published statement, he or she will give an explanation to the prisoner concerned, in writing if the prisoner so requests" (SO 4: 5).

The Chief Inspector of Prisons criticised the fact that association may be limited: "Regimes are determined by staff attendance systems. These embrace rigid shift patterns. The net result is a reduction in time out of cell during evenings and weekends in many establishments because the regime moves towards programming everything between 8 am and 4 pm on weekdays for the convenience of staff. The priority should be to maximise time out of cell first and then construct shift patterns to complement these arrangements" (1991: 3.26). He also noted marked differences between establishments, even of the same category, in the length and quality of facilities for association.

Circular Instruction 75/1995 introduced the Incentives and Earned Privileges Scheme. This Scheme links five main earnable privileges (private cash, extra or improved visits, enhanced earning schemes, earned community visits if eligible, and in-cell television) directly to a prisoner's behaviour. Other local privileges and, where prisoners on different privilege levels share the same accommodation, the possibility for convicted prisoners to wear their own clothes and increased time out of cell for association may also be part of the Scheme. The Incentives Scheme varies between prisons, even those of the same type. The Chief Inspector of Prisons argued strongly against such inequality between prisons generally: "If there is one word that covers my concerns about current treatment and conditions of prisoners it is 'inconsistency'.... This is manifest in every prison up and down the country with the notable exception of the Dispersal estate, which has its own Director" (1999: 21).

In the case of Incentives and Earned Privileges, the Court of Appeal in *Bowen* (1998) judged that such differences between establishments did not constitute unlawful delegation of the Secretary of State's powers under the Prison Act. The Divisional Court also ruled in *Hepworth* (1997) that, "it would take an exceptionally strong case to justify review of the criteria on which earned privileges could be granted or removed..." (Livingstone and Owen (1999: 5.36). However, Livingstone and Owen go on to explain that "once a set of criteria has been adopted, a prisoner acting consistently with them can argue that he has a legitimate expectation that, at the very least, any privilege accorded to him should not be removed without a hearing" (para. 5.38).

While the Incentives and Earned Privileges Scheme is linked with a prisoner's behaviour and was designed to give prison staff increased discretion and control without having to resort to formal disciplinary procedures, the Scheme is *not* part of the formal disciplinary system in prisons. The danger is that, as with other administrative controls, prisoners will *feel* as though the Scheme can be a punishment, and prison staff may use it as such.

The Rules are quite specific about the privileges which may be forfeited directly. Rule 55(b) provides that privileges subject to forfeiture are those made under r 8. Privileges which the Rules create directly, as opposed to those resulting from delegation under r 8, are apparently not forfeitable under rule 55(b). For unconvicted prisoners, these may include forfeiture of the 'right' to be supplied with their own books, newspapers, writing materials, and other means of occupation provided for in r 43(1) (forfeiture authorised by r 55(g)). For convicted prisoners forfeiture of rule-created privileges includes exclusion from associated work (r 55(c)), and stoppage of earnings (r 55(d)).

The Rules do not recognise a right for convicted prisoners to have property of their own for use in prison. They are only permitted it as a privilege under r 8 or because of an exercise of the governor's discretion in their favour, under r 43(2) or r 44(4).

(See also r 25(2) Alcohol and tobacco, and r 55 Governors' punishments.)

Temporary release

9.   (1) *The Secretary of State may, in accordance with the other provisions of this rule, release temporarily a prisoner to whom this rule applies.*

(2) *A prisoner may be released under this rule for any period or periods and subject to any conditions.*

(3) *A prisoner may only be released under this rule:*

(a) *on compassionate grounds or for the purpose of receiving medical treatment;*

(b) *to engage in employment or voluntary work;*

(c) *to receive instruction or training which cannot reasonably be provided in the prison;*

(d) *to enable him to participate in any proceedings before any court, tribunal or inquiry;*

(e) *to enable him to consult with his legal adviser in circumstances where it is not reasonably practicable for the consultation to take place in the prison;*

(f) *to assist any police officer in any enquiries;*

(g) *to facilitate the prisoner's transfer between prisons;*

(h) *to assist him in maintaining family ties or in his transition from prison life to freedom; or*

(i) *to enable him to make a visit in the locality of the prison, as a privilege under rule 8.*

(4) *A prisoner shall not be released under this rule unless the Secretary of State is satisfied that there would not be an unacceptable risk of his committing offences whilst released or otherwise failing to comply with any condition upon which he is released.*

(5) *The Secretary of State shall not release under this rule a prisoner serving a sentence of imprisonment if, having regard to:*

(a) *the period or proportion of his sentence which the prisoner has served or, in a case where paragraph (10) does not apply to require all the sentences he is serving to be treated as a single term, the period or proportion of any such sentence he has served; and*

(b) *the frequency with which the prisoner has been granted temporary release under this rule, the Secretary of State is of the opinion that the release of the prisoner would be likely to undermine public confidence in the administration of justice.*

(6) *If a prisoner has been temporarily released under this rule during the*

relevant period and has been sentenced to imprisonment for a criminal offence committed whilst at large following that release, he shall not be released under this rule unless his release, having regard to the circumstances of this conviction, would not, in the opinion of the Secretary of State, be likely to undermine public confidence in the administration of justice.

(7) For the purposes of paragraph (6), "the relevant period":

(a) *in the case of a prisoner serving a determinate sentence of imprisonment, is the period he has served in respect of that sentence, unless, notwithstanding paragraph (10), the sentences he is serving do not fall to be treated as a single term, in which case it is the period since he was last released in relation to one of those sentences under Part II of the Criminal Justice Act 1991 ("the 1991 Act")[4];*

(b) *in the case of a prisoner serving an indeterminate sentence of imprisonment, is, if the prisoner has previously been released on licence under Part II of the Crime (Sentences) Act 1997[5] or Part II of the 1991 Act, the period since the date of his last recall to prison in respect of that sentence or, where the prisoner has not been so released, the period he has served in respect of that sentence; or*

(c) *in the case of a prisoner detained in prison for any other reason, is the period for which the prisoner has been detained for that reason; save that where a prisoner falls within two or more of sub-paragraphs (a) to (c), the "relevant period", in the case of that prisoner, shall be determined by whichever of the applicable sub-paragraphs produces the longer period.*

(8) A prisoner released under this rule may be recalled to prison at any time whether the conditions of his release have been broken or not.

(9) This rule applies to prisoners other than persons committed in custody for trial or to be sentenced or otherwise dealt with before or by any Crown Court or remanded in custody by any court.

(10) For the purposes of any reference in this rule to a prisoner's sentence, consecutive terms and terms which are wholly or partly concurrent shall be treated as a single term if they would fall to be treated as a single term for the purposes of any reference to the term of imprisonment to which a person has been sentenced in Part II of the 1991 Act.

(11) In this rule:

(a) *any reference to a sentence of imprisonment shall be construed as including any sentence to detention or custody; and*

(b) *any reference to release on licence or otherwise under Part II of the 1991 Act includes any release on licence under any legislation providing for early release on licence.*

Prison Rule 9 has no equivalent European Prison Rule, although European Rule 70.2 discusses home leave.

Sentenced young offenders held in prisons and remand centres and civil prisoners are also subject to Rule 9 (CI 36/1989:5). Those who are not eligible for temporary release include unconvicted and convicted unsentenced prisoners, sentenced prisoners who are remanded on further charges, those detained under the Immigration Act 1971, foreign nationals and Commonwealth citizens who are to be deported at the end of their sentence, prisoners subject to extradition proceedings, those considered mentally ill or suffering from mental disorder or who have been committed to prison as a place of safety, and prisoners who are in category 'A' or on the escape list (SO 7E: 7a-g). These prisoners may, however, be allowed the alternative of escorted absences in certain circumstances.

The White Paper *Custody, Care and Justice* extended the number of opportunities for home leave in open prisons from three times per year to six and planned to "consider the further extension of home leave arrangements" (1991: 7.37). Prison Service Instruction 46/1998 sets out the provisions for release on temporary licence and recall. (See also sec. 103 - 105 of the Crime and Disorder Act 1998 regarding recall to prison.)

Ethnic monitoring of temporary release decisions is described as best practice in the Annex to AG 32/1995 on Race Relations.

Information to prisoners

10.   (1) *Every prisoner shall be provided, as soon as possible after his reception into prison, and in any case within 24 hours, with information in writing about those provisions of these Rules and other matters which it is necessary that he should know, including earnings and privileges, and the proper means of making requests and complaints.*

(2) *In the case of a prisoner aged less than 18, or a prisoner aged 18 or over who cannot read or appears to have difficulty in understanding the information so provided, the governor, or an officer deputed by him, shall so explain it to him that he can understand his rights and obligations.*

(3) *A copy of these Rules shall be made available to any prisoner who requests it.*

According to Livingstone and Owen, "The Prison Service does not regard [r 10] as including the provision of copies of all Orders and current Instructions, though a refusal to do so in the face of a direct request by a prisoner could be challenged by means of an application of judicial review" (1999: 1.41). Prison Service Instruction 1/1997, however, states that "as a general principle, prisoners will be allowed access, through libraries in Prison Service establishments, to all Orders and Instructions which affect them", though "some parts... will, for security reasons, not be accessible to prisoners."

The Prisoners' Information Book (F 2311), produced jointly by the Prison Service and the Prison Reform Trust, should be issued on first reception to all prisoners and young offenders. Prisoners are then issued with updated copies or informed that they may request one. Remand prisoners are required to return the Information Book when they go to court; if they are subsequently re-committed to prison, another copy is issued only to those prisoners who handed in their previous copy (IG 83/1995).

Sentenced prisoners will be asked to return their Prisoners' Information Book on discharge, but will not be punished if it is lost or destroyed (CI 32/1991). Further copies are not issued upon transfer unless the prisoner has handed in the original copy, so a prisoner's original copy should generally stay with his or her personal property.

Prison libraries must keep spare copies of the Prisoners' Information Book for reference. Prisoners who have difficulty understanding the Book must have their rights and obligations explained to them, especially regarding the requirements of the Prison Rules. Rule 10(2) and European Rule 41.2 require information to be conveyed orally to prisoners with reading difficulties. There is in addition a pressing need for written information to prisoners to be supplied in languages other than English and in clearer and simplified language: evidence suggests that 15 percent of prisoners have a reading age below the age of 10 (Education, Science and Arts Committee 1991, q.16). If prisoners cannot read English and the Prisoners' Information Book is not available in the appropriate language, "the Governor will ensure that the necessary information is explained to them..." (SO 1A 50). A cassette with a summary of the information should be in each prison library, and the Book is also available in 16 foreign languages. Operating Standard A3 states that facilities for interpretation should be available for essential communication with prisoners.

Standing Order 1A requires that the Reception Board must ensure that prisoners know what further information can be available to them and how they can obtain them, including all the documents listed in SO 7B as stocked by the library (para. 52). Although governors are encouraged to supply local information in addition to the Prisoners' Information Book, this is not mandatory.

Like r 10, European Prison Rule 41.1 states only that prisoners should be provided with "written information about the regulations governing the treatment of prisoners", and not the regulations themselves. It does not specify a time limit within which this information is to be supplied, merely "on admission". Rule 10(3) provides that the Prison Rules shall be made available to any prisoner who requests them. The Prison Service Operating Standards state not only that information should be provided personally to prisoners on reception (including the Prisoners' Information Book within 24 hours of reception; N11), but also throughout the period of custody "unless there is a clear and justifiable reason to deny access to such documents" (commentary to Op. Std. A2). The Standards also recommend an induction programme for all prisoners to introduce them to an establishment and to assess prisoners' needs (Section O).

European Rule 41.1 requires the prison administration to inform prisoners of "the authorised methods of seeking information and making complaints, and all such other matters as are necessary to understand the rights and obligations of prisoners and to adapt to the life of the institution". In practice, sources of crucial information may be constructively withheld, simply because prisoners are not made aware of their right to ask for such documents. The Prisoners' Information Book informs prisoners of their right to such material, but the Prison Rules have not yet incorporated a guarantee to such information as the European Rules do. The Prison Service Operating Standards specify that establishments should provide information and advice about legal aid and representation, bail, and contact with solicitors (Op. Std. E1). (See also rr 38-39 Legal advisers and correspondence with legal advisers and courts.)

European Rule 41.1 requires prisoners to be informed of the disciplinary requirements of the institution; r 10 does not, and should do so. The Prisoners' Information Book contains r 51 in its entirety, and explains other relevant Rules, then refers prisoners to the Prison Discipline Manual for more detailed information. As the commentary following r 51 demonstrates, there has been considerable legal debate of the disciplinary rules, and it is unreasonable to expect a prisoner to know and understand them, or indeed to require the ordinary prison officer to explain and interpret them, on the basis of the language of the Rules alone. Members of Boards of Visitors may share the same difficulty (see commentary to r 78).

Operating Standard A4 emphasises the recommendation in the Woolf Report (1991) and in the White Paper *Custody, Care and Justice* (1991) that reasons should be given to prisoners for decisions which affect them.

According to the Criminal Justice Act 1991 Detailed Guide, "Ministers have now given a firm commitment to give prisoners meaningful reasons for parole decisions and to let prisoners have access to the information on which the reasons were based" (para. 23). Information held about a prisoner should be disclosed to that prisoner on request (Op. Std. A5). Exceptions to this include "security grounds; when necessary to prevent crime; to protect third parties; and where authorised by the medical officer" (commentary to Op. Std. A4). The Standards also recommend consultation with prisoners about matters which affect them (A6).

The Court of Appeal decision in *Wilson* (1992) allows prisoners to have access to the reports against them in order to represent themselves adequately at parole hearings. Lord Justice Taylor explained that "Since *Payne, Gunnell*, and *Bradley* were decided, the approach of the Home Office to procedures before the Parole Board has greatly changed and new statutory provisions are in place. When they come into force, there can be no doubt that the appellant will be entitled by statute to the disclosure he now seeks. The authorities therefore believe that prisoners such as this appellant should be so entitled. In my judgement it would be unjust that he should have to wait for many months to obtain disclosure and that he should be deprived of it on the current review." In *Georghiades* (1992), the High Court quashed a decision to refuse parole after it ruled that important information had wrongly been withheld from the plaintiff. Lord Justice Watkins confirmed the ruling in *Wilson*, stating that applicants should see any information about them so they can adequately defend themselves.

The Court of Appeal decision in *Walsh* (1992) established that prisoners serving discretionary life sentences are entitled to know the length of their tariff. From October 1992, "discretionary lifers... who have completed their tariffs will have the right to appeal to specially constituted panels of the Parole Board at formal hearings where they will have the right to appear in person and to see reports about them shown to the panels. If they can establish they are not dangerous, they will be entitled to release as of right" (Fitzgerald 1992: para. 6).

Further, the Court of Appeal decision in *Doody, Pierson, Smart and Pegg* (1992) gives mandatory lifers the right to know the length of their tariff, the reason for the length of their tariff, and whether the Home Secretary increased the tariff period which the judges recommended. The Home Secretary is under no obligation to give reasons for setting a higher tariff, though "if the disparity between the two periods is considerable, and he gave no reasons, it might well be that his decision would be open to challenge by way of judicial review on the grounds that it was irrational" (*The Guardian* 13 May 1992). The High Court confirmed this in *Doody* (1994), among other cases. The cases of *Wilson, Georghiades*, and *Doody* entitle prisoners to have access to all relevant information regarding their case in order to make adequate representation to the Home Secretary or Parole Board. Circular Instruction 85/1992 entitles prisoners to a note of the Parole Board's detailed reasons for refusing parole.

(See r 11 Requests and complaints, rr 20-21 Medical attendance, r 33 Library books, and r 78 Particular Duties [of Boards of Visitors].)

Requests and complaints

11. *(1) A request or complaint to the governor or board of visitors relating to a prisoner's imprisonment shall be made orally or in writing by the prisoner.*
(2) On every day the governor shall hear any requests and complaints that are made to him under paragraph (1).
(3) A written request or complaint under paragraph (1) may be made in confidence.

Prisoners have no absolute right to see the No. 1 Governor but only the governor grades in general or "a senior member of staff" (Prisoners' Information Book). Prison Rule 80 states that governors may delegate any of their duties, which includes the duty to hear applications.

Standing Order 5C mentions the right to petition the Monarch and Parliament. Prisoners may take up grievances at any time with people outside the prison management, including the Boards of Visitors, parliament, the European Court of Human Rights, and so on, though prisoners should use the internal procedures as a starting point because it is generally faster (Prisoners' Information Book). Prisoners should receive a written reply from the prison within seven days of submitting a Requests/Complaints form (F2059A), either with a full answer or an indication of when they can expect a full reply.

Prison Service Instruction 30/1997 introduced a time limit for prisoners to submit a request/complaint form. Prisoners must submit the form within three months of the matter under complaint coming to light. If a complaint is submitted outside this time limit, a prisoner must show good reason why this was the case, and only in exceptional circumstances will the complaint be eligible for consideration.

Requests or complaints about certain subjects, called "reserved subjects", may only be handled by Headquarters. These subjects are parole, allocation to or removal from mother and baby units, allocation to category A, life sentence prisoners, transfers and deportation, wrongful conviction or sentence, special remission, artificial insemination, and allocation and reallocation of people sentenced under the Young Persons Act. Both Standing Order 5C and the Prisoners' Information Book set out the various procedures for making requests and complaints, as does the booklet *How to Make a Request or Complaint: Information for Prisoners*, which is available in prison libraries.

The area manager deals with all appeals against adjudications. Otherwise since 1996 the Prisoner Casework Unit (PCU) handles all casework previously dealt with in area offices. Replies from the area manager will be sent to prisoners via the PCU, but should be worded to show that the decision is clearly the area manager's; the PCU will only say they are *replying* on behalf of the area manager if the he/she has actually seen the case and agreed to the reply (IG 47/1996).

Rule 11 does not deal with the timeliness of response to requests or complaints, as European Rule 42.4 requires. Grievance procedures require that oral applications receive a response within two days (though the Operating Standards say that responses should be within 24 hours; R2) and that formal written complaints made inside the prison receive a response within seven days, as mentioned above. Complaints to Headquarters should receive a reply within six weeks. The Rules have incorporated none of these time limits, and they are not enforceable. The Rules have also not

acknowledged the role of the Prison Ombudsman, though the original intention was that the Ombudsman should be included (Peddie 1999).[1]
Each decision should include a written explanation of the reasons behind the decision.

The Rules make no provision for a prisoner to make a request to an inspector of prisons as European Prison Rule 42.2 requires. In practice, the hearing of such complaints is the province of the Board of Visitors. The Inspectorate has no jurisdiction with respect to individual grievances. It is up to the Inspectors whether they will talk to any prisoner wishing to see them during visits to establishments. Rule 78(1) provides that the Board of Visitors and any member of the Board "shall hear any complaint or request which a prisoner wishes to make to them or him".

European Rule 42.2 provides that the prisoner's complaints may be made out to an authorised visitor to the prison "without the director or other members of the staff being present". This is an important protection, which has no equivalent in r 11. Instead, r 79(2) gives Boards of Visitors the right to conduct private interviews: "A member of the Board shall have access at any time to every part of the prison and to every prisoner, and he may interview any prisoner out of the sight and hearing of officers." The Rules make no mention of the circumstances in which interviews with visiting officers of the Secretary of State are to take place.

No proper grounds exist for refusing a prisoner a request to have his application heard by the full Board. The Association of Members of Boards of Visitors (AMBoV) has suggested a quorum of not fewer than three members for this purpose. The Prison Rules do not specify how soon applications should be heard. However AMBoV commented that, "the spirit of the Rules is that visiting members should hear any application any prisoner wishes to make at some stage during that same visit. A prisoner who wishes to put his case at a clinic or to the Board should be heard at the next available clinic or Board meeting". Members of Boards should ask prisoners if they wish to make an application in confidence, and there should be compelling and over-riding reasons for refusing such a request. "A prisoner requesting a confidential hearing should be told at the outset the degree to which confidence can be respected" (1991 AMBoV Handbook, 4.2.3 f). Full Boards or application clinics should hear applications in private.

Of concern is that records of applications are not always kept in a place which ensures confidentiality. If prison staff have authorised or un-authorised access to Board records then members should be aware of the fact. Members should know if prison staff have access to their records, and unauthorised access should be stopped (1991 AMBoV Handbook, 4.2.3 j).

Prisoners may write directly to the governor, area manager, Chairman of the Board of Visitors,[2] or Prison Ombudsman, under confidential cover if the request or complaint regards an issue which they cannot raise with

---

[1] The Office of the Ombudsman therefore has no statutory footing as yet, though this was the original intent, and the Ombudsman renewed his call for it in his 1998 Annual Report.

[2] The Board of Visitors Handbook (1993) states that oral complaints about members of staff are not their duty to investigate. Rather, these should be submitted formally in writing and can be sent to the governor or Area Manager via confidential access. The governor then investigates, "unless there are exceptional circumstances", and the Board of Visitors should monitor the progress of these complaints.

prison staff. Prisoners have similar protection under Standing Order 5B 32(3) when corresponding with legal advisers about legal proceedings or forthcoming adjudications unless the governor has reason to believe a prisoner is abusing this practice. European Rule 42.3 requires that the prisoner also be allowed to make a confidential complaint to "the judicial authority or other proper authorities". The Council of Europe's Committee for the Prevention of Torture recommended that envelopes for confidential access be available in a place which is generally accessible to prisoners so they do not have to ask staff for the envelopes and be able to transmit them without having to hand them to staff (1991: para. 184). The Home Office disagreed with this recommendation and stated instead that the current system of central registration and sealing of numbered confidential access forms was a better safeguard against the possibility of staff blocking complaints (Home Office response to the CPT, p. 35). Confidential access to the area manager is only for those issues which cannot be raised locally (IG 47/1996).

The system of requests and complaints includes a means of appeal against the decisions of prison managers. If a prisoner is unhappy with any decision, he or she may submit an appeal form (F2059B) to the area manager. Further, since the decision in *Hague and Weldon* (1991), all administrative decisions in prisons are susceptible to judicial review. This expands on the judgements in *St. Germain* (1979) and *Leech* (1988), which opened up Boards' and governors' disciplinary decisions to judicial review. (See commentary to r 45 for a further discussion of *Hague*.)

In *King* (1984), although the Court of Appeal concluded that the applicant had been wrongfully convicted, it held that the courts had no jurisdiction to quash a governor's decision and that the only remedy was against the Secretary of State. If the governor then fails to correct the error, the prisoner should seek judicial review of this decision, not that of the governor. A prison governor's decision on disciplinary matters was not open to judicial review at that time, and the court was not anxious to undermine a governor's authority. Lawton L J stated that all prisons "are likely to have [prisoners] who delude themselves that they are the victims of injustice. To allow such men to have access to the High Court, whenever they thought that the Governor abused his powers, failed to give them a fair hearing *or misconstrued the Prison Rules*, would undermine and weaken his authority and make management very difficult indeed" (emphasis added). Browne-Wilkinson L J concurred: "[T]he practical repercussions of holding that the disciplinary decisions of prison governors are subject to review by the courts are frightening. It would be to shut one's eyes to reality to ignore the fact that, if prisoners are able to challenge in the courts the disciplinary decisions of the governor, they are likely to try to do so in many often unmeritorious cases, and the maintenance of order and discipline in prisons is likely to be seriously undermined".

The Court of Appeal in Northern Ireland took the opposite view to *King* in *McKiernan* (1985). House of Lords judgements in the cases of *Leech and Prevot* (1988) subsequently granted prisoners the right to challenge governors' decisions in the courts. Disciplinary hearings are now therefore open to judicial review.

The office of the Prisons Ombudsman started its operations in October 1994 to supplement the existing avenue of external complaints. According to its original terms of reference, all complaints are eligible to go to the Ombudsman except the following: decisions of bodies other than the Prison

Service (e.g. the police, courts, or Parole Board); complaints subject to civil or criminal proceedings; complaints relating to the clinical judgement of prison doctors; and Ministerial decisions regarding the review or release of lifers (although related administrative action by the Prison Service is eligible for complaint). Envelopes going to the Ombudsman should be sealed and marked 'Prisoner's Confidential Access' and addressed to the Prisons Ombudsman's Office; staff may only check the contents if they have reasonable grounds to suspect it would be a criminal offence to send it (e.g. if it contained indecent or obscene material). The prison pays the postage for letters to the Ombudsman. Complaints should go through internal channels first, then must be submitted to the Ombudsman within a month of receiving a substantive reply from the Prison Service (although this is open to discretion).

In 1997, the Ombudsman received 1,960 letters (an increasing number every year since its inception), 553 of which were eligible for investigation. Most ineligible complaints were because prisoners did not use internal complaints procedures first. Disciplinary adjudications made up the largest proportion of complaints (169, or 30.5 per cent of eligible complaints, of which 36 were upheld. Complaints regarding prisoners' property are the most likely to be upheld (60 per cent of such complaints in 1997).

The Home Office issued new terms of reference for the Prisons Ombudsman in May 1996, which gave the Home Secretary the power to determine the eligibility of a complaint and excluded all Ministerial decisions on any subject from the Ombudsman's remit. The revised terms of reference give a limited account of what lies within the Ombudsman's remit, then states that "all other matters are excluded". Finally, the revised terms of reference require the Ombudsman to submit the draft results of any investigation to the Director General for scrutiny. "By acting in this way, the Home Secretary [Michael Howard]was clearly motivated by a desire to muzzle what was becoming an effective and enthusiastic watchdog on the actions of the Prison Service" (Livingstone and Owen 1999: 2.29).

However, in 1999 the terms of reference were liberalised (IG 41/1999), suggesting a more positive view of the Prisons Ombudsman's work and role on the part of the New Labour administration.

Prison staff must not prevent the submission of complaints to the Ombudsman or judge the eligibility of such complaints. Replies to prisoners should be given to them unopened, unless staff have reason to believe it did not come from the Ombudsman's Office (in which case, it should be passed unopened to the governor). The Prisons Ombudsman has unfettered access to Prison Service documents, including classified information, provided this is solely for the purpose of investigations within his terms of reference. Interviews with the Ombudsman or representative do not count against a prisoner's normal visit allowance and should take place in the sight but out of the hearing of staff (including calls on official telephones from the Ombudsman's office to the prisoner, unless the Ombudsman requests otherwise).

The Woolf Report recommended the establishment of a prisoner's 'contract', which "...should identify what kind of regime the establishment should provide for the inmates within each of its units. There is no reason why a prisoner should not be informed of the terms of that 'contract' or at least, in simple terms, those parts that are relevant to him" (para. 12.120). This would mean that prisoners who wish to complain "...could also take up the matter through the grievance procedure on the basis that the establishment had not included in his 'contract' those matters which the establishment should. This could even amount to maladministration, which could give redress before the Parliamentary Commissioner. Finally.... there is a possibility in an extreme case that judicial review would be of assistance" (para. 12.126). The Prison Service agreed to establish such 'contracts' or 'compacts' on a pilot basis, and has embodied this aim in Operating Standard O8. In practice, the use of compacts is most relevant to voluntary testing (drug-free) units or enhanced regimes and, while commonplace, they are not consistently in place across the prison estate.

Circular Instruction 8/1989 sets out the procedure for making allegations against staff and includes an information sheet for prisoners who wish to make an allegation (CI 8/1989 Annex A). Staff should inform prisoners who make oral allegations of the proper procedures for making allegations and should give them a copy of the information sheet. (This sheet only mentions making complaints to the governor or Secretary of State and fails to mention recourse to the Board of Visitors or to other external bodies.) However, if a prisoner continually makes an oral allegation against a member of staff in the presence of other officers or members of the Board of Visitors, but fails to make a written application or such an application has been investigated and found to be unsubstantiated, the prisoner may be given a formal order not to repeat the allegation orally and subsequently punished for disobeying a direct order if the prisoner persists (CI 8/1989, paras. 7, 8, and 25). This does not apply to repeated *written* allegations, such as if a prisoner takes the same complaint to several bodies for investigation. Complaints against the Prison Service of racial discrimination should be dealt with through normal complaints proce-dures, though such complaints eventually lead to civil action for damages against the Service and/or against named individuals for up to three years after the incident which gave rise to the complaint. "Both prisoners and staff are entitled to take such action under the Race Relations Act 1976, either through their solicitors or with the assistance of the Commission for Racial Equality" (AG 20/1993). Ethnic monitoring of requests and complaints is recommended 'best practice' according to the Annex of AG 32/1995 on Race Relations.

Information about how to petition the European Commission on Human Rights should be "freely available" in prison libraries (SO 7B 32).

The High Court in *Doody* (1994) concluded that mandatory lifers should have the opportunity to make written representations to the Home Secretary about the length of their tariffs before the Home Secretary has set the tariff period. (See commentary to r 10 Information to prisoners for a further discussion of mandatory and discretionary lifers.)

Standing Order 16 is available for prisoners who wish to become parties in legal proceedings. Prisoners may conduct litigation in person without the services of a solicitor and "may be allowed reasonable special facilities for this purpose at the discretion of the Governor..." (CI 18/1991: 4).

(See also r 39 Correspondence with legal advisers and courts.)

WOMEN PRISONERS

Women prisoners

12. *(1) Women prisoners shall normally be kept separate from male prisoners.*
    (2) The Secretary of State may, subject to any conditions he thinks fit, permit a woman prisoner to have her baby with her in prison, and everything necessary for the baby's maintenance and care may be provided there.

Both European Rule 11.2 and r 12(1) provide for the separation of male and female prisoners. Children may be permitted to stay with their mothers by virtue of r 12(2) and European Rule 28.2, but neither specifies the age limits involved: the European Rule makes reference only to "infants". The Council of Europe's Committee for the Prevention of Torture stated that "whether a mother should be allowed to keep her baby with her in prison and, if so, for how long, are controversial issues. The fundamental principle must be the respect of the baby's best interests. This may require the adaptation of different approaches in different cases" (1991: para. 124).

In a 1985 case reported in the *Guardian* (10 and 21 August 1985), the High Court ruled that a prison governor acted lawfully when he separated an 18-year old mother from her nine month old baby. Although the Secretary of State may technically exercise discretion under r 12, such decisions can be delegated to Prison Service officials. Only Styal, Askham Grange, New Hall, and Holloway have mother and baby units, all 'drug free', with a total of 64 places, with a possible four more at Holloway for short-term emergencies.

Because of the limited number of spaces in such units, some prisoners suitable for open conditions may have to be allocated to a closed establishment in order to be placed in such a unit (CI 2/1991:14). In addition, women who are foreign nationals are not located in open prisons as a matter of policy. Holloway and Styal prisons currently run a scheme providing for day visits by children to their mothers, which is under consideration for expansion to other prisons.

European Rule 62 marks a significant change from its predecessor (ESMR 54) which, far from encouraging the deployment of staff of the opposite sex, demanded that "special care" should be taken in the appointment and supervision of such staff.

(See also rr 20-21 Medical attendance, r 28 Hygiene, r 41 Search, r 49 Restraints, and r 58 Cellular confinement.)

RELIGION

Religious denomination

13. *A prisoner shall be treated as being of the religious denomination stated in the record made in pursuance of section 10(5) of the Prison Act 1952[6] but the governor may, in a proper case and after due enquiry, direct that record to be amended.*

Special duties of chaplains and prison ministers

14.　(1) The chaplain or a prison minister of a prison shall -
　　　(a) interview every prisoner of his denomination individually soon after
　　　　the prisoner's reception into that prison and shortly before his release;
　　　　and
　　　(b) if no other arrangements are made, read the burial service at the funeral
　　　　of any prisoner of his denomination who dies in that prison.

(2) The chaplain shall visit daily all prisoners belonging to the Church of England who are sick, under restraint or undergoing cellular confinement; and a prison minister shall do the same, as far as he reasonably can, for prisoners of his denomination.

(3) The chaplain shall visit any prisoner not of the Church of England who is sick, under restraint or undergoing cellular confinement, and is not regularly visited by a minister of his denomination, if the prisoner is willing.

Regular visits by ministers of religion

15.　(1) The chaplain shall visit the prisoners belonging to the Church of England.

(2) A prison minister shall visit the prisoners of his denomination as regularly as he reasonably can.

(3) Where a prisoner belongs to a denomination for which no prison minister has been appointed, the governor shall do what he reasonably can, if so requested by the prisoner, to arrange for him to be visited regularly by a minister of that denomination.

Religious services

16.　(1) The chaplain shall conduct Divine Service for prisoners belonging to the Church of England at least once every Sunday, Christmas Day and Good Friday, and such celebrations of Holy Communion and weekday services as may be arranged.

(2) Prison ministers shall conduct Divine Service for prisoners of their denominations at such times as may be arranged.

Substitute for chaplain or prison minister

17.　(1) A person approved by the Secretary of State may act for the chaplain in his absence.

(2) A prison minister may, with the leave of the Secretary of State, appoint a substitute to act for him in his absence.

Sunday work

18.　Arrangements shall be made so as not to require prisoners of the Christian religion to do any unnecessary work on Sunday, Christmas Day or Good Friday, or prisoners of other religions to do any such work on their recognised days of religious observance.

Religious books

19.　There shall, so far as reasonably practicable, be available for the personal use of every prisoner such religious books recognised by his denomination as are approved by the Secretary of State for use in prisons.

The Rules themselves contain no provision for pastoral visits in private as in European Prison Rule 47.2. However, Circular Instruction 51/1989 specifies that the pastoral visits granted under paragraph 19 of Standing Order 7A "must be allowed to take place in privacy and not in the public

Visits Room. If a prisoner wishes to make his confession then conditions of absolute privacy must be provided." The language of European Rule 47.3, which provides prisoners access to qualified representatives of all denominations, is stronger than that of r 15(3), which states that the governor should "do what he reasonably can" to arrange such visits if requested.

European Rule 46 endorses the possession of "necessary" religious books; r 19 requires that the Secretary of State approves these books. Circular Instruction 24/1992 cites 27 Standard Religious Books which prisons should have available for prisoners, at least 17 of which are for Christian denominations. Prisoners should also, with the permission of their Chaplain or Visiting Minister, be allowed to possess a prayer stool. This includes category A prisoners and those on the 'E' list (CI 17/91). Rule 13 does not indicate what grounds a governor would have for inquiring into a prisoner's stated religious denomination; one could argue that this violates European Rule 2 guaranteeing religious freedom. As the commentary to r 3 indicated above, the Prison Rules have no equivalent to European Prison Rule 2. However, the Prison Service Race Relations Policy Statement reads: "Members of minority religious groups have the same right to practise their faith as those of the majority faith. Wherever feasible in prison circumstances arrangements are made to give them the practical opportunity to do so." Prison Service Operating Standard T9 states that prisoners should be able to request visits from their local clergy or religious leader.

The prison chaplain must be a member of the Church of England. The governor must provide any visiting prison minister with a list of those prisoners declaring themselves to belong to his denomination, but he may visit only those prisoners. However, prisoners not belonging to the Church of England must be allowed to attend chapel or to receive visits from the chaplain (Prison Act 1952, s.7(4), and s.10(4), (5)). Paragraph 8 of Standing Order 7A also states that "Prisoners do not forfeit the right to attend the main service of their religion because they are undergoing punishment, segregated under the Rules, on the escape list, in Category 'A', or in hospital." Prisoners may only be barred from these services if the Medical Officer advises against it (in the case of a hospital patient), the governor judges that they have misbehaved at a service or that their presence would be likely to cause a disturbance or threat to security or control, or if they are located in a special unit which normally has its own services and in which attendance at the main service is exceptional (SO 7A 9a-c; also Op. Std. T6). Governors may bar prisoners from services for security reasons (SO 7A 9b) for up to one month, though they may renew this period. "The Governor will inform the appropriate chaplain or visiting minister after each such decision" (SO 7A 10). Prisoners barred from main services are still entitled to "pastoral care and such private acts of worship as may be arranged" (SO 7A 11). Religious worship for prisoners housed in Special Secure Units (SSUs) must take place within the Unit.

HM Chief Inspector of Prisons stated in his 1991 Annual Report that the Inspectorate was "disappointed to find that inmates on Rule 43 [now r 45]...were sometimes unable to attend chapel services because officers could not be found to escort them. Regrettably the facilities for those non-Christian faiths still vary considerably. Muslims are poorly served in many establishments" (para. 3.95).

Prisoners should not receive visits from ministers of religion against their wishes (Op. Std. T12).

The Home Office does not recognise Rastafarianism as a religion, though the Prisoners' Information Book specifies that "those following the Rastafarian faith are entitled to have their needs met, such as a vegetarian diet, retaining locks and wearing suitable headwear etc." Circular Instruction 51/1989 also refuses such "doubtful religious registrations" as Scientology and Black Muslim. Transcendental meditation is not regarded as a religion, but the previous ban on teaching it in establishments to those who request it has been relaxed to some extent (CI 18/1992). Annex A.3 to Circular Instruction 51/1989 cites some permitted considerations such as services, food, dress, and work for certain religious minorities, while the *Directory and Guide on Religious Practice in HM Prison Service* (1988) specifies other facilities.

(See also r 3 Purpose of prison training and treatment, and commentary to r 24 Food.)

MEDICAL ATTENTION

Medical attendance

20. (1) *The medical officer of a prison shall have the care of the health, mental and physical, of the prisoners in that prison.*

(2) *Every request by a prisoner to see the medical officer shall be recorded by the officer to whom it is made and promptly passed on to the medical officer.*

(3) *The medical officer may consult a medical practitioner who is a fully registered person within the meaning of the Medical Act 1983[7]. Such a practitioner may work within the prison under the general supervision of the medical officer.*

(4) *The medical officer shall consult another medical practitioner, if time permits, before performing any serious operation.*

(5) *If an unconvicted prisoner desires the attendance of a registered medical practitioner or dentist, and will pay any expense incurred, the governor shall, if he is satisfied that there are reasonable grounds for the request and unless the Secretary of State otherwise directs, allow him to be visited and treated by that practitioner or dentist in consultation with the medical officer.*

(6) *Subject to any directions given in the particular case by the Secretary of State, a registered medical practitioner selected by or on behalf of a prisoner who is a party to any legal proceedings shall be afforded reasonable facilities for examining him in connection with the proceedings, and may do so out of hearing but in the sight of an officer.*

Special illnesses and conditions

21. (1) *The medical officer or a medical practitioner such as is mentioned in rule 20(3) shall report to the governor on the case of any prisoner whose health is likely to be injuriously affected by continued imprisonment or any conditions of imprisonment. The governor shall send the report to the Secretary of State without delay, together with his own recommendations.*

(2) *The medical officer or a medical practitioner such as is mentioned in rule 20(3) shall pay special attention to any prisoner whose mental condition appears to require it, and make any special arrangements which appear necessary for his supervision or care.*

The Prison Service Health and Safety Policy Statement (PSO 3801) states that, "The Prison Service will take all reasonably practicable steps to safeguard the health and safety of ... those in custodial care." Despite this, the Chief Inspector stated in his 1999 Annual Report that "No part of prison life gives me greater or more consistent cause for concern than the way in which Healthcare is delivered, and it gives me no pleasure at all to find myself reporting the same failings over and over again, with there seeming to be little improvement ... The Prison Service states that it aims to deliver Healthcare of an equivalent standard to that provided by the NHS, which it patently fails to do in three particular respects: 1) Equivalence in health policy; 2) Equivalence in the standard of care provided, [and] 3) Equivalence in access to care" (p. 36).

European Rule 26.1 provides for prison medical services to be organised "in close relation with the general health administration of the community or nation". "In close relation" is not specific, but even so it is scarcely an accurate description of the healthcare service for prisoners in England and Wales, which is not part of the National Health Service. Prison doctors are not responsible to and hence cannot be censured by the Regional Health Authority, which has no power to investigate complaints. "A separate state system for any minority group (let alone one like prisoners) often becomes a system of the lowest standards, recruiting the worst categories of staff and perpetuating less freedom of choice, more felt discrimination and unfairness and - above all - less public accountability" (Cohen and Taylor 1978: 63).

The Chief Inspector of Prisons has stated that, "Prisoners are entitled to the same level of health care as that provided in society at large. Those who are sick, addicted, mentally ill or disabled should be treated, counselled, and nursed to the same standards demanded within the National Health Service. Failure to do so could not only damage the patient but also put society at risk" (1996: 1). He also argued that health care in the Prison Service should be supported by a patient's charter. Similarly, the report of the Working Party on the Education and Training of Doctors in the HCSP (1994) noted that medical care for prisoners should not only be appropriate to their needs but equal to that found in the NHS. The White Paper *Custody, Care and Justice* stated that "the Prison Medical Service [as it then was] should become a Prison Health Service much more closely aligned to the National Health Service..." (1991: 6.24).

The *Report on an Efficiency Scrutiny of the Prison Medical Service* recommended that medical practitioners should provide clinical care under contract to prisons, and that the Prison Health Service "should be a purchaser, not a provider of medical services" (1990: 16.4). The Report also recommended a separation of clinical and managerial duties. Doctors in prisons would therefore be part of the wider medical community, independent from the managerial and disciplinary structure of the prison. The European Committee for the Prevention of Torture argued for this in its visit to UK prisons in 1991. The Chief Inspector of Prisons argued in a discussion paper entitled *Patient or Prisoner?* that "It is no longer sensible to maintain a health care service for prisoners separate from the National Health Service. There is an immediate need for the Home Office and the Department of Health, together with the Prison Service and the National Health Service to agree a timetable for the NHS to assume responsibility for the commissioning and provision of health care and health promotion in prisons" (1996: 7).

In 1999, the first steps were taken to establishing a new healthcare partnership model between the Prison Service and the NHS. A Prison Health Policy Unit and Prison Health Care Task Force are to be based within the NHS Executive. The Prison Service Directorate of Health Care will be phased out.

The Association of Members of Boards of Visitors (AMBoV) makes the point that "Prisoner patients have no access to the NHS complaint system and have no internal specialist avenues of complaint yet credible safeguards are important as prisoners cannot choose or change doctors. The 1986 Social Services Committee inquiry into the [Prison Medical Service] recommended that a nurse or doctor be appointed to each board and that boards should have the powers to seek a second opinion, a right currently held by remand prisoners..." (1991 AMBoV Handbook, 5.5.1 c). The BoV Handbook (1993) specifies that Board members should check whether a) ante-natal and post-natal care compare favourably with what would be available outside; b) a female prisoner may be seen by a female doctor should she so choose; and c) the dignity of prisoners is respected throughout reception and induction procedures. The Prison Service recognises the right of female prisoners to be treated by a female doctor, but in practice they may find considerable delays in doing so (HMCIP 1997b).

In the case of female prisoners, para. 60.28 of the Prison Service Security Manual states that no prison staff should be present in the delivery room or where an intimate examination is taking place unless the prisoner requests it. A birthing partner should be allowed, at the woman's request, if the governor believes this is not a risk to the security or safety of staff or the public, and (for category A prisoners) if the partner is an approved visitor.

In 1991, the Committee for the Prevention of Torture (CPT) commented that, "Hospital officers have both a health care and a disciplinary role. The delegation had the impression that the latter would often take precedence over the former. This dual role must also complicate relations between hospital and medical officers" (1991 para. 180). With this in mind, the CPT recommended that prison doctors should not be asked to certify whether a prisoner is fit to undergo punishment, nor should he or she carry out body searches or other examinations requested by an authority except in an emergency where no other doctor can be called (1993: para. 71). This guidance directly conflicts with the Prison Rules.

The prison officers' industrial action in 1979-80 illustrated the effects of the relationship between general prison conditions and incidence of reported ill-health among prisoners. The Prison Department (as it was then) noted: "Medical officers in several establishments reported that the incidence of inmates requesting to see the medical officer fell during the period of industrial action. This was attributed to a lessening of tension as a result of the reduction in overcrowding coupled with an increase in free association due to the closure of workshops" (1980 Report: 210). Over-crowding also has an impact on prison medical services: "The physical and psychological well-being of a prisoner - already at risk by virtue of the very fact of incarceration - will be seriously prejudiced under conditions of this sort. The health care services of such a prison will tend to become overwhelmed by the day to day requests for medical attention; they will simply react to events, having no time to pursue a health policy of a preventive nature" (CPT 1991: para. 141).

The Prison Reform Trust has pointed out that the medical officer is expected to advise on food, hygiene, working conditions, the suitability of candidates for employment in the prison service, fitness of members of the service, accidents to prisoners and staff, fitness for adjudication, self-injury, food refusal, petitions to the Home Secretary, and fitness of prisoners for transfer (*Prison Medicine* 1985: 7-8). Rule 20(2) emphasises these responsibilities. This section, similar to European Rules 100.2 and 100.3, appears to justify the use of medical criteria to modify the conditions of imprisonment and is related to the Home Secretary's power to transfer a prisoner to hospital under sections 47 and 48 of the Mental Health Act. Standing Order 13 sets out the specific duties of medical staff in prisons.

Three types of doctors work in the Health Care Service for Prisoners: full-time medical officers who are civil servants, GPs working part-time, and visiting specialists. The Director of Healthcare has said that doctors from outside the service carry out two-thirds of medical work in prison. Nurses and other paramedical staff are employed, but hospital officers carry out much of the routine care. The full-time prison medical officer is not subject to any sort of audit or peer scrutiny, and, apart from the assistance of part-time GPs, acts in isolation from professional colleagues (*Prison Medicine* 1985: 15-17). The Chief Inspector of Prisons has recommended that, "Virtually every prison could benefit from civilianising most of its hospital administration work to allow trained Hospital Officers to concentrate on clinical duties" (1991: 4.08).

In *R v Ashdown* (1973), the Court of Appeal considered that a life-sentence prisoner's release on licence depended on his co-operation in various behaviour modification schemes being tested by the visiting psychotherapist at Wormwood Scrubs. Standing Order 13(25) states: "In general prisoners are free to accept or decline any medical or psychiatric treatment offered to them. Invasive medical procedures (including procedures necessary for the administration of medicine) should not be carried out without a prisoner's consent (or of a prisoner's parent or guardian if he or she is under 16 years of age) unless without such procedures the prisoner's life would be endangered, serious harm to him or her or to others would be likely, or there would be an irreversible deterioration in the prisoner's condition" (also Op. Std. K3). Circular Instruction 4/1988 further specifies that no radiographs may be taken without the consent of the patient, but neither the Prison Rules nor European Prison Rules deal directly with the issues of consent to treatment or the relationship between a prison medical officer and the prison administration.

The case of *Freeman v Home Office* (1984) raised both issues. Freeman alleged that he had been held down and injected, and claimed damages in trespass. He argued that he could not have consented since he was neither told what was wrong with him nor the effect of the medication and its likely side-effects. The Court of Appeal took into consideration the difficulties that would follow from a decision that lawful consent was impossible under the present system, and held that the prison doctor was acting, within the prison, as a doctor and not as a senior manager. The argument of the absence of informed consent was rejected on the grounds that no such doctrine exists in English law. Because consent was found as an issue of fact, the court did not rule on whether the Prison Rules should treat the issue of consent as being within the gambit of s. 58 of the 1983 Mental Health Act (which would have required the doctor to certify in writing that

Freeman did not consent, and then to obtain a second psychiatric opinion agreeing to the administration of the proposed drugs).

The Criminal Evidence (Amendment) Act 1997 introduced an exception to the principle of consent to medical procedures. The Act extends the power of police under the Police and Criminal Evidence Act 1984 (PACE) to take non-intimate body samples (e.g. saliva, hair other than pubic hair) without consent for DNA testing and to be kept on a national DNA data base. This Act applies specifically to prisoners charged with or convicted of burglary, violence, or sexual offences and is detailed in the Appendix of PSI 40/1997. The power to take such samples without consent lapses on the prisoner's release.

According to PSI 40/1997, any requests for prisoners to delay sampling in order to consult a legal adviser or to have a legal adviser present during sampling should be denied because the 1997 Act makes no provision for such requests; the powers of the police in this case are very clear. In fact, the police may use 'reasonable force' to take a prisoner to the sampling room, as long as they first issue a direct order and a charge for disobeying that order. Prison officers may assist the police in this, "using such reasonable force as may be necessary to restrain a prisoner while a sample is taken. This is considered a legitimate use of force to assist the police in the execution of their duties" (PSI 40/1997). Female prisoners must have a female prison officer present and the sample taken by a female police officer; particular care must be taken with the use of force if the female prisoner is known or thought to be pregnant.

The Chief Inspector commented in his second (1990) report on the prevention of suicides in prison that "There will always be a number of patients who refuse medication; they may be very disturbed, violent, self-neglecting and perhaps paranoid ... Whilst Common Law permits treatment against a patient's will in extreme situations, doctors are loathe to effect it as the legal boundaries are unclear. In most cases the patient will be persuaded to accept medication. With the few who do not, or who subsequently do not respond to treatment, arrangements are made for transfer to a psychiatric hospital under Section 48 of the Mental Health Act 1983. Such transfers are often difficult to arrange and the tradition to date in prisons is not to transfer out except as a last resort" (1990: 3.64).

The Committee for the Prevention of Torture expressed concern about such difficulties with transfers, noting that "consequently, [staff] could find themselves with a seriously mentally disordered patient in their custody for a considerable time without having the possibility to provide him with the treatment he required" (1991: para. 162). The Chief Inspector suggested the possibility of upgrading the training of staff and the facilities in prisons to qualify certain wings as psychiatric hospitals under the definition of the Mental Health Act, though admitted that this would require significant improvements in training and in co-operation with the NHS, plus may bring with it the risk of having more mentally ill patients allocated to prisons (1990: 3.65).

Of concern is that, according to Fawcett (1985: 71), the European Commission of Human Rights has said that the forced administration of medicine to a detainee is not contrary to the Convention. Further, several cases have alleged that inadequate medical treatment amounts to a violation of Article 3 of the Convention, but none have been declared admissible.

The Access to Health Records Act 1990 specifies that prisoners have the right of access to their health records (and may have copies made on request) "unless in the opinion of the record holder, the disclosure would cause serious harm to the physical or mental health of the patient" (Home Office response to the CPT, p. 9, and now incorporated into Op. Std. K12, though subject to payment of a prescribed fee). Reports to the Parole Board or to the courts are not included in this directive, though the Court of Appeal in *Wilson* (1992) gave prisoners access to copies of any reports against them (see r 7 for a further discussion of this case).

The same codes of confidentiality which bind the medical profession general also apply to the Prison Service. Circular Instruction 30/1991 states that "personal health data are to be protected and must not be disclosed for other than specifically defined purposes" (para. 27). The same confidentiality applies for prisoners who are HIV positive, though if "it seems desirable in the inmate's interest" to inform a third party, a member of staff must discuss the issue with the inmate and *must obtain the prisoner's consent* before disclosing the information (emphasis added) (CI 30/1991: 28). Unfortunately in practice many staff members either do not know about or do not always follow these directions. During the course of preparing the third edition of this book, an officer informed me, in front of several other members of staff, that the prisoner I was about to interview was HIV and Hepatitis B positive. It was not "in the inmate's interest" to inform me of this, nor had I asked for the information, nor had the prisoner been consulted, let alone given his consent. HM Chief Inspector of Prisons specifically addressed this point, saying that "The standards of medical confidentiality available within the National Health Service should apply within the Prison Service. Information should be limited to those clinically involved with a particular patient and any decision to inform others about HIV positive/Hepatitis B status should rest with the individual prisoner" (1991: 4.49). Disclosure of a prisoner's HIV status may be justified for the protection of the rights and freedoms of others (*TV v Finland* 1994), but would be less justified if disclosure was by staff to other prisoners.

Circular Instruction 30/1991 makes a further proviso that "It may also be prudent to explain to the inmate that confidentiality (medical or otherwise) is not easily achieved or maintained in prison and that while members of the care team will do everything possible to respect his/her wishes strict confidentiality cannot be assured" (CI 30/1991: 28). In other words, doctors employed by the Prison Service have the same codes of confidentiality as the general medical profession but are not necessarily expected to be able to follow those codes.

The Committee for the Prevention of Torture recommended that medical examinations of prisoners be conducted without the presence of non-medical staff. The Home Office rejected this recommendation, stating that security has a higher priority than a prisoner's privacy: "... it is essential to guard against the possibility of a potentially violent prisoner assaulting members of the medical staff during the course of an examination. It is not appropriate, therefore, to preclude in all circumstances the presence of non-medical staff" (Home Office response to the CPT, 1991: 9).

Mental disorder
So far as mentally disturbed offenders are concerned, r 21(2) merely requires the medical officer to make "any special arrangements which appear necessary" for the care or supervision of "any prisoner whose

mental condition appears to require it". *The Guardian* reported in March 1991 that Sir Montague Levine, a South London coroner now retired, had demanded a time limit for psychiatric examinations and reports for prisoners. The limits should be a maximum of 14 days, but ideally within a week of remanding a prisoner for such examination. European Rule 100, though phrased in outmoded language, states specifically that "insane" prisoners shall be removed to appropriate establishments for the mentally ill, and those "suffering gravely" from other types of mental illness or abnormality should be treated in specialised facilities. It is surprising that this terminology was not amended when the European Rules were revised.

The 1979 May Report noted its inability to establish precisely the number of mentally disturbed offenders in prison cells. However, many studies indicate that rates of both mental illness and mental impairment are much higher in prison than outside. The Home Office estimated the figure of acute cases to be over 20 percent in December 1990 for young and adult males in prison and 35 percent for female prisoners (*The Observer*, 2 December 1990). Recent research in England and Wales (Singleton et al. 1998) identified a vast range of mental disorder amongst prisoners, estimated at 70 per cent of the population when substance abuse was taken into account. These included personality disorders amongst 50 - 78 per cent of prisoners (with male remands the highest), as well as 7 - 14 per cent with psychoses (most common amongst female prisoners), and 39 - 75 per cent with neurotic symptoms (also more common amongst females). Relatively few of these prisoners are likely to meet the more stringent standards of mental disorder under the Mental Health Act

Gunn, Maden, and Swinton found in their study of mentally disordered prisoners that almost a third of the prisoners in their sample of what they considered to be "hospital cases" were receiving no treatment for their particular disorders (1991: 59, table 7.7). They commented that, "Frequent reference has been made to the inadequate facilities within which medical officers are required to carry out their work" (p. 95). The researchers further stated that, "A constant theme of our description of prison medical services is the extreme variation in standards between prisons and individual doctors ... We have already referred to the failure of the prison medical service to develop an explicit policy on the degree to which it will accept responsibility for managing psychiatric disorder" (p. 96). They recommended adequate funding and training for health services and staff in prisons, a development of clear policies on the management of psychiatric problems, and a clarification of the roles of the prison and health services in managing mental disorder. It is clear that the overall provision of service falls short of that set out by European Rule 32: "The medical services of the institution shall seek to detect and shall treat any physical or mental illnesses or defects which may hamper a prisoner's resettlement after release. All necessary medical, surgical and psychiatric services including those available in the community shall be provided to that end."

Custody, Care and Justice stated that, although prisoners who are mentally ill need special care, some "cannot for security reasons be given hospital treatment in the outside community. Such prisoners may be able to be accommodated within normal living units with other prisoners, at least for some parts of their sentences, if particular care is given to their allocation and their programme. Others, for at least some part of their time in prison, will need more specialist care and attention. At present, such prisoners may be allocated to a prison hospital. The Prison Service will consider the case for establishing a small number of special care centres in selected prisons which would specialise in the care of such prisoners" (1991: 7.41).

The Committee for the Prevention of Torture noted the problem of housing mentally disordered people in prisons. Some wings house large numbers of persons in need of psychiatric observation and care, but have neither the physical facilities or the staff of psychiatric hospitals (1991: para. 151). HM Chief Inspector of Prisons noted his concern that, according to the decision in *Knight v Home Office* (1990), the standard of care for mentally ill persons detained in prison hospitals does not have to be as high as that provided in psychiatric hospitals outside prisons. "Accordingly the facilities and numbers of staff for the provision of medical care for persons detained in prison did not have to be the same as for psychiatric hospitals" (1991: 4.54). The case further stated that prison officers are not liable for the suicides of prisoners, though Farquharson LJ in *Kirkham v Chief Constable of the Greater Manchester Police* (1990) stated that the police are liable for the suicides of prisoners in their custody. One challenge to the ruling in *Knight* came from the Queen's Bench Division in *Brooks v Home Office* (1999). In this instance, Mr. Justice Garland held that a pregnant woman in prison is entitled to the same standard of obstetric care and observation as if she were at liberty (a recurring shortfall in the standard of prison health care; HMCIP 1996).

In the meantime, the Chief Inspector continues to state his concern over the care for prisoners with mental disorders: "One group for whom [the Prison Service] certainly does not provide equivalence of service [with the NHS] is the large number of mentally disordered offenders (MDOs) ... Previously we have reported that the condition of mentally disordered prisoners deteriorates in prison, because they are not given access to appropriate treatment. Not only is there no strategy for dealing with MDOs; I now believe that the way that they are treated actually damages them, which adds urgency to the need to rectify the situation" (1999: 36).

Suicidal behaviour
The European Prison Rules do not deal with suicidal prisoners. The suicide rate in English prisons is roughly four times the rate for the general population (Liebling 1992). Sixty-eight self-inflicted deaths (65 men and three women) took place in prisons in 1997, and 82 in 1998 with a fairly stable rate of 1.16 per 1,000 prisoners from 1995 - 97 (Home Office 1998b).

The 1984 Inspectorate Report *Suicides in Prison* criticised the then extant Standing Orders and Circular Instructions on suicide and its prevention. Following the Report of the Working Group on Suicide Prevention, Circular Instruction 20/1989 introduced new strategies including early identification and referrals, self-help forms, and annual reviews. The subsequent Chief Inspector's Report *Suicide and Self-Harm in Prison Service Establishments* (1990) recommended a 'user-friendly' guide to the Instruction and set out a detailed analysis of suicides in prison and possibilities for prevention. The Report emphasised the need not to view suicides only as a medical issue but that the Prison Service needs instead to address several related factors such as medical resources, reception procedures, prisoner accommodation, staffing levels, the needs of young offenders, the role of prison officers, and facilities for counselling. The Chief Inspector's most recent (third) thematic review on suicides, which includes a survey of performance in every prison (conducted by the Boards of Visitors) is entitled *Suicide is Everyone's Concern*

(1999). It places particular emphasis upon induction and the treatment of prisoners in local prisons.

All staff have a role in identifying people at risk and in preventing suicide (IG 1/1994). Prison Service Operating Standards recommend that local policies on the care of prisoners at risk of suicide and self-harm, and on measures to reduce the likelihood of self-harm, should be published and given to prisoners (W1). In addition, "Prisoners should be made aware of matters relating to suicide and self-harm, and provided with information about counselling and support services" (W7).

Other issues

Standing Order 13(26) provides that in addition to cases where consultation is desirable under r 20(3), a medical officer "has the authority to call another medical practitioner into consultation, and shall do so if time permits before carrying out any invasive medical procedure in the absence of the prisoner's consent. A medical officer should also whenever possible consult the doctor or hospital previously responsible for a patient's treatment where the diagnosis or previous medical history of a patient is in doubt, or where the prisoner is considered liable to commit acts of violence against him or others." This is more limited in scope than in the previous Standing Order 13, but is still wider than actual practice may suggest. Circular Instruction 34/1988 requires, however, that "in all cases where it is medically indicated, and irrespective of whether the inmate is unconvicted or serving a custodial sentence, the medical officer will endeavour to obtain a copy or summary of the medical history from the relevant GP, clinic or hospital" (CI 34/1988: 2c(i)).

The prisoner's prison medical record should contain all relevant information regarding examinations and treatment while in custody, and the medical officer is responsible to ensure, by telephone if necessary, that all receiving establishments (in the case of transfer) or external GP, clinic, or hospital (when a prisoner is discharged) if a prisoner "is receiving medical treatment or otherwise has a medical history" (CI 34/88: 2c(iii and iv)). Governors should therefore advise the managing medical officer sufficiently in advance of impending transfers or discharge. If a prisoner's history includes mental disorder, "the medical officer should invite the appropriate physician to the establishment for the purpose of making his own assessment of the prisoner's medical needs on release" (CI 34/88: 2c(iv)). The Instruction emphasises that an accurate prison medical record is particularly important if a prisoner is identified (e.g. during the reception process) as belonging to an HIV risk group, is mentally disturbed, potentially suicidal, or a drug misuser.

Condoms should be made available to prisoners on request. However, the legal status of consensual homosexual activity in prisons remains uncertain. One view is that homosexual sex is necessarily illegal in that the law only acknowledges sexual activity "between consenting adults in private. Nowhere in a prison legally constitutes a private place" (1991 AMBoV Handbook, 5.5.3; see also Livingstone and Owen 1999: 5.39, which states that virtually no privacy rights remain in prison). However, the AIDS Advisory Committee (1995), which recommended that condoms be made available through prison health centres, pointed out that no criminal prosecutions or disciplinary proceedings had ever resulted from consensual sexual activity in prisons. The Chief Inspector has found that condoms are becoming increasingly available for men going on home leave, which "may well prove a useful contribution to public health" (1994: para. 5.39).

The JUSTICE report *Justice in Prison* (1983) recommended that the Rules should give convicted prisoners similar rights to those of unconvicted prisoners under r 20(5). It also recommended that the Rules make provision for cases where a prisoner needs treatment for a condition which was treated by his own doctor before his imprisonment. It suggested the following: "If a prisoner needs medical attention for a condition for which he had been previously treated by a registered medical practitioner, and he makes this fact known to the medical officer and gives him the name and address of the practitioner, it shall be the duty of the medical officer, if reasonably practicable, to communicate with the practitioner and obtain from him the prisoner's previous medical history and information about the treatment he was given" (para. 41).

Interestingly, the only reference to drug use in the Prison Rules is in the context of discipline and punishment. The Rules do not take into account the special needs of addicted prisoners. However, the Operating Standards state that prisoners suffering from addiction or dependency should have access to multi-disciplinary support throughout their sentence, including clinical detoxification, management of withdrawal, maintenance of a drug-free lifestyle, and preparation for release (Op. Std. K10). The Standards also recommend programmes for the prevention of HIV, including basic education, trained staff, voluntary testing free of charge with pre- and post-test counselling, and a small supply of condoms prior to home leave or release (K13).

Among other rules, the medical officer has veto power over the use of restraints under r 49 and of solitary confinement for breaches of discipline under r 56 Cellular confinement. See also rr 24-25 Food, alcohol and tobacco, r 29 Physical education, r 31 Work, and r 45 Removal from association. The NACRO Code (1984) proposed inspection responsibilities for the medical officer in relation to sanitary facilities, hair care, clothing, bedding, and exercise and recreation (Codes B and D).

Notification of illness or death

22. (1) *If a prisoner dies, becomes seriously ill, sustains any severe injury or is removed to hospital on account of mental disorder, the governor shall, if he knows his or her address, at once inform the prisoner's spouse or next of kin, and also any person who the prisoner may reasonably have asked should be informed.*
    (2) If a prisoner dies, the governor shall give notice immediately to the coroner having jurisdiction, to the board of visitors and to the Secretary of State.

The Prison Rules contain no equivalent to European Prison Rule 49.2, providing that a prisoner is to be informed immediately of the death or serious illness of any near relative. In 1990, HM Chief Inspector of Prisons reported: "We found overall that little thought is given to the next of kin and we have received reports of difficulties encountered by families and relatives trying to obtain information or ascertain details from a prison. The general practice is for the local police to break the news to the next of kin. Officers undertaking such a duty may not have full information on the case ... We have heard of parents being told to wait until the following morning for information" (1990: 5.06-07). The Chief Inspector recommended that the next of kin have the option of identifying the body (a duty usually left to the

Medical Officer) and that at the earliest possible opportunity the details of the death be given to the next of kin (1990: 5.08-09).

The Home Office reported to the Council of Europe that prisoners are not allowed to "see the deceased" as this is not customary practice in the UK, but prisoners will normally be allowed to attend the funeral of a close relative.

Prison Service Order 2710 sets out specific procedures following deaths in custody. These procedures include a requirement for immediate action and reporting, contact with the press office and media, support for staff and prisoners as well as follow-up support for the prisoner's family, preparations for internal investigations and inquests, funeral arrangements, and information to the family and their legal representatives. The Order requires that the prisoner's next of kin are informed before anything is reported or confirmed to the media.

PHYSICAL WELFARE AND WORK

Clothing
23. (1) *An unconvicted prisoner may wear clothing of his own if and in so far as it is suitable, tidy and clean, and shall be permitted to arrange for the supply to him from outside prison of sufficient clean clothing:*
Provided that, subject to rule 40(3):
> (a) *he may be required, if and for so long as there are reasonable grounds to believe that there is a serious risk of his attempting to escape, to wear items of clothing which are distinctive by virtue of being specially marked or coloured or both; and*
> (b) *he may be required, if and for so long as the Secretary of State is of the opinion that he would, if he escaped, be highly dangerous to the public or the police or the security of the State, to wear clothing provided under this rule.*

(2) *Subject to paragraph (1) above, the provisions of this rule shall apply to an unconvicted prisoner as to a convicted prisoner.*
(3) *A convicted prisoner shall be provided with clothing adequate for warmth and health in accordance with a scale approved by the Secretary of State.*
(4) *The clothing provided under this rule shall include suitable protective clothing for use at work, where this is needed.*
(5) *Subject to rule 40(3), a convicted prisoner shall wear clothing provided under this rule and no other, except on the directions of the Secretary of State or as a privilege under rule 8.*
(6) *A prisoner may be provided, where necessary, with suitable and adequate clothing on his release.*

European Rule 31.1 requires the medical officer to inspect and advise regularly on the suitability and cleanliness of prisoner clothing; r 23 has no such provision. European Rule 22 states that clothing is to be kept clean and in proper condition, and that underclothes are to be changed and washed as often as necessary for the maintenance of hygiene. Other than the vague requirement that a convicted prisoner is to be provided with clothing "adequate for ... health", r 23 makes no provision for frequent clothing changes in the interest of hygiene. The Standing Orders require clothing issued to be clean, aired and in reasonable condition; underclothing and socks to be changed regularly and as frequently as practicable; prisoners allowed to wear their own clothes but lacking sufficient clean underwear are to be supplied with it; and governors are responsible for ensuring a high standard in the cleanliness and condition of clothing, which is to be laundered at prescribed intervals. Prisoners engaged in especially dirty tasks are afforded the opportunity for change of clothing. The Standing Orders make reference to an unspecified pattern and scale of clothing; weather-protective clothing for prisoners discharged, temporarily released or transferred; and necessary protective clothing for health and hygiene for prisoners engaged in work requiring it (SO 2C and 14; see also Section M of the Operating Standard).

Unlike the regulations for unconvicted prisoners in r 23(1), neither the Prison Rules nor European Prison Rules address the wearing of private clothing by convicted prisoners (although this is an area of discretion for governors). The only exception is r 40(3) which concerns the wearing of personal or non-prison clothing to court. The Prison Rules do not acknowledge the practice that women prisoners are permitted to wear their own clothes, subject to certain restrictions. Section 39 of the Prison Service Security Manual requires that convicted category A prisoners wear prison clothing at all times, except when they go to court. Unconvicted category As should wear their own 'sterile' clothing on all escorts.

The 1991 White Paper *Custody, Care and Justice* expressed the then Government's intent gradually to allow convicted prisoners more of a choice of clothing and to wear their own clothes. The White Paper states that, "The extent of these provisions and the pace at which they can be introduced will depend on the experience of the pilot schemes; on finding suitable alternative work for prisoners [for those currently employed in the manufacture and laundering of Prison Service clothing]; and on identifying acceptable arrangements for laundering prisoners' own clothes. The changes are therefore likely to be phased and will take some years to implement in full" (para. 6.31). The Operating Standards state that prisoners should have access to facilities where they may wash and dry items of personal clothing (H9).

The NACRO Code made detailed proposals, including changes of underclothing and socks at least three times a week, so as to coincide with bathing whenever possible, and provision for items worn and reissued to other prisoners to be properly cleaned first (1984: Code B1(f)). Four changes of underwear should take place each week in most prisons. The Chief Inspector of Prisons has recommended a daily change of underwear and socks as well as adequate facilities for prisoners to wash, dry, store, and return their clothing (1990: 3.13).

If upon release a prisoner's clothes no longer fit or are not warm enough for the time of year, the Prison Service must provide 'liberty clothing'. Prisoners should ask about this a few days prior to release, as the day of release will probably be too late (Prisoners' Information Book).

Food
24. (1) *Subject to any directions of the Secretary of State, no prisoner shall be allowed, except as authorised by the medical officer or a medical practitioner such as is mentioned in rule 20(3), to have any food other than that ordinarily provided.*
    (2) *The food provided shall be wholesome, nutritious, well prepared and served, reasonably varied and sufficient in quantity.*

(3) The medical officer, a medical practitioner such as is mentioned in rule 20(3) or any person deemed by the governor to be competent, shall from time to time inspect the food both before and after it is cooked and shall report any deficiency or defect to the governor.
(4) In this rule "food" includes drink.

Alcohol and tobacco

25. *(1) No prisoner shall be allowed to have any intoxicating liquor except under a written order of the medical officer or a medical practitioner such as is mentioned in rule 20(3) specifying the quantity and the name of the prisoner. (2) No prisoner shall be allowed to smoke or to have any tobacco except as a privilege under rule 8 and in accordance with any orders of the governor.*

European Rule 25.1 requires that food be provided in accordance with the standards laid down by the health authorities, and takes into account "so far as possible, religious or cultural requirements"; there is no equivalent in r 24, which states that dietary modifications are subject to the directions of the Secretary of State and as authorised by the medical officer. (As long ago as 1977, the Home Office was saying that arrangements were made for prisoners to comply, within reason, with the dietary tenets of their faith; *Prisons and the Prisoner* 1977: 58). Annex A.3 to Circular Instruction 51/1989 describes the dietary requirements for certain religious minorities, while the *Directory and Guide on Religious Practice in HM Prison Service* (1988) discusses the requirements for several other religions. Members of some religions, in particular Jewish prisoners, must be "able to demonstrate an adherence" to the dietary laws of their religion in order to qualify for special diets (CI 37/1991). Governors retain the discretion under Circular Instruction 2/1983 to allow visiting ministers to bring in items of food for religious festivals and holy days to unconvicted prisoners who belong to religious minorities (CI 10/1988:7). Advice to Governors 32/1995 on Race Relations states that prisons should be able to cater for pork-free, rice-based, vegetarian, vegan, Halal, and Kosher diets.

European Rule 25.2 provides for the availability of drinking water; r 24(4) does not. The Prison Rules provide for food to be inspected "from time to time" by the medical officer (r 24(3)), and "at frequent intervals" by a member of the Board of Visitors (r 78(2)). Standing Order 2B provides further that authorised dietary scales will be strictly observed, and that details of meals served are to be inspected and signed by the medical officer. Meals for prisoners in Crown Court Custody areas must also meet standards of food handling and hygiene (CI 57/1989). Standing Order 14.1(a) and (b) calls for governors to ensure proper observance of the relevant provisions of the Food Act 1984 and the Food Hygiene (General) Regulations 1970. Standing Order 14.28 provides for formal inspections by Regional Catering Managers and independently by the Home Office Health and Safety Officers, and Standing Order 14.30 opens each establishment to "unannounced random independent validation checks by an Environmental Health Officer from the Department of Health." The Food Safety Act 1990 is binding in Crown establishments, which includes prison kitchens.

Although not provided for in the Rules or in Standing Order 4 on privileges, prisoners may purchase food from the canteen (now usually called the prison shop). However, the Chief Inspector of Prisons has noted that "We have not seen the evidence of promised expansion of canteen facilities to replace the withdrawal of the daily food parcels once allowed to remand prisoners" (1990: 3.15). The Operating Standards include an aspiration for prisoners to have facilities to prepare drinks and snacks adjacent to association areas (H11). The Learmont Report was very critical of the practice of allowing category A prisoners to be able to cook their own food and recommended that this only be available as an earned privilege under the Incentives Scheme (1995: 2.216).

AMBoV has advised its members: "In addition to the quality, quantity, and variety of the food, attention should be paid to whether hot meals are hot for everyone when served, whether the same prisoners always have last and therefore least choice, whether prisoners on special diets (including religious minorities) are well catered for, and that prisoners on punishment or r 43 are receiving their food in its proper condition. The absence of prisoner complaints does not always signify that all is well. Inspection [by members of Boards of Visitors] should mean asking as well as listening" (1984 AMBoV Handbook, para. 3C(12)).

In the early 1990s, the Inspectorate found at HM Prison Canterbury that food for prisoners in the hospital and Reception Unit was carried in canvas bags, with no use of heated trolleys (1992: 4.25). The Chief Inspector commented in his 1991 annual report that "Trolleys which did not heat food properly or were damaged in some way or which had not been pre-heated were commonly found. Dilapidated and unhygienic wooden trolleys were in use at Channings Wood and Wormwood Scrubs among other places. In older establishments, many inmates faced a long walk from wing serveries to cells on the upper landing carrying lukewarm food on cold metal trays. We found little evidence of efforts to improve matters. Food is often delivered from the kitchen to the wing far too early" (1991: 3.11). The Woolf Report included a similar passage: "The poor quality of the food served in prisons was a recurrent theme of the letters we received from prisoners. It featured in over a third of all the letters we received from prisoners in the prisons whose disturbances were not investigated. This was more than any other complaint" (para. 14.198). Prison Service Operating Standards have tried to address these issues (Op. Stds. L7-10), but again these Standards are currently aspirational rather than enforceable.

Woolf believed that "there is a substantial problem in the timing and the serving of meals.... We know from our own visits that the mid-day meal is served around 11.00. The last meal of the day is often around 16.00" (para. 14.212). The Committee for the Prevention of Torture (1991) further commented that diabetic prisoners may have difficulty with the long hours between meal-times at many prisons, especially at weekends. Woolf recommended a return to the practice of communal dining and that meals should be served at more sensible hours. The Prison Rules address neither matter, and the European Rules make no recommendation for communal dining.

The NACRO Code's recommendations include the availability of drinking water; that no more than 14 hours should pass between the evening meal and breakfast; that special medical diets shall be provided as prescribed; that special diets should be provided on philosophical and religious grounds as far as possible and failure to make such provision must be recorded and reported; and that frequent inspections should be made by local authority environmental health officers (1984: Code C). Prescribed meal times in the Operating Standards are for breakfast between 7:30 and 9:00 a.m., lunch between noon and 2:00 p.m., and the evening meal between 5:00 p.m. and 7:30, with a minimum of four and a half hours between meals (Op. Std. L4 and commentary).

The Committee for the Prevention of Torture commented that special diets, particularly in overcrowded establishments, are often difficult for kitchens to prepare, which in turn seems to discourage doctors from prescribing them (e.g. fat-free diets for heart patients). The Inspectorate noted in its report on Canterbury prison that some medical diets, for example 'fried only', seem inappropriate at best and should be justified (1991: 4.24).

Operating Standard L6 states that prisoners in segregation should receive the same menu as other prisoners.

Standing Order 4 limits the amount of tobacco which prisoners may retain in their possession to 62.5 grams of loose tobacco, or 80 cigarettes, cigars, or a combination of both. The limit for unconvicted prisoners is 137.5 grams or 180 cigarettes. Sentenced prisoners under sixteen years of age may not smoke or possess tobacco (SO 4: 9). Prisoners may take tobacco, cigarettes, and cigars to court and smoke them in places where smoking is permitted, and those in hospital or under observation may smoke at such times as the medical officer directs (SO 4: 49-50).

(See also r 26 Sleeping accommodation, regarding the use of tobacco in prisons, and commentary to rr 13-19 Religion.)

Sleeping accommodation

26. (1) *No room or cell shall be used as sleeping accommodation for a prisoner unless it has been certified in the manner required by section 14 of the Prison Act 1952 in the case of a cell used for the confinement of a prisoner.*

(2) A certificate given under that section or this rule shall specify the maximum number of prisoners who may sleep or be confined at one time in the room or cell to which it relates, and the number so specified shall not be exceeded without the leave of the Secretary of State.

Neither r 26 nor European Rule 14 refers to the length of time to be spent in cells; this is a significant omission as it is self-evident that space and length of occupancy are inextricably linked to the appropriate level for other basic requirements such as hygiene, sanitation and ventilation. Neither rule makes any reference to noise, "one of the most disruptive aspects of prison life. It interferes not only with normal living but with the effective running of an establishment, since it affects everyone within range and is a primary cause of increased tension and stress. Those who have lived and worked in prisons testify to the importance of noise as a disturbing factor in prison life" (Casale 1984: 21).

Neither the European Rules nor Prison Rules make any specifications for minimum cell contents. The NACRO Code included this element in its Code of Minimum Standards: "...efforts to maintain at least these levels of cell contents are all the more urgent in light of the many hours spent in cells, the lack of opportunity for work and the necessity in some instances for eating meals in cells" (1984: 23).

European Prison Rule 14.1's preferred norm of single cell accommodation, even with the proviso "except in cases where it is considered that there are advantages in sharing" is clearly at variance with the situation in many British prisons. Prison Rule 26 provides no redress for prisoners housed in overcrowded and insanitary conditions. The Woolf Report quoted the Director General of the Prison Service as saying that "the life and work of the Prison Service have, for the last 20 years, been distorted by the problems of overcrowding. That single factor has dominated prisoners' lives, it has produced often intolerable pressure on the staff, and as a consequence it has soured industrial relations. It has skewed managerial effort and it has diverted managerial effort away from positive developments. The removal of overcrowding is, in my view, an indispensable pre-condition of sustained and universal improvement in prison conditions" (1991: para. 11.135). Woolf stated "We unreservedly endorse the Director General's assessment of the effect of overcrowding and of the importance of resolving the overcrowding problem in the future... Nothing is, however, static. Even if overcrowding is banished in accordance with the Director General's timetable, it is necessary to ensure that there is no return to the present situation. Once banished, it must not return. Inmates and staff must in future be protected from the corrosive consequences of overcrowding ..." (paras. 11.137 and 11.140).

The Woolf Report recommended a new Prison Rule to allow no establishment to hold prisoners in excess of its Certified Normal Accommodation except by three per cent for a period of no longer than one week in any three calendar months. The Home Secretary would have the power to increase this limit in exceptional circumstances, but would have to issue a certificate specifying the maximum increase and the conditions of that increase. Such a certificate would have to be renewed every seven days and would be laid immediately before the Houses of Parliament. If such a Rule were introduced, levels of overcrowding would be susceptible to judicial review. The Government responded only that, "Once the system comes into equilibrium, it will consider the possible substance of a Prison Rule and of any formal procedure to notify Parliament of any significant instance of overcrowding..." (*Custody, Care and Justice* 1991: 6.13).

Such "equilibrium" seems even more distant now than it was then, with a 40 per cent increase in the overall prison population since 1992-93 (including an increase of over 100 per cent in the female prison population) and numbers topping 62,500 on an average day in 1997-98 (Home Office 1999a). According to the Chief Inspector of Prisons, "Overcrowding still remains a problem ... [Local prisons] are the most overcrowded, on average holding 26% more prisoners than they are resourced to do" (1999: 7 and 10).

Neither domestic nor European Rules deal with the issue of smokers and non-smokers sharing cells; the only Prison Rule dealing with smoking notes simply that smoking and the possession of tobacco are privileges exercised in accordance with governor's instructions (r 24(2)). However, governors have been instructed that they can create no smoking areas within establishments "if this is appropriate in local conditions" (CI 17/ 1985). Many visiting areas now enforce no-smoking rules. Circular Instruction 3/1989 asked "for non-smokers not to be compelled to share living accommodation with smokers [and] for non-smoking areas to be available in visiting accommodation and association rooms so long as this does not reduce access to visiting and association facilities. If this is not possible in the short-term, Governors should consider the installation of smoke extractors or filtering equipment" (CI 3/1989 2a and b. See also SO 14.26 a and b; also Op. Std. K14). Given the possibility of harmful effects of passive exposure to tobacco smoke, the segregation of accommodation for smokers and non-smokers is an appropriate area for health regulations in prisons.

Rule 26 makes no reference to the requirements of European Rule 15, namely "requirements of health ... and especially the cubic content of air, a reasonable amount of space, lighting, heating and ventilation". No technical standards specifically address prison lighting in the Standing Orders, only that "all parts of the establishment where prisoners live or work have adequate heating, lighting and ventilation" (SO 14.57). European Prison Rule 31.1(c) provides that the medical officer or competent authority should inspect and advise the director (i.e. the governor) on lighting and heating. Standing Order 14.59 contains approved temperatures, which are identical to those set out in the NACRO Code. It requires only that "ventilation should be provided to ensure a fresh atmosphere, subject to security requirements" (para. 58). Standing Order 14.1 refers to observation of the relevant statutory provisions, including the Health and Safety at Work Act 1974, the Factories Act 1961, and the Offices, Shops and Railway Premises Act 1963.

The Prison Service Operating Standards set out more specific criteria for cell accommodation. According to these Standards, the minimum size of a cell should be 5.5 square metres, or 1.3 times that size for double cells (Op. Std. H2). Cells should have natural ventilation, with artificial supplements where necessary, which meet Health and Safety guidelines (H5). Prisoners should be able to open and close cell windows, with the exception of certain special cells (H5, commentary). Prison Service Building Standards specify standards of heating, lighting, and sanitation facilities. Certified Normal Accommodation should have natural light (H6; the amount of light is not specified), and prisoners should have a light switch in their cells for the artificial light (H6, commentary). All cells should have alarm call bells (H7). Cell furniture should be "in a safe and serviceable condition" (H14) and (with the exception of special cells or segregation cells) should consist of at least a bed, storage cupboard/wardrobe, chair, and use of a table, mirror, and pin board (H13).

Prisons do not need a fire certificate. Inspectors under the Fire Precautions Act 1971 have no jurisdiction over prisons and no right of entry to them (Halsbury: 1148). AMBoV has long pressed for the independent inspection of safety standards by independent expert bodies. "There seems to be no good reason why fire inspectors ... should not have full access to prisons and be able to enforce standards" (*AMBoV Quarterly*, July 1983: 6).

The NACRO Code covered the relationship between time in cell and size of accommodation, lighting, heating, ventilation, noise, contents of cells, and safety (including inspection by local authority environmental health officers) (1984: Codes A1-6 and E).

JUSTICE has cited r 26 as an example of a situation in which the rule should recognise the prisoner's unconditional right to a benefit, as it was clearly the intention of Parliament by virtue of s. 14 of the Prison Act, 1952 that every prisoner should have adequate and hygienic accommodation. The relevant section of the Prison Act reads as follows: "(1) The Secretary of State shall satisfy himself from time to time that in every prison sufficient accommodation is provided for all prisoners; (2) No cell shall be used for the confinement of a prisoner unless it is certified by an officer (not being an officer of a prison) acting on behalf of the Secretary of State that its size, lighting, heating, ventilation and fittings are adequate for health..." Instead, the rule empowers the Secretary of State to withhold that benefit as he thinks fit. Thus, "the officer to the Secretary of State may certify a cell as adequate in respect of its size etc. for the accommodation of one prisoner, but the authority may house in it two or three prisoners if the Secretary of

State gives them leave". JUSTICE believed the exercise of this discretion had made s. 14 of the 1952 Prison Act "a dead letter" (1984: 3(c)).

In the early 1990s, the Prison Service came under intense criticism for prison conditions, primarily brought on by overcrowding and inadequate physical facilities (e.g. Woolf 1991). By April 1996, 'slopping out ended in all Prison Service establishments, and by March 1997 no prisoners were held three to a cell designed for one (Prison Service 1997-8). However, these improvements are not universal or irreversible, as the Chief Inspector's damning reports on (for example) Holloway in 1995, Glen Parva in 1997 (regarding exercise), and Dartmoor in 1998 (regarding sanitation) have shown. The housing of two prisoners in cells designed for one is not unusual, as shown by the use of 96 single cells in a new housing block at HMYOI Werrington to house 192 children. Key Performance Indicator 4 lists cases in which two or three prisoners are held in cells designed for one, but makes no mention of prisoners being held three to cells designed for two, or of prisoners held in cells of less than minimum size (HMCIP 1999). The increasing prison population makes prison conditions particularly vulnerable to decay and to reductions in standards.

The Committee for the Prevention of Torture recommended that each prison have an enforceable ceiling put on the prisoner population (1991: para. 61). However, the Home Office replied that "... the Government does not think that it would be right to impose a ceiling on the number of prisoners any particular establishment should hold. This is because the Prison Service has an absolute obligation to hold accused and sentenced persons committed by the courts" (1991: 7). In practice, prison governors agree an 'operational capacity' in their annual 'contracts' with area managers. In local and remand prisons, these 'operational capacities' are invariably greater than the prison's Certified Normal Accommodation, albeit less than the population levels which were commonplace before the series of prison riots in 1990.

In *Williams v Home Office (No. 2)* (1981), the Court considered the plaintiff's allegations about the conditions of his physical surroundings in the control unit at Wakefield Prison. Williams stated that there was insufficient daylight by which to read, and referred to r 11(a) of the UN Minimum Standard Rules that windows should be large enough to enable prisoners to read or work by natural light. The judge found no evidence of sensory deprivation. However, the judge firmly rejected the Home Office's contention that s. 14(3) of the Prison Act is express Parliamentary authority for indefinite confinement. Tudor Evans J stated: "Counsel's submission, as I understood it, is that since s. 14(3) provides that a certificate may limit the period for which a prisoner may be separately confined, it presupposes that he may be confined for an unlimited number of hours if there is no certificate. Therefore, since there was no certificate in respect of the plaintiff, he could be indefinitely confined even for 24 hours a day in the cell ... I cannot accept this argument. Section 14 of the Act has all the appearance of a health and welfare provision, and, in my judgement that is all it is dealing with".

Tudor Evans J held that no authority in modern law supports the submission that although a detention may be lawful it can become unlawful if the nature (meaning the conditions) of the imprisonment changes. "There is in fact in the administration of prisons of this country ample safeguard against abuse ... s. 4(2) of the [Prison] Act provides comprehensively for supervision of the conduct of prison officers, the treatment and conduct of prisoners and all matters concerning the management of prisons. The subsection provides a duty in terms that officers of the Secretary of State shall ensure compliance with the Prison Act and Rules. Conditions vary from prison to prison, according to the category of the prisoner and his behaviour in prison". In *Middlewick v Chief Constable of Merseyside* (1990) the Court of Appeal rejected this approach and followed the precedent in *Nahar* (1983) in which the Divisional Court said there must be some minimum standard to render detention lawful because it was possible to conceive of circumstances in which the conditions of detention would be such as to make it unlawful. The Court of Appeal accepted this and held that a detention which was initially lawful could become unlawful by reason of changes in the conditions of imprisonment. For example, a person's lawful detention in a prison cell would cease to be lawful if the conditions in that cell were seriously prejudicial to health, and thereby provide a remedy to the prisoner in damages for false imprisonment.

The House of Lords' decision in *Hague and Weldon* (1991) held that "no cause of action, either in false imprisonment or for breach of statutory duty, arose at the suit of a prisoner in respect of allegedly unlawful conditions of confinement," and that the dictum of Lord Justice Ackner in *Middleweek* was an incorrect statement of the law. "To say that detention became unlawful when its conditions became intolerable was to confuse conditions of confinement with the nature of confinement. If a prisoner at any time had no liberty to be in any place other than where the regime permitted, he had no liberty capable of deprivation by the regime so as to constitute the tort of false imprisonment. An alteration of conditions therefore deprived him of no liberty because he had none already" (*Independent*, 4 Sept. 1991).

Not only ordinary cells must be certified: punishment and special cells (see r 48) must also be certified in accordance with s. 14 of the Prison Act 1952.

The prison at Belmarsh (S.E. London) incorporates a large proportion of double cells in the living blocks. As a result of this policy decision, 60 per cent of the prisoners (most of them untried) are subject to compulsory cell-sharing. Other new prisons at Bullingdon, Swaleside, Lindholme, and the Wolds, amongst others, also contain double cells. Despite the evident breach of European Rule 14.1 ("Prisoners shall normally be lodged during the night in individual cells..."), some evidence suggests that many prisoners may prefer to share accommodation even when they cannot choose their cellmate (McGurk and Fludger 1987; HM Chief Inspectors of Prisons and Social Work Services for Scotland 1998). In 1997-98, an average of 11,548 prisoners were held two to a cell designed for one, a 22 per cent increase over the previous year (Home Office 1998b).

Custody, Care and Justice recognised that, "A decent [prison] service depends on the end of overcrowding ... the Government accepts therefore that the objective should be that no prisoner should have to be accommodated in overcrowded conditions" (1991: 6.10 and 6.11). It also said it would consider the possibility of a Prison Rule to regulate overcrowding and a formal procedure to notify Parliament of any significant overcrowding (1991: 6.13), as recommended in the Woolf Report. The Home Office put forward no time scale for these proposals, and no further public reference to them has been made since the White Paper was published. The Home Affairs Committee too made no mention of a new Prison Rule to control overcrowding, but stated: "We consider that the prevention of prison overcrowding must remain a major priority, so

that progress made towards the proper accommodation of all prisoners can be maintained, and that there should be no return to trebling, to use of police cells, or to use of cells without adequate access to sanitation" (1997: xv).
(See also rr 20-21 Medical attendance.)

Beds and bedding

27. *Each prisoner shall be provided with a separate bed and with separate bedding adequate for warmth and health.*

Standing Orders provide that issued bedding must be clean, aired and in reasonable condition, and that the mattress and bedding will be aired at least an hour once a week (SO 14: 27).
The NACRO Code (B1(g)) included recommendations that clean sheets and a pillowcase be issued at least weekly; clean blankets should be issued annually; and that all bedding be cleaned before reissue to other prisoners. The Code incorporated safety standards for the composition of bedding and mattress covers. Prison Service Operating Standards state that bedding sufficient for warmth should comprise two sheets, a pillow case, bed cover, and two blankets (I8). These should meet fire retardant standards and be laundered weekly (blankets and bed covers should be laundered monthly; I8-9). Towels should be laundered at least weekly (I9).

Hygiene

28. *(1) Every prisoner shall be provided with toilet articles necessary for his health and cleanliness, which shall be replaced as necessary.*
     (2) Every prisoner shall be required to wash at proper times, have a hot bath or shower on reception and thereafter at least once a week.
     (3) A prisoner's hair shall not be cut without his consent.

One of the most significant omissions in the entire Prison Rules is that it makes no mention of adequate sanitation. Considering that 24-hour access to sanitation has only recently become available for all prisoners, this seems a significant oversight. European Rule 17 provides that sanitation shall be "adequate to enable every prisoner to comply with the needs of nature when necessary and in clean and decent conditions". On this issue, the Prison Rules cannot be said to be "broadly consistent with the principles" embodied in the European Rules. The only references in the Standing Orders concern regular inspection of sanitary installations, washing facilities, and drainage systems and maintenance of sanitary installations "in a clean and decent condition" (SO 14.53 and 14.55). Rule 28(1)(c) stipulates regular inspection and advice by the medical officer on sanitation.
Standing Order 14 directs governors to ensure proper observation of relevant parts of the Public Health Acts 1936 and 1961, the Factories Act 1961, and the Offices, Shops and Railway Premises Act 1963. The Order provides for the supply of all the toilet items stipulated in NACRO's Minimum Standards, and also expands on r 28(2), providing for hand-washing facilities before meals, arrangements to ensure against unnecessary exposure when dressing, general staff supervision of baths and showers, and a 'reasonably warm' bathing temperature. The prescribed standards for men and women are now relatively similar since "it is thought inappropriate to maintain the distinction between provisions for

male and female prisoners" (CI 56/1989: 4a). The distinction between men and women in the previous Rules regarding having their hair cut has been removed; the reference to 'hair' in r28(3) includes facial hair, so prisoners are no longer required to shave or be shaved (PSI 27/1999).

Women are to be "provided with sanitary towels and/or tampons and the means to dispose of them as necessary" (SO 14 12; also Op. Std. J6), but female prisoners are not always allowed to keep sanitary towels in their cells and may have to ask for one each time they need it. One researcher observed that while staff claimed to be becoming more sensitive to the needs of female prisoners, they simultaneously ignored or delayed responding to requests for sanitary supplies when the prisoner needed them (Liebling 1992).

The Prison Rules do not refer to the cleanliness of the prison establishment; European Rule 19 requires it to be "properly maintained and kept clean at all times". Standing Order 14 provides for the weekly cleaning of floors, twice yearly washing of interior paint-work, and maintenance and cleaning of drains. The Prison Service Operating Standards also state the need to maintain the standards of health, hygiene, and safety laid out in the Prison Design Briefing System (PDBS). Prisoners should also have daily access to cleaning materials and equipment to clean their cells (I7).

Integral Sanitation
Although they agree that integral sanitation is an improvement over slopping out, both prisoners and staff have expressed concern over the implications that in-cell toilets may have on both hygiene and association. Many prisoners must eat in their cells and dislike the idea of 'living and eating in a toilet'. Some have suggested that the toilets should at least be in an alcove with a cover or curtain. Ideally, three cells should be converted into two with the middle cell used as the toilet and washroom. HM Inspectorate of Prisons recommended this particular method of integral sanitation in its report on HMP Gartree since the cells were "too small to allow the fitting of individual toilets," though stated that a system of electronic locking could also be considered (1990: 2.16). The Committee for the Prevention of Torture (CPT) advocated such a remedy during their first visit to prisons in the UK in 1991. The Chief Inspector for Prisons believes that though the latter alternative is ideal, it is financially and physically impractical in the majority of prisons. The CPT stressed in its report that "the objective should be to avoid prisoners having to comply with the needs of nature in the presence of other persons in a confined area that is used as their living quarters" (1991: para. 49).

The Prison Service Operating Standards state that prisoners should have access to toilets and hand washing facilities of an approved standard 24 hours a day (I2).

Bathing
The European Committee for the Prevention of Torture commented during its visit in 1991 that "access for prisoners to bathing facilities at least once a week is an absolute minimum requirement (reference can also be made in this context to Rule 18 of the European Prison Rules) in any prison; further, the particular circumstances in a given prison may mean that simply meeting that requirement is not enough. In an establishment where prisoners do not have ready access to either toilet facilities or running

water, a shower a week cannot be considered as sufficient" (para. 74). The Operating Standards aspire to showers or baths for prisoners a minimum of three times per week (I3), with access to hot showers or baths available on the cessation of activities for those prisoners involved in heavy or dirty work or "other energetic activities" (I4). All recesses and showers should be cleaned twice per day (I5).

HM Chief Inspector of Prisons stated in his 1990 report on the prevention of suicide and self-harm in prisons that, "There can be few more degrading or depressing conditions for a human being than not having access to a toilet or wash basin when required, and not to be able to rid oneself of the prison smell by a daily shower ... The majority of prisoners in local prisons can expect only one shower per week. This is unacceptable and every inmate should have a chance to shower daily" (para. 3.12).

The NACRO Code proposed separate sets of standards on personal and general hygiene. Personal hygiene standards include hair care; the provision of bathing facilities (preferably showers) at least weekly; a sufficient supply of wash-basins; access to WCs at all times; a minimum of one WC and wash-basin per 10 prisoners; and inspection of sanitary facilities by environmental health authorities (1984: Code B1). The general hygiene standards cover the cleanliness and good repair of the entire facility, including bathing and toilet areas; rubbish disposal; pest control; inspection and reporting of inadequate conditions; and inspection by environmental health authorities (Code B2). The Prison Service Operating Standards state that prisoners should be provided with toilet articles necessary for "cleanliness, hygiene and self-esteem"; prisoners should not be expected to use articles previously used by others (J4).

Circular Instruction 8/1992 introduces required training packages for food handling and hygiene in prisons. Meals for prisoners in Crown Court Custody areas must also meet standards set out in Circular Instruction 57/1989.

(See also commentary to rr 20-21 Medical attendance and rr 24-25 Food, alcohol and tobacco.)

Physical education

29.   (1) *If circumstances reasonably permit, a prisoner aged 21 years or over shall be given the opportunity to participate in physical education for at least one hour a week.*

(2) *The following provisions shall apply to the extent circumstances reasonably permit to a prisoner who is under 21 years of age -*

   (a) *provision shall be made for the physical education of such a prisoner within the normal working week, as well as evening and weekend physical recreation; the physical education activities will be such as foster personal responsibility and the prisoner's interests and skills and encourage him to make good use of his leisure on release; and*

   (b) *arrangements shall be made for each such prisoner who is a convicted prisoner to participate in physical education for two hours a week on average.*

(3) *In the case of a prisoner with a need for remedial physical activity, appropriate facilities will be provided.*

(4) *The medical officer or a medical practitioner such as is mentioned in rule 20(3) shall decide upon the fitness of every prisoner for physical education and remedial physical activity and may excuse a prisoner from, or modify, any such education or activity on medical grounds.*

Time in the open air

30. If the weather permits and subject to the need to maintain good order and discipline, a prisoner shall be given the opportunity to spend time in the open air at least once every day, for such period as may be reasonable in the circumstances.

Rule 30 and Prison Service Order 4275 'Time in the Open Air' reduce the standards stated in previous Standing Orders. Instead of the one hour of time in the open air previously allocated, 'time' is left unspecified except what is "reasonable in the circumstances". Health care advice in the PSO continues to state that "ideally prisoners should have the opportunity to spend at least an hour in the open air each day and that the period allowed should not normally be less than half an hour." 'Time in the Open Air' in a given day does not have to refer to a single period, though the intent for this direction seems to be to break up longer periods rather than to decrease already short periods. However, time prisoners spend outside moving between buildings is, according to the Order, "reasonable" to be included as time spent in the open air.

The Order goes on to say that prisoners should not have to choose between time outside and other purposeful activities or entitlements. Cancellation or curtailment of time outside should only be when the weather makes it unreasonable or, "exceptionally", for security or control (the reason should be recorded clearly). If time outside is cancelled, then prisoners on normal location should be able to substitute it with a period of association, recreation, or physical education. Further, "every effort should be made to provide for some time in the open air" before or after time in court. According to the Prisons Inspectorate, exercise is of special relevance for the well-being of prisoners but is particularly vulnerable to staffing variations (1982 Report: 4.02-08). Key Performance Indicators did nothing to ensure that 'time unlocked' (KPI 6) included time spent in the open air: "... no differentiation between types of prison or prisoner are made [in the KPI], so that it will not highlight that we found some children in Feltham locked up for at least 23 hours per day, nor that they did not see the fresh air for days on end. What is more it does not indicate what happens at weekends" (HMCIP 1999: 24). The KPIs no longer make reference to time prisoners spend unlocked.

Prisoners segregated for punishment or under rr 45 or 55 should spend a minimum of one hour in the open air each day (also the case for remands who choose not to work or to participate in other activities; PSO 4275). Exercise is related to work and association: if prisoners work indoors, they are to have half an hour's exercise daily on workdays if they have evening association and one hour's exercise if there is no evening association (SO 6A 24(a)). This order also provides for half an hour of exercise indoors on the third consecutive day when weather prevents outdoor exercise and daily thereafter until the weather permits outdoor exercise. Unconvicted prisoners are allowed a daily hour of exercise out of doors, weather permitting, and at least half an hour of exercise on the day they are produced at court (SO 8A 24).

Prison Service Operating Standards state that prisoners not in outdoor work or in an open prison should have the opportunity to spend at least an hour each day out of doors, weather permitting (U3). NACRO Code D also stated this, but with the proviso that this should be in addition to the minimum time out of cell. The NACRO Code also covered the minimum size of the exercise area, alternative indoor facilities, and inspection by the medical officer.

European Rules 83, 84, and 85 regarding physical exercises have no previous equivalent ESMR, nor do they have equivalents in the domestic Prison Rules. However, Standing Order 7C now requires the Medical Officer to assess a prisoner's level of fitness for physical education at reception: "Physical education staff should ensure that those classed as in need of remedial or compensatory exercise regularly receive appropriate exercise under the general direction of the Medical Officer" (SO 7C 7). Prisoners over age 35 must be passed as fit by the Medical Officer in order to participate in PE. The Order also states that "Physical education staff should take all reasonable steps to ensure the safety of prisoners taking part in physical exercise..." (SO 7C 15). PE should last at least one hour, though this may include showering time. Convicted adults should be able to participate in at least one session per week, and young offenders a minimum of two sessions per week.

Work

31.   (1) *A convicted prisoner shall be required to do useful work for not more than 10 hours a day, and arrangements shall be made to allow prisoners to work, where possible, outside the cells and in association with one another.*

(2) *The medical officer or a medical practitioner such as is mentioned in rule 20(3) may excuse a prisoner from work on medical grounds, and no prisoner shall be set to do work which is not of a class for which he has been passed by the medical officer or by a medical practitioner such as is mentioned in rule 20(3) as being fit.*

(3) *No prisoner shall be set to do work of a kind not authorised by the Secretary of State.*

(4) *No prisoner shall work in the service of another prisoner or an officer, or for the private benefit of any person, without the authority of the Secretary of State.*

(5) *An unconvicted prisoner shall be permitted, if he wishes, to work as if he were a convicted prisoner.*

(6) *Prisoners may be paid for their work at rates approved by the Secretary of State, either generally or in relation to particular cases.*

The most significant omission in r 31(1) is the fact that it provides for a maximum working day of not more than 10 hours, but not a minimum. In contrast, European Rule 71.3 refers to "a normal working day". To some extent the Prison Service Operating Standards do this in its reference to organised activities reflecting "the outside working day" (U6), but this is not enforceable.

Circular Instruction 1/1983 notes that a prison, in its entirety, constitutes a workplace within the meaning of the Health and Safety at Work Act 1974, and instructs governors to afford access to inspectors of the Health and Safety Executive to all areas of the establishment. The Medical Officer should assess prisoners for work and allocate them to a particular category (1-heavy, 2-medium, 3-light work). Prisoners should not be required to work outside the category allocated to them (SO 6A 9). Ethnic monitoring of work distribution is also 'best practice' (AG 32/1995, Annex). Standing Order 14.1 requires governors to observe not only the Health and Safety at Work Act 1974, which it regards as binding, but also any other statutory provisions relevant to the working conditions for prisoners and staff.

The Prison Reform Trust pointed out a fundamental difference between the European Rule and r 31(1) in that no onus is placed on the Prison Service in Britain to provide work. This implies no sanction against prison management when work is not provided, but prisoners are punished if they decline to work on those occasions when it is available (*Working their Time* 1984: 12).

The JUSTICE report pointed out that r 31(5), which provides that "an unconvicted prisoner shall be permitted, if he wishes, to work as if he were a convicted prisoner", should be made effective. "It would be wrong if an unconvicted prisoner were worse off in any respect than one who has been convicted. He has at least an equal right to have his time occupied while he is being detained against his will" (1983: 17). However, in response to the Committee for the Prevention of Torture's criticism that many unconvicted prisoners had no work available, the Home Office stated that "Since convicted inmates are required to work, the Prison Service has taken the view that they should have a degree of priority in regime provision, including the availability of industrial work" (1991: 2). The Home Office used the excuse that workshops for remand prisoners may be under-used since unconvicted prisoners are not required to work. Such a view directly opposes the statement in the JUSTICE report, as well as more recent reports such as Casale and Plotnikoff 1990 and the reports of the CPT. The Operating Standards suggest that the Prison Service aspires to sufficient provision of work, including work for remands (U5).

The Home Office also acknowledged that as far as opportunities for work are concerned, "...lack of resources prevents the department from fully achieving the proposed standards in all establishments". In November 1991, the House of Commons Employment Committee called for more relevant work for prisoners, longer working hours, and realistic rates of pay. It stressed the need for vocational training and education and called for an end to the practice of paying lower wages for education compared with industrial work (House of Commons Paper 495, 1991). The Chief Inspector followed up this theme, saying that "... .some prisons pay a wage for attending education and some only pay the minimum for those unemployed. It is inappropriate to consider education as unemployment" (1999: 33).

European Prison Rule 76.1 refers to an "equitable system of remuneration". The Committee for the Prevention of Torture expressed concern that, at their current rates of pay, prisoners in England have no prospect of being able to save money as European Prison Rule 76 states. The domestic Prison Rules make no reference to payment. The Woolf Report argued that present levels of prison pay are "a very substantial cause of disquiet and dissatisfaction within prisons" and said that prisoners "should be able to earn more realistic pay levels" (1991: 14.162-163). The Chief Inspector of Prisons stated that if a prisoner earns "... a realistic wage, the inmate can be reasonably expected to contribute towards his keep, send money home to his family, and possibly open a savings account" (1990: 3.28). Describing prisoners as "the poor men of Europe," Woolf proposed an increase of pay to an average of £8 per week. This was in 1991; eight years later, average pay has increased to £7 a week, with variations according to the type of work and level on the Incentives and Earned Privileges Scheme (Prisoners' Information Book).

(See also r 18 Sunday work, and r 51(21) intentionally fails to work properly or, being required to work, refuses to do so.)

EDUCATION AND LIBRARY

Education

32. *(1) Every prisoner able to profit from the education facilities provided at a prison shall be encouraged to do so.*
(2) Educational classes shall be arranged at every prison and, subject to any directions of the Secretary of State, reasonable facilities shall be afforded to prisoners who wish to do so to improve their education by training by distance learning, private study and recreational classes, in their spare time.
(3) Special attention shall be paid to the education and training of prisoners with special educational needs, and if necessary they shall be taught within the hours normally allotted to work.
(4) In the case of a prisoner of compulsory school age as defined in section 8 of the Education Act 1996[8], arrangements shall be made for his participation in education or training courses for at least 15 hours a week within the normal working week.

Rule 32 makes special provision for the education of prisoners of compulsory school age. Operating Standard U10 states that education of this group should be for at least 15 hours per week; U11 states that such opportunities should be available for prisoners over school leaving age as well, again for at least 15 hours per week (though part-time education should also be an option; U9). However, it still contains no equivalent to the requirement in European Rule 81(a) for integration of prison education with the "educational system of the country so that after their release they may continue their education without difficulty". Rule 32 also fails to meet the requirement of European Rule 77 for a "comprehensive education programme in every institution" or for it to have the same status and pay as work (European Rule 78). In fact, the Prison Reform Trust found that less than half of prisons paid prisoners as much for education as for work or training (Flynn and Price 1995).

NACRO in a submission to the Education, Science and Arts Committee stated that "The Prison Rules make no provision for education for remand prisoners, although the Young Offender Institution Rules have been extended, by Circular Instruction, for *sentenced* young offenders held in local prisons and remand centres. *We believe that it can only be to the benefit of prisoners, education and other prison staff for an explicit policy on education to be set down. This matter is of considerable importance in view of the proposals for private sector involvement in the remand system*" (1991: 9) (**emphasis** in original).

Under the current Standing Orders, "All prisoners will normally be eligible to take part in education classes and courses" (SO 7B 8). Prison Service Operating Standards further state that education should be available year-round, as well as in mornings, afternoons, and evenings (see details in Op. Std. O8), though the new Prison Rules removed the requirement for evening classes, previously r 29(2). In practice, evening classes are becoming an increasing rarity. Education is voluntary for all prisoners except those of compulsory school age (who are denied education only as a last resort; SO 7B 10-11). Governors have discretion under Standing Order 7B 14 and 15 to refuse or terminate a prisoner's attendance at a class or course if the governor believes it necessary due to the risk of disruption, for the needs of security, or if a disciplinary punishment (e.g.

segregation) prevents it (although removal from education may not be used as a disciplinary punishment). Advice to Governors 32/1995 encourages the ethnic monitoring of access to and distribution of education.

The 'eligibility' of prisoners in the Standing Orders to participate in education does not necessarily match the availability of education. The Chief Inspector of Prisons noted in 1999 that, "It was ... with some alarm that I drew attention in each of my previous annual reports to the numbers of prisons where education provision had been reduced in order to achieve what are euphemistically called 'efficiency savings'. I have mentioned some deplorable situations in adult prisons ... but the problem is seen at its most acute in YOIs. For example our inspection of HMYOI and RC Feltham showed that much of the available education money was being spent on the few juveniles who were still under school leaving age, for whom 15 hours of compulsory education has to be provided by law each week. As a result only 10 per cent of all young prisoners in Feltham were attending education classes" (1999: 30). He further commented that, "Adults in prison have far too limited access to education, in many cases only one in five being able to participate. Few prisoners have adequate induction interviews to diagnose their educational needs and inform them about what is on offer" (1999: 31).

Prison Service Order 4200 requires that education providers in prison must assess the need of prisoners using the Basic Skills Agency screening test, which should be offered to all prisoners. The result of this test should be recorded and transferred with the prisoner. In practice, this does not always happen. The PSO also states that any records of achievement such as certificates for the completion of a course or training programme must not have the name of the prison or any other reflection of the prison environment on it.

While prison education contractors are required to have BT Connect installed on their computers, this must be in an office or other secure room; prisoners are not allowed access.

Educational provision in prisons lacks a clear set of national guidelines for objectives and standards (Livingstone and Owen 1999). Variations in the curriculum at different prisons may also create difficulties for prisoners in continuing courses in a new prison after transfer (Prison Reform Trust 1992). This is a particular problem where prisoners are trying to earn qualifications. HM Chief Inspector of Prisons has written: "There is one practice ... covering both work and education, that I wish the Prison Service would eliminate, namely moving prisoners to other prisons while they are in the middle of courses leading to qualifications. Much time is wasted, and irritation caused, by poor communication between establishments. For example some prisoners have to do identical tests each time they are moved between establishments ... This is a waste of public money invested not only in course provision but also in the prisoner undertaking it. It also denies others the opportunity. It is, in fact, a complete negation of all that prisons allege that they are trying to do to achieve the overall aim" (1999: 33).

(See also r 4 Outside contacts, r 5 After care, r 31 Work, and r 43 Prisoners' property.)

Library

33. *A library shall be provided in every prison and, subject to any directions of the Secretary of State, every prisoner shall be allowed to have library books and to exchange them.*

European Prison Rule 82 makes provision for "instructional" text books as well as recreational books; r 33 does not define what may be provided, though Standing Order 7B 29 mentions "both recreational and instructional books." The Standing Order states that, "where there is sufficient demand, the provision includes books suitable for ethnic minorities and books printed in foreign languages. Facilities should also be provided for prisoners to request books not held in stock at the establishment." The Annex to AG 32/1995 continues this theme, requiring that libraries have foreign language and black interest sections. Standing Order 4 states that each establishment may specify the maximum number of books, newspapers, and periodicals which prisoners may retain in their possession, but this number must allow for at least six newspapers and periodicals and at least three books.

Neither the Prison Rule nor the European Prison Rule makes provision for the prison library to hold specific works of reference, though Circular Instruction 20/1991 and Standing Order 7B 32 directs establishments to make available the current Prison Rules and Young Offender Institution Rules, European Prison Rules, documents relating to parole and life sentences, data protection, repatriation of foreign prisoners, and the Police and Criminal Evidence Act, advice on petitioning the European Court of Human Rights, the International Covenant on Civil and Political Rights, the Prison Discipline Manual, and published Standing Orders. Libraries should also hold copies of the Prisoners' Information Book, as well as copies of prisoners' dietary scales and 'Wiping the Slate Clean', regarding the employment of people with a criminal record. AMBoV has suggested that prisoners have access to Boards of Visitors annual reports (see r 80). Some prison libraries obtain materials from Citizens' Advice Bureaux. Prison Service Operating Standards aim for prisons to carry a minimum of 2,000 titles or 10 books per prisoner, whichever is higher, and to cater for a wide range of needs and tastes (U23). This should include up to date copies of standard legal reference works and other required publications (U24). The Standards suggest the opportunity of at least one visit to the library a week of at least 20 minutes (U25).

In the US, it is a legal requirement that prisoners have access to legal materials (*Bounds v Smith*, 430 US 817, 1977). Instruction to Governors 73/1996 specifies that prison libraries must keep certain legal texts and materials to assist prisoners in filing appeals and legal challenges and understanding aspects of imprisonment.
(See r 10 Information to prisoners.)

COMMUNICATIONS

Communications generally

34. *(1) The Secretary of State may, with a view to securing discipline and good order or the prevention of crime or in the interests of any persons, impose restrictions, either generally or in a particular case, upon the letters or other communications to be permitted between a prisoner and other persons.*
(2) Without prejudice to the generality of paragraph (1), the Secretary of State may require that any visit, or class of visits, shall be held in facilities which include special features restricting or preventing physical contact between a prisoner and a visitor.

(3) *Without prejudice to sections 6 and 9 of the Prison Act 1952[9], and except as provided by these Rules, a prisoner shall not be permitted to communicate with any outside person, or that person with him, without the leave of the Secretary of State or as a privilege under rule 8.*

(4) *Except as provided by these Rules, every letter or other communication to or from a prisoner may be read, listened to, logged, recorded or examined by the governor or an officer deputed by him, and the governor may, at his discretion, stop any letter or other communication on the ground that its contents are objectionable or that it is of inordinate length.*

(5) *Every visit to a prisoner shall take place within the sight of an officer, unless the Secretary of State otherwise directs.*

(6) *Except as provided by these Rules, every visit to a prisoner shall take place within the hearing of an officer, unless the Secretary of State otherwise directs.*

(7) *The Secretary of State may give directions, generally or in relation to any visit or class of visits, concerning the day and times when prisoners may be visited.*

(8) *In this rule:*

"communications" includes communications during or by means of visits or by means of a telecommunications system or telecommunications apparatus, and "telecommunications apparatus" has the meaning assigned by paragraph 1 of Schedule 2 to the Telecommunications Act 1984[10].

Personal letters and visits

35. (1) *Subject to paragraph (8), an unconvicted prisoner may send and receive as many letters and may receive as many visits as he wishes within such limits and subject to such conditions as the Secretary of State may direct, either generally or in a particular case.*

(2) *Subject to paragraph (8), a convicted prisoner shall be entitled -*
>   (a) *to send and to receive a letter on his reception into a prison and thereafter once a week; and*
>   (b) *to receive a visit twice in every period of four weeks, but only once in every such period if the Secretary of State so directs.*

(3) *The governor may allow a prisoner an additional letter or visit as a privilege under rule 8 or where necessary for his welfare or that of his family.*

(4) *The governor may allow a prisoner entitled to a visit to send and to receive a letter instead.*

(5) *The governor may defer the right of a prisoner to a visit until the expiration of any period of cellular confinement.*

(6) *The board of visitors may allow a prisoner an additional letter or visit in special circumstances, and may direct that a visit may extend beyond the normal duration.*

(7) *The Secretary of State may allow additional letters and visits in relation to any prisoner or class of prisoners.*

(8) *A prisoner shall not be entitled under this rule to receive a visit from:*
>   (a) *any person, whether or not a relative or friend, during any period of time that person is the subject of a prohibition imposed under rule 73; or*
>   (b) *any other person, other than a relative or friend, except with the leave of the Secretary of State.*

(9) *Any letter or visit under the succeeding provisions of these Rules shall not be counted as a letter or visit for the purposes of this rule.*

Police interviews

36. A police officer may, on production of an order issued by or on behalf of a chief officer of police, interview any prisoner willing to see him.

The Police and Criminal Evidence Act 1984 (PACE) and the *Codes of Practice* which govern the conduct of interviews at police stations do not generally apply to those conducted in prisons, although "the spirit of the provisions must be observed as though the interview were at a police station" (CI 10/ 1989: 2). Copies of the *Codes of Practice* must be available in all establishment libraries.

The room in which the interview takes place must have adequate heating, lighting, and ventilation. Interviews should not take place in a cell unless the prisoner is sick in the cell or is otherwise unable to leave. Prisoners must not be required to stand, and female prisoners should not be interviewed solely in the presence of males (CI 10/1989: 16). Prisoners must be provided with refreshments and have a short break at least every two hours, and they must not miss a main meal (CI 10/1989: 17).

Prisoners have the right to consult a legal adviser before any such interview and may have an interpreter present (SO 5A 39(5)). Interviews should normally take place in the sight but out of the hearing of a prison officer unless the prisoner requests the presence of an officer; if only one police officer and no other person is present; if, in the case of female prisoners, no other female is present, in which case a female officer should be present; or if an officer is acting as the 'appropriate adult' (for prisoners under the age of 17 or who is mentally ill or mentally handicapped) (CI 10/ 1989: 28).

Standing Order 5A sets out further provisions relating to police interviews in prison.

Securing release

37. A person detained in prison in default of finding a surety, or of payment of a sum of money, may communicate with and be visited at any reasonable time on a weekday by any relative or friend to arrange for a surety or payment in order to secure his release from prison.

European Rule 92.1 provides: "Untried prisoners shall be allowed to inform their families of their detention immediately..." The Prison Rules have no equivalent to this. Standing Orders state that unconvicted prisoners may write and receive unlimited letters at their own expense (SO 5B 8 and 10). They are also allowed two second-class letters a week from the prison at public expense and may send "special letters" regarding defence of their case, to inform visitors of any transfer, or "In urgent domestic or business situations" first-class at public expense if they have no private cash (Prisoners' Information Book).

In the case of *McVeigh, O'Neill, Evans v UK*, the Committee of Ministers of the Council of Europe confirmed the Commission's report and finding of violation of the "right to family life" under Article 8. Two of the applicants were held for 45 hours under the Prevention of Terrorism (Temporary Provisions) Act 1976, without being able to contact their wives. The Committee accepted the UK's new arrangements for such contacts, which were incorporated into s. 62 of the Criminal Law Act 1977, under which there must be a full record of all requests for notification of detention to a person named by the detained persons. Under the Police and Criminal

Evidence Act (1985), persons arrested and in custody are entitled to have someone notified of their whereabouts as soon as is practicable. If detained in connection with a 'serious arrestable offence' then a police super-intendent can authorise delay in exercise of this right for up to 36 hours under certain specified circumstances.

Significantly, the Prison Rules omit a crucial element from European Rule 49.3: "All prisoners shall have the right to inform at once their families of imprisonment or transfer to another institution." Prison Rule 34(2) provides that a convicted prisoner is entitled to send and receive a letter on his reception into prison, and Standing Order 5B 8 states: "Accordingly a letter should be issued as part of the normal reception procedure on the day that an inmate is received into custody. An extra letter should be issued on the day of his reception into a new establishment on transfer or allocation if a letter has not been issued prior to his transfer and the postage of such letters will be at public expense." Circular Instruction 5/1987 extended this provision so that the extra first class letter should normally be issued from the dispatching establishment. In addition, convicted prisoners should on request be granted as many first class letters (at public expense) as they have visiting orders outstanding to prevent visitors from making wasted journeys. If a letter has insufficient time to reach an intending visitor, staff at the dispatching prison should offer to telephone anyone with an out-standing Visiting Order.

Unconvicted prisoners are allowed one extra letter at public expense, but the governor has the discretion to allow more for likely visitors. Again a member of staff may make a telephone call to at least one likely visitor if there is insufficient time for notification by post. The only exception to these provisions are category A prisoners, who receive no prior notification of transfer for security reasons. If the prisoner has attempted to ensure that intending visitors are notified of transfer, visitors can claim from the Prison Service the cost of any abortive visit.

Rule 34 vests extensive discretion in the Home Secretary to restrict communications. The detailed contents of PSO 4400, which replaces Standing Order 5 and all Circular Instructions on communications, explain most of this. The preface to Standing Order 5 states: "It is one of the roles of the Prison Service to ensure that the socially harmful effects of an inmate's removal from normal life are as far as possible minimised, and that contacts with the outside world are maintained. Outside contacts are therefore encouraged, especially between an inmate and his or her family and friends. At the same time, the Prison Service has an overriding duty to hold inmates in lawful custody in well ordered establishments; and to have regard to the prevention of crime and similar considerations; and some regulation of inmates' communications is therefore necessary."

Certain groups of prisoners are subject to specific restrictions on correspondence. These include prisoners remanded in custody for or convicted of offences under the Protection from Harassment Act 1997 (stalking), sexual offences against children, or of making or attempting to make obscene telephone calls or other communication. In these cases prisoners are subject to routine monitoring of all outgoing mail and telephone calls, except for official and legally privileged communications and those with the Criminal Cases Review Commission or Samaritans. Their visits too may be subject to closer supervision, including being in the direct hearing of an officer. These prisoners should not normally be transferred to open conditions if they are still being monitored, and they can be transferred from open to closed conditions if they are caught making restricted correspondence while in open conditions (IG 73/1995). Governors also have the discretion to place these restrictions on prisoners who have past convictions for obscene correspondence, even if this is not part of their current offence.

For all prisoners, governors have the discretion to decide whether to disclose the contents of a prisoner's correspondence to the police and other investigating or prosecuting authorities (IG 87/1995). Disclosure should only take place if it prevents escape; helps prevent or detect a crime or convictions of an offender; helps prevent or reveal a miscarriage of justice; helps in the recovery of proceeds of a crime; or if it affects national security or public safety. In the case of telephone calls, which fall under the terms of the Data Protection Act 1984 (unlike letters), the recovery of the proceeds of crime alone is not a valid reason for disclosure. An investigating authority may request the routine monitoring of a prisoner's non-privileged correspondence, and the governor has the discretion to decide whether to comply. Any such request must be for specific information, however, and not just a 'fishing expedition'.

On request, prisoners have the right to listen to a recording or to have a copy of the transcript of their telephone calls submitted for disclosure except where this would prejudice the prevention or detection of a crime or apprehension of offenders.

Visits
Convicted prisoners are allowed visits as frequently as circumstances at establishments permit, with a minimum of one visit after reception and one every two weeks thereafter, of 30 minutes minimum duration on the weekends and ideally at least one hour on weekdays, "but where circumstances permit, governors should allow longer" (CI 11/1991: 15). Operating Standard Q3 adds that at least one weekend visit should be possible every four weeks, and visits of at least an hour should be available. Visits should take place under "the most humane conditions possible" (SO 5A 3 and 24(1)). Unconvicted prisoners may have daily visits of fifteen minutes, but the governor has the discretion to organise visiting arrangements to accommodate the needs of their establishments and the wishes of prisoners and visitors, "subject to certain limitations. No reduction in the aggregate minimum allowance of 1 1/2 hours a week may be made without the express consent of the Home Secretary" (CI 11/1991: 20). Operating Standard Q2 increases this minimum to three hours per week, including at least one at weekends, and visits of not less than thirty minutes. The Operating Standards also aspire to flexible visiting hours, including evening visits (Q5-7). In its evidence to the Woolf Inquiry, the Prison Service stated: "Inmates generally prize visits above all other privileges" (para. 14.225). Woolf himself said that the Service "should work towards providing convicted prisoners with at least one visit each week" (para. 14.229).

Visits from probation officers, legal advisers, priests or ministers, MPs, and special visits (for prisoners who are seriously ill or who have serious welfare problems) do not count against a prisoner's visits entitlement (Home Office response to the CPT 1991: 13). Governors do however have the discretion to refuse visits on the grounds of "security, good order or discipline and in the interests of the prevention or discouragement of crime" (SO 5A 31), though for close relatives of the prisoner this should only be done in exceptional circumstances.

Under the Assisted Prison Visits Scheme, close relatives of prisoners may be eligible to have the cost of their visits paid for by the government (see PSO 4400). All prisoners, both unconvicted and convicted, are eligible to receive assisted visits as soon as they are taken into custody as long as the relative(s) qualify for the scheme, which is based on income.

Prisoners may accumulate up to 26 visits per year and are eligible for temporary transfer to take these visits twice a year starting six months after allocation (CI 11/1991: 17). Transfers for accumulated visits may be to any suitable prison provided that the receiving governor is content (CI 7/1992: 2).

Following the case of *Simms and O'Brien* (1999), journalists may visit prisoners in their official capacities if the purpose of the visit is to assist a prisoner who claims to have been wrongfully convicted.

Official Prison Visitors may also visit prisoners who request it. These are "officially appointed volunteers who visit establishments to befriend inmates ... Prison Visitors are a valuable local resource to establishments for voluntary visiting and can provide inmates, particularly those who have no other visitors, with an independent and informal contact with the outside world" (CI 16/1989: 1 and Annex A (also SO 7D 2)).

Following the highly publicised escape from HMP Parkhurst and the subsequent Learmont Report (1995), all exceptional risk category A prisoners (those held in the Special Secure Unit at Whitemoor and the Belmarsh Category A Unit) must have closed visits for all visits (originally including legal visits). Such prisoners may apply for open visits via the governor and area manager, though the governor and area manager have no discretion to grant open visits and may only comment on the merits of the application. Open visits for exceptional risk prisoners are allowed "only in the most exceptional circumstances" (IG 72/1995).

Prison Service Order 4400 requires that all children under the age of 18 accompanying visitors on a visiting order must also be named on that order. Further, prisoners identified as presenting a risk to children should only be permitted visits from their own children and siblings (legitimate and natural children, step-children, adopted children, and children of the prisoner's partner if they were living with that partner prior to prison), unless the governor believes it is in the best interest of a child outside these categories to visit. Unescorted children are not normally allowed to visit prisoners identified as a risk.

HM Chief Inspector of Prisons has reported that, "The provision of visiting facilities is unsatisfactory. The worst conditions for visits tend to be found in urban prisons, which are relatively accessible, while better conditions exist in training prisons, many of which are difficult to reach by public transport" (1991: 3.68). He further commented that, "The reduction in censorship and ... introduction of card phones for convicted and unconvicted inmates are welcome developments. However, prisoners who are located a long way from home are disadvantaged by the consequent cost of making telephone calls within the allowance from their private cash ... There remains considerable scope to improve assistance to inmates in maintaining ties with their families. For those without private cash, card phones are of no use while wages remain as low as they are" (1991: 3.73). This exemplifies the fact that what the Prison Rules provide in principle is not always feasible in practice, which again demonstrates the need for more specific Rules and the incorporation of minimum standards (e.g. for physical facilities, allocation, wages, and so on).

The JUSTICE report *Justice in Prison* (1983) recommended that the principle stated in the Standing Orders - that prisoners should be allowed as many visits as the circumstances of the prison permit - should be stated in the Rules; that r 34(4) be amended "to provide that visits should be within the hearing of an officer only if the governor considers, in particular cases and on grounds clearly specified by him, that this restriction is necessary. In this way the Rule would be brought into line with the existing practice"; and that the Rules take into consideration the distance of a prisoner from his home in the allocation decision. *Custody, Care and Justice* acknowledged the fact that, "Location nearer to home is likely to lead to greater stability in prisons" and that, "prisoners should be located in prisons suitable to their status and security category as near to their home as possible, unless they request otherwise, or their behaviour or the management of their sentences requires it" (1991: 5.13).

(See also rr 13-19 Religion, r 41 Search, and r 73 Visitors.)

Letters

The Home Office commented to the Council of Europe that in its view, the restrictions on communications which ESMR 37 (now European Prison Rule 43.1) permits "in the interests of treatment" contravene Article 8 of the European Convention on Human Rights and that restrictions on communications should only be allowed "in the interests of security and good order".

As with visits, "The governor has discretion to disallow correspondence with a person or organisation if there is reason to believe that the person or organisation concerned is planning or engaged in activities which present a genuine and serious threat to the security or good order of the establishment or other Prison Department establishments" (SO 5B 26). Standing Order 5B also prohibits prisoners' correspondence with minors (where the parent or guardian objects to it), convicted prisoners in other establishments or ex-offenders (where the governor believes this is undesirable), and victims of the offence (unless the victim is a close relative or the prisoner is unconvicted). Writing to box numbers or receiving anonymous letters is also generally not allowed. The governor should consult Headquarters before disallowing correspondence with 'close relatives' as defined in the Standing Order.

Reading prisoners' letters is justified as follows: "The examination and reading of correspondence to and from inmates is undertaken to prevent its use to plan escapes or disturbances or otherwise jeopardise the security or good order of establishments, to detect and prevent offences against prison discipline or the criminal law and to satisfy other ordinary and reasonable requirements of prison administration. Accordingly the extent to which correspondence needs to be read will vary according to the nature of the establishment, inmate and correspondent. Limits have to be placed on the amount of correspondence that inmates may send and receive, if such correspondence has to be examined and read, because the staff resources available to supervise correspondence are limited: otherwise the diversion of staff to censorship duties will inevitably cause other aspects of the prison regime to suffer, to the detriment of all inmates" (SO 5B 1).

The White Paper *Custody, Care and Justice* announced the abolition of the routine reading of letters in all establishments except maximum security prisons and for all category A prisoners or people held in category A units, and for prisoners on the Escape List. "Incoming mail is still searched for contraband such as drugs, while governors retain the right, and may be required, to read an individual's mail for security reasons" (1991: 7.36). The European Court of Human Rights decided in *McCallum* (1990) that the censorship of mail while the plaintiff was in the segregation unit in Inverness Prison was a breach of Article 8 of the Convention, and as a result the UK had to pay £3,000.

Despite the end of routine screening of correspondence for most prisoners, r 34(3) maintains the governor's right to read and stop any letter or communication considered objectionable or of inordinate length. The Court of Appeal in *R v Home Secretary, ex p Leech (No. 2)*(1994) declared that this Rule was *ultra vires* with regard to correspondence between prisoners and solicitors. The test for reading correspondence between prisoners and solicitors is whether a "self-evident and pressing need" exists for the interference; if this is the case, then the intrusion must be the "minimum necessary to ensure that the need is met" (Steyn LJ). Rule 34(3) therefore does not sanction the *routine* reading of a prisoners' privileged correspondence. The European Court of Human Rights made a similar ruling in *Campbell v UK* (1993), in which a Scottish prisoner claimed (successfully) that the routine reading of correspondence between prisoners and their lawyers was a breach of Article 8 of the European Convention.

The Court of Appeal in the case of *O'Dhuibhir* (1997) attempted to limit the Court of Appeal's ruling in *Leech (No. 2)* to the powers of r 34 rather than extending it to the approach of the court "whenever a fundamental right is interfered with without express Parliamentary approval ..." (Livingstone and Owen 1999: 19, fn 70). However, Lord Browne-Wilkinson in *Pierson* (1997) confirmed the correctness of approach in *Leech (No. 2)* to acts which interfere with a person's legal rights or basic principles of UK law, and not just to correspondence with solicitors.

The minimum allowance of one letter permitted to be sent out weekly, as stated in r 35, is misleading. Prisoners may write one letter a week (the 'statutory' letter) for which postage is paid, and at least one 'privilege' letter a week, for which the prisoner must pay the postage out of his or her prison earnings. "At establishments where all or most correspondence is not censured, there are no restrictions on the number or length of letters which inmates may receive" (SO 5B 10). Statutory letters may not be withdrawn or withheld as part of a disciplinary punishment (SO 5B 5).

Prisoners may also send 'special letters', which are not counted against their allocation of statutory or privilege letters, if they have been granted special permission to send such a letter for a special reason. Special letters should be granted to convicted prisoners when they are about to be transferred or upon reception at the new establishment after transfer; immediately after conviction to settle business affairs if necessary; where necessary for the welfare of the prisoner or his or her family; in connection with legal proceedings to which the prisoner is a party; where necessary to enable a prisoner to write to a home probation officer or to an agency which is arranging employment or accommodation for him or her on release; where necessary to enable a prisoner to write to the Parliamentary Commissioner for Administration; or at Christmas. Governors have the discretion to limit the number of special letters allowed (SO 5B 5(3) and 7(1-7)). Unconvicted prisoners may send such letters in the case of transfers (as for convicted prisoners) or in connection with their defence if they cannot afford the costs of a privilege letter for this purpose (SO 5B 8 3(a) and (b)).

At Christmas a convicted prisoner can send one additional letter to be paid for from his or her prison earnings, and the governor has the discretion to allow more. In addition a prisoner is permitted to buy up to twelve cards with stamps from the prison canteen with prison earnings or private cash (SO 5B 15). Prisoners are allowed to receive stamped addressed envelopes from their correspondents to help defray costs (CI 10/1991: 34). If a correspondent makes a practice of sending a prisoner an 'excessive number' of letters (undefined), the governor has the discretion to return these. If incoming letters are often 'overlong', correspondents may be asked to confine themselves to four sides of A5. If they ignore the request, their letters may be returned. In both cases, the prisoner should be informed (SO 5B 11). In practice these restrictions apply only to institutions such as maximum security prisons which regularly censor mail. Prison Service Operating Standards state that prisoners, except those in maximum security prisons, should be able to receive as many letters as they wish, irrespective of length, as long as the contents do not break Prison Rules. Further, letters should be issued within one working day of their receipt in the establishment (Q27; or within two days in maximum security prisons, unless translation is necessary; Q29).

The Rules do not indicate in what respect a letter will be considered objectionable, but the Standing Order lists twelve categories of subjects not to be included in general correspondence. The Standing Order no longer includes a prohibition on complaints about prison treatment since the reform of the complaints procedures in 1990. (See commentary to r 11 Requests and complaints for a discussion of current grievance procedures.) The European Court declared that stopping or censoring letters because they contain what are perceived as derogatory remarks about prison authorities is not justified (*Pfeifer and Plankl v Austria* 1992).

The European Court of Human Rights decided in *Boyle and Rice* (1988) that stopping letters on the grounds that the recipient was a media personality contravenes Article 8 of the European Convention.

The Committee for the Prevention of Torture recommended that letters sent by prisoners should not be recognisable to outsiders as having been sent from a prison (1991: para. 113). Many prisons already follow such a policy, such as allowing prisoners to use the street address of the prison as their postal address with no reference to their prison number or to the name of the prison, for example when prisoners are corresponding with their children.

(See also r 73 Visitors.)

Telephones

Prisons have installed card phones "to encourage prisoners to take more responsibility for maintaining close and meaningful family ties ... to respect the privacy of calls made by prisoners so far as this is reasonably practicable without compromising the interests of security and the good order of the prison ... [and] to help alleviate tension and reduce the depressive effects of prison life by normalising the environment" (CI 21/1992). Prisoners may use official telephones for special reasons such as bereavement or urgent welfare needs at the Governor's discretion (Home Office response to the CPT 1991: 23). Standing Order 5G sets out the guidelines on prisoners' use of telephones. Some restrictions include calls to mobile telephones and any calls to the media where the call itself or the information from it is intended for publication or broadcast (e.g. calls to radio programmes). The European Commission has, however, found this restriction on telephone communication with the media to be an infringement of Article 10 of the European Convention (*Bamber v UK* 1997).

All calls may be monitored and will be recorded, and all prisoners must be made aware of this in order to comply with the legal requirements of the Interception of Communications Act 1985. Telephones should be available in reception, where ideally two short calls should be allowed at public expense (Op. Std. N14 and commentary).

Calls for legal purposes to a legal adviser and calls to the Samaritans and "other reputable organisations" will not be monitored (CI 21/1992: 41 and 44). "Although it is not possible to guarantee the confidentiality of such calls made using the card phone system, governors should take steps to ensure so far as reasonably practicable that staff who realise that a genuine call to the Samaritans is being made or a call to some other reputable organisation of a personal sensitive nature should switch off the monitoring equipment. The officer may alert other staff (e.g.. the prisoner's personal officer) that a call to the Samaritans has been made, but no details of the conversation should be disclosed. Nor should any recording be played back or any use of the tape made" (CI 21/1992: 45). Letters to and from the Samaritans also should not be read and need not be opened for examination unless absolutely necessary (CI 10/1991: 26).

The governor has the discretion to prohibit prisoners from using the telephone for a period, take appropriate disciplinary action, or to suspend the facility altogether for a period in the case of widespread abuse of the privilege (SO 5G 7). Monitored calls may be terminated if they are abusive, offensive, or a threat to the good order and discipline of an establishment (Op. Std. Q23). However, "A prisoner should not normally be prohibited from using a card phone in any case where his or her disciplinary offence is not related directly to the misuse of a card phone or phone card" (CI 21/1992: 22).

Prisoners may not consult telephone directories and must apply to the governor or legal aid officer (if a solicitor's number is needed) to obtain a particular number (SO 5G 8 and CI 21/1992: 19). Certain prisoners may also not be allowed to possess phone cards, but only to have access to them through the wing office, namely a) all category A prisoners, b) all prisoners on the escape list, and c) at the discretion of the governor, any vulnerable prisoners who it appears are liable to be compelled by other prisoners to pass on their phone cards (CI 21/1992: 9). (See Standing Order 5G or Circular Instruction 21/1991 for further regulations on the use of card phones.)

According to Operating Standard Q26, prisoners who normally live abroad should be allowed one five-minute telephone call to their home country from an official telephone every calendar month, unless they have received a domestic visit in the previous month.

Prison Rule 33(6) affords the Board of Visitors (though not individual members) executive powers to grant additional letters and visits, the use of which do not require a prisoner to have made a formal application. The AMBoV Handbook points out that as the Rules grant both the governor and the Secretary of State power to grant letters and visits in r 35(3) and (7), an application to the Board may follow a refusal from elsewhere (para. 3D (6)c).

Legal advisers

38. *(1) The legal adviser of a prisoner in any legal proceedings, civil or criminal, to which the prisoner is a party shall be afforded reasonable facilities for interviewing him in connection with those proceedings, and may do so out of hearing but in the sight of an officer.*

(2) A prisoner's legal adviser may, subject to any directions given by the Secretary of State, interview the prisoner in connection with any other legal business out of hearing but in the sight of an officer.

Correspondence with legal advisers and courts

39. *(1) A prisoner may correspond with his legal adviser and any court and such correspondence may only be opened, read or stopped by the governor in accordance with the provisions of this rule.*

(2) Correspondence to which this rule applies may be opened if the governor has reasonable cause to believe that it contains an illicit enclosure and any such enclosures shall be dealt with in accordance with the other provision of these Rules.

(3) Correspondence to which this rule applies may be opened, read and stopped if the governor has reasonable cause to believe its contents endanger prison security or the safety of others or are otherwise of a criminal nature.

(4) A prisoner shall be given the opportunity to be present when any correspondence to which this rule applies is opened and shall be informed if it or any enclosure is to be read or stopped.

(5) A prisoner shall on request be provided with any writing materials necessary for the purposes of paragraph (1).

(6) In this rule, "court" includes the European Commission of Human Rights, the European Court of Human Rights and the European Court of Justice; and "illicit enclosure" includes any article possession of which has not been authorised in accordance with the other provisions of these Rules and any correspondence to or from a person other than the prisoner concerned, his legal adviser or a court.

Following numerous legal challenges such as *Golder v UK* (1975), *Silver v UK* (1983), *Anderson* (1984), and *Raymond v Honey* (1982), regarding access to outside courts, prisoners may now correspond with legal advisers, members of Parliament, the Monarchy, the European Parliament, the European Commission of Human Rights, the Parliamentary Commissioner for Administration, and so on at any time. (See r 11 Requests and complaints for more details about the procedures.)

Circular Instruction 48/1984 explains prisoners' contact with legal advisers about possible legal proceedings. A prisoner who wishes to have a visit from a legal adviser to discuss the possibility of litigation (or other legal business, such as drawing up a will) is entitled to this without disclosing the substance of the matter to be discussed, and all such visits should be out of the hearing of staff. Prisoners are not entitled to a visit out of hearing on demand: they must state that the purpose is to discuss possible legal business or about a forthcoming adjudication, but they cannot be required to disclose details of the matter to be discussed (SO 5A 34).

The Divisional Court in *Anderson* held that a prisoner should be allowed to correspond with a legal adviser about possible proceedings relating to a complaint about treatment or allegation against staff without first making the complaint through internal procedures. Such correspondence may be read, since r 39(1) does not apply until proceedings have been instituted, but it should not be stopped unless it is clear from the context that the prisoner is writing for some purpose other than obtaining legal advice about possible proceedings; even then it should not be stopped on these grounds without reference to Headquarters. Standing Order 5B 35 clarifies that correspondence with a solicitor about any disciplinary charge which has been preferred against the prisoner should not be read or stopped.

According to Standing Order 5F 8, "An inmate should not be placed on report on account of anything contained in an application to the European Commission of Human Rights or in a letter to his or her legal adviser with a view to or in regard to an application to the Commission." Despite this implication in the Standing Order that such correspondence is read, "An inmate may correspond with his or her legal adviser ... in regard to an application [to the Commission] or any proceedings resulting from it. Such correspondence should not be read unless the governor has reason to suspect that it contains other matter" (SO 5F 7).

Instruction to Governors 13/1995 clarified this guidance, stating that all correspondence between prisoners (including category 'A' prisoners) and legal advisers, courts, or European bodies must be treated as privileged and cannot be opened, read, or stopped except in the circumstances specified in r 38. Even then, such correspondence may only be opened in the prisoner's presence, unless the prisoner waives this right and signs a form stating so. If staff suspect that correspondence contains an illicit enclosure or is a threat to security they should pass the letter, unopened, to the governor, who will take the decision personally as to whether to examine the correspondence. Prisoners must be informed if their correspondence, or any enclosure, is to be read or stopped. Any decision to and reasons for examining privileged correspondence must be recorded clearly on the prisoner's record. "Any breach, even if accidental, is likely to lead to legal challenge in both the domestic and international courts" (IG 113/1995).

In *Guilfoyle v Home Office* (1981), the Court of Appeal held that a prisoner should have free access to his or her legal adviser for the purpose of any proceedings which have a legal content, even though they might not qualify as legal proceedings under the Rules. Instruction to Governors 113/1995 states that privileged correspondence may be handed in sealed if prisoners write "Prison Rule 38" (or the equivalent YOI Rule) and their name on the back. Even if correspondence is not marked this way but is clearly addressed to a legal adviser, it should be treated as though it were marked properly.

The Convention considered a broad range of issues, including that of correspondence, in *Campbell and Fell v UK* (1984). The applicants had been involved, along with four other prisoners, in an incident at Albany Prison in September 1976 in which members of staff and the two applicants were injured. Both were charged with mutiny, or incitement to mutiny, or gross personal violence to an officer. Both stated they had been repeatedly refused permission by the authorities to seek legal advice in connection with claims for compensation for injuries they sustained in the altercation. Fell also alleged that he had later been refused permission to consult his solicitors out of the hearing of prison officers. The Court concluded that as regards both claims there had been breaches of Articles 6(1) and 8. The Court agreed with Fell's claim that the refusal of permission to correspond with certain individuals on the grounds that they were not relatives also constituted a violation of Article 8.

In *McAvoy* (1984), a remand prisoner charged with participation in a gold bullion robbery was transferred without warning from London to Winchester. As a result, his invalid parents, solicitor and counsel all found it extremely difficult to visit him due to the distance and the poor visiting facilities. McAvoy claimed that the transfer was unlawful, relying on his general 'rights' to freedom of association and to a fair trial, as reflected in rr 35(1) and 38(1) (then rr 34 and 37). Webster J rejected the Secretary of State's claim that his exercise of powers granted by s. 12(2) of the Prison Act was not subject to review by the courts and held that transfer decisions are reviewable and the obligations contained in the Prison Rules must be taken into account. However, if, as in this case, 'operational and security' reasons are claimed for the transfer, the court should not look behind those reasons which will almost invariably outweigh the prisoner's right to visits, lay or legal. The sudden removal of a remand prisoner to a prison where his or her lawyers can no longer visit or take adequate instructions is arguably a breach of Article 6 of the European Convention.

The European Court of Human Rights determined in *Campbell v UK* (1992) that screening correspondence between prisoners and their solicitors breached prisoners' rights. The Court ruled that the need to respect confidentiality between the lawyer and client outweighs the possibility of abuse.

The Court of Appeal decided in *Barrow* (1991) that, "A litigant in person in civil proceedings is entitled to receive assistance in the presentation of his case before the court from an adviser who is not exercising rights of audience. The court can object to the assistance if it disrupts or abuses the processes of the court" (*Independent*, 7 August 1991).

Conversations between prisoners and prison officers acting as Legal Aid Officers are *not* privileged for the purposes of evidence which may be used in legal proceedings. This judgement relates solely to discussions about the substance of an application for legal aid and does not affect interviews to assist prisoners on other matters related to the legal process (e.g. applications for bail or advice on appeal procedures) (*R v Mfongbong Umoh* (1987); C.I. 22/1987).

Any information that prisoners give to Legal Aid Officers about legal aid, bail applications, or appeals should be treated as confidential unless it is a threat to security or contains information about criminal activity (Op. Std. E2). Legal Aid Officers should advise prisoners of any circumstances in which confidentiality cannot be kept.

Since July 1997, all visits with lawyers take place in open conditions. This followed concern from a UN Special Rapporteur (1996 Annual Report) that closed visits hampered unfettered access of prisoners to legal advice. Visits by legal advisers should not be refused without consulting Headquarters (CI 11/1991: 47).

Prisoners who are preparing their own defence or legal proceedings may purchase photocopies. They may also interview another prisoner (with that prisoner's consent) in the sight of and in or out of the hearing of staff, at the governor's discretion. They may interview a prisoner at another establishment if they contribute to the cost of the transfer and obtain authorisation for this.

(See also rr 34-35 Communications generally and r 41 Search.)

REMOVAL, SEARCH, RECORD AND PROPERTY

Custody outside prison

40. *(1) A person being taken to or from a prison in custody shall be exposed as little as possible to public observation, and proper care shall be taken to protect him from curiosity and insult.*

(2) A prisoner required to be taken in custody anywhere outside a prison shall be kept in the custody of an officer appointed or a police officer.

(3) A prisoner required to be taken in custody to any court shall, when he appears before the court, wear his own clothing or ordinary civilian clothing provided by the governor.

Rule 40 does not contain the proviso in European Rule 50.1 protecting a prisoner in transit from "publicity in any form", or the prohibition of unnecessary physical hardship due to the condition of the transport used in European Rule 50.2.

Standing Order 1G(8) states that prisoners may be handcuffed in court (which includes "any court of law, coroner's court or other tribunal") only if there is danger of escape or violence and the judge is satisfied that handcuffing is necessary. An application for the use of handcuffs must be made in open court (CI 26/1991:50). Standing Order 1F sets out general standards for the use of handcuffs during escorts outside prison.

The Home Office reported to the Council of Europe: "Practice in England and Wales requires prisoners to pay for the cost of their transport in certain circumstances. This includes transport and escort costs for attendance at their own weddings and for the purpose of attending court in civil proceedings. This is not thought to be unreasonable." The Court of Appeal has since clarified in *Wynne* (1992) that prisoners cannot be asked to meet the costs of their imprisonment, including transport costs for court appearances.

The Prison Service Operating Standards give guidance for custody outside prison beyond that in r 40. First, the Standards require "proper provision" of meals, clothes, hygiene, health, and shelter (Op. Std. G2). Escorts should also be in approved vehicles under "safe and secure conditions" (G4). Professional visits should be allowed at court, within the sight but out of the hearing of escorting staff (G5). Finally, escorting officers should seek immediate medical attention for prisoners who appear to be ill and should escort the prisoner to hospital if necessary (G6).

Search

41. *(1) Every prisoner shall be searched when taken into custody by an officer, on his reception into a prison and subsequently as the governor thinks necessary or as the Secretary of State may direct.*

(2) A prisoner shall be searched in as seemly a manner as is consistent with discovering anything concealed.

(3) No prisoner shall be stripped and searched in the sight of another prisoner, or in the sight of a person of the opposite sex.

No European Prison Rule deals with searches. Rule 41(1) gives the governor complete discretion to schedule searches as he or she thinks necessary. As establishment-wide searches are very time-consuming, this has implications for other aspects of the regime, e.g. restrictions on the quantity of prisoners' property. In fact, restrictions on prisoners' property through volumetric control followed a recommendation of the Woodcock Report (1994) specifically to increase the ease of searching. The Woodcock Report also recommended the creation of Dedicated Search Teams to reduce the possibility of intimidation and 'conditioning' of staff during cell searches. The Report directed that "A clear written policy on searching procedures should be available to all staff, inmates and visitors" (1994: rec. 11).

Following Woodcock and Learmont, cell searches take place without the prisoner present. One prisoner alleged in *Main* (1998) that a cell search conducted in his absence created a risk that his legal papers and correspondence would be read by prison staff, contrary to r 39 (then r 37A). The Court of Appeal rejected this, concluding that: "any interference with confidential communication between a prisoner and his lawyer was the minimum necessary to ensure that security was maintained" (Livingstone and Owen 1999: 5.13). The extension of searching to privileged documents in a prisoner's possession may however be considered disproportionate under Article 8(2) of the European Convention (Kaufmann 1998). Operating Standard B7 states that prisoners and accommodation should be searched on a regular basis, and that searches "should be carried out with proper regard for the prisoner's privacy and dignity".

Circular Instruction 1/1992 states that a prisoner is "in the sight" of another prisoner or an officer if they could see him or her if they looked in the prisoner's direction. Simply looking away does not suffice for the purpose of the Rule. A prisoner is "in the presence" of an officer if the officer is close enough to be able to overhear the proceedings, even if out of sight. No prisoner may be stripped in the sight of any other person for any reason other that searching. Although officers must sometimes assist in restraining a prisoner of the opposite sex, such assistance must not be provided while the prisoner is being stripped. The Circular Instruction also states that no more than two officers should be present during a strip search except in "the most exceptional circumstances" (CI 1/1992:9(b)). This guidance seems confusing in light of the subsequent Operating Standard (B8), which states that "*at least* two officers of the same sex as the prisoner" must carry out a strip search (emphasis added). Circular Instruction 49/1992 gives more specific guidance on staff searches of the opposite sex.

CI 1/1992 stated that prisoners should not be required to bend forward, squat, or crouch, and no mirror or probe should be used during strip searches. This guidance has changed since Woodcock and Learmont: the Manual on Security now states that prisoners may in fact be asked to squat. The Prisoners' Information Book explains that this may be done for visual inspection only, and that "standards of modesty and decency should be maintained at all times".

Recent examples show that this guidance is not always followed. While the situation at HMP Highpoint has since improved, an inadequate proportion of female staff meant that male staff strip searched a female prisoner and, after delayed results of internal inquiries, have still made no apology to the prisoner (HMCIP 1999: 16). Following a forced strip search of all the female prisoners in Maghaberry Prison in March 1992, groups such as the Irish Women's Defence Campaign, the Committee for the Administration of Justice, and the Northern Ireland Association for the Care and Resettlement of Offenders called for an end to the practice of strip-searching, describing it as "an outrageous assault on women prisoners" (*Irish News*, 19 June 1992). The Home Affairs Committee recommended in

1997 that the new Security Manual should take into account "the particular difficulties associated with strip searching in women's prisons" (1997: xxvii).[3]

The Prisons Ombudsman questioned Prison Service practice in relation to intimate (internal) searches. The Prison Service considered it reasonable to ask a prisoner to conduct an intimate body search on himself, though legal advice said that such an order was likely to be judged unlawful. This has not yet been tested in court. The Ombudsman commented in his Annual Report, "I believe prison managers may need to do more to ensure that officers are following properly the instructions on the conduct of strip searches so that prisoners are not subjected to such searches in circumstances which are not justified" (1998: 2). The European Commission found that close body searches in which a prisoner was required to squat and a mirror was used did not violate Article 3 of the Convention (*McFeely v UK* 1981). However the Commission's decision, "leaves room for argument that where prisoners are required to squat in the absence of any substantial evidence that a security threat is posed, the requisite level of debasement and humiliation will be reached" (to qualify as a violation of Article 3; Kaufmann 1998).

Intimate searches may only be conducted by a medical practitioner, with the consent of the prisoner. A doctor may only conduct the search without consent if he or she believes this is necessary to prevent death or serious harm to the prisoner. In such cases the doctor must have the agreement of the governor and obtain a second medical opinion (Security Manual, paras. 66 and 67).

Prison Service Instruction 35/1997 states that prisoners should normally be strip searched prior to being handed over to contracted out staff for an escort "unless medical arrangements make this impractical". The Divisional Court in *Mohammed Zulfikar* (1995) held that the policy of routine strip searches before and after visits was lawful. However, while random strip searches of prisoners for drugs following visits "should be encouraged", blanket strip searching of all prisoners should not take place without good reason (Home Affairs Committee 1997: xxvii).

Certain civilian staff have powers to conduct rub-down searches of prisoners. These staff include civilian instruction officers, industrial staff, stores persons, civilian catering staff, agricultural or horticultural craftsmen, night patrols, prison auxiliaries, nursing grades ("in a health care context"), and other civilian grades whose duties involve the custody or supervision of prisoners (IG 42/1995). Contract staff or seconded staff such as teachers or probation staff generally do not have this power, though the head governor may authorise them to do so. Staff cannot be forced to conduct searches; rather, it must be an agreed part of their duties stated in their contract, and they must be trained for it. Prisoners must be notified of which staff have the power to search them.

For rub-down searches, prisoners are not required to remove clothes other than an outer coat, jacket, headgear, gloves, and footwear. Staff may use reasonable force where necessary and may seize and detain any unauthorised property found on a prisoner during a search (sec. 152, Criminal Justice and Public Order Act 1994).

---

[3] Presumably the "particular difficulties" the Committee had in mind were, for example, the possibility of retraumatisation due to high rates of physical and sexual abuse amongst female prisoners prior to custody (see for example Loucks 1998).

Operating Standard B10 states that visitors may be searched prior to visits, but that they too must be searched by an officer of the same sex and that the search "should be carried out with proper regard for the visitor's privacy and dignity". In *Bayliss and Barton* (1993), a county court ruled that a strip search of a visitor gave rise to an action for damages when such standards were not followed. Visitors should not be strip searched without consent (though in this case they may be offered a closed visit or denied a visit), nor may prison staff conduct intimate searches of visitors.

Tudor Evans J rejected a complaint by the plaintiff in *Williams v Home Office (No. 2)* (1981) that he was subject to excessive surveillance (including being watched in the shower and lavatory) and searches by the prison staff while held in the control unit at Wakefield Prison. The judge accepted that by r 41(1) the frequency of searches depends on the governor, and that it is necessary to carry out searches in the prison system for security reasons and to ensure compliance with the rules.

(See also r 8 Privileges, r 58 Cellular confinement, and r 73 Visitors.)

Record and photograph

42. (1) *A personal record of each prisoner shall be prepared and maintained in such manner as the Secretary of State may direct.*

(2) *Every prisoner may be photographed on reception and subsequently, but no copy of the photograph shall be given to any person not authorised to receive it.*

Unconvicted prisoners, civil prisoners, fine defaulters, and Immigration Act detainees should not routinely be photographed (CI 2/1990: 13), and civil prisoners should be fingerprinted only in exceptional circumstances (SO 17 13). Sentenced prisoners should have their fingerprints taken on reception after sentence (Op. Std. B15). Standing Order 17 sets out the specific provisions for records, reference photographs, measurements, identification procedures, and so on. Operating Standard B16 states that convicted prisoners should be photographed on reception and at least once every two years while in custody. Unconvicted prisoners may be photographed "where there are justifiable security grounds", as may immigration detainees (though this is exceptional).

The Home Office reported to the Council of Europe that details are also kept of prisoners' medical requirements, their family, and their education as well as any previous convictions. The Access to Health Records Act 1990 specifies that prisoners have the right of access to their health records and may have copies made on request (see rr 20-21 Medical attendance).

Prisoners' property

43. (1) *Subject to any directions of the Secretary of State, an unconvicted prisoner may have supplied to him at his expense and retain for his own use books, newspapers, writing materials and other means of occupation, except any that appears objectionable to the board of visitors or, pending consideration by them, to the governor.*

(2) *Anything, other than cash, which a prisoner has at a prison and which he is not allowed to retain for his own use shall be taken into the governor's custody. An inventory of a prisoner's property shall be kept, and he shall be required to sign it, after having a proper opportunity to see that it is correct.*

(3) *Any cash which a prisoner has at a prison shall be paid into an account under the control of the governor and the prisoner shall be credited with the amount in the books of the prison.*

(4) Any article belonging to a prisoner which remains unclaimed for a period of more than 3 years after he leaves prison, or dies, may be sold or otherwise disposed of; and the net proceeds of any sale shall be paid to the National Association for the Care and Resettlement of Offenders, for its general purposes.

(5) The governor may confiscate any unauthorised article found in the possession of a prisoner after his reception into prison, or concealed or deposited anywhere within a prison.

Money and articles received by post

44.   *(1) Any money or other article (other than a letter or other communication) sent to a convicted prisoner through the post office shall be dealt with in accordance with the provisions of this rule, and the prisoner shall be informed of the manner in which it is dealt with.*

(2) Any cash shall, at the discretion of the governor, be -

   (a) dealt with in accordance with rule 43(3);
   (b) returned to the sender; or
   (c) in a case where the sender's name and address are not known, paid to the National Association for the Care and Resettlement of Offenders, for its general purposes:
   Provided that in relation to a prisoner committed to prison in default of payment of any sum of money, the prisoner shall be informed of the receipt of the cash and, unless he objects to its being so applied, it shall be applied in or towards the satisfaction of the amount due from him.

(3) Any security for money shall, at the discretion of the governor, be -

   (a) delivered to the prisoner or placed with his property at the prison;
   (b) returned to the sender; or
   (c) encashed and the cash dealt with in accordance with paragraph (2).

(4) Any other article to which this rule applies shall, at the discretion of the governor, be -

   (a) delivered to the prisoner or placed with his property at the prison;
   (b) returned to the sender; or
   (c) in a case where the sender's name and address are not known or the article is of such a nature that it would be unreasonable to return it, sold or otherwise disposed of, and the net proceeds of any sale applied in accordance with paragraph (2).

According to the 1984 AMBoV Handbook, questions arising under r 43(1) should be dealt with by the full Board: "...it would be quite improper to use r 43 for the purposes of moral censorship over and above the provisions of the criminal law" (para. 3D (6)b).

Although European Rule 48.4 provides for the exercise of the prison medical officer's discretion regarding a prisoner's own personal medications brought in on admission, the Prison Rules make no such provision. This often causes enormous difficulties for prisoners who have been receiving regular medication outside. Standing Order 13 gives the medical officer discretion to deal with any medicine, drugs, and prescriptions which prisoners have with them on reception as part of their private property. Wherever possible medicine dispensed in prison is administered in liquid rather than pill form.

The Home Office reported to the Council of Europe in 1991: "In England and Wales there is provision for the destruction or disposal of any articles of a prisoner's private property which could be used for the commission of offences on release, e.g. flick-knives, rubber gloves etc. This will normally only be done with the consent of the prisoner."

Standing Order 1C (amended in Annex C of CI 22/1990) sets out the specific regulations regarding a prisoner's property. The Operating Standards recommend that establishments should log any property or money in a prisoner's possession at reception (N6), that governors should publish a statement of property which prisoners may keep in their possession (N7), that property not in prisoners' possession should be stored securely in conditions which prevent loss or damage (N8), and that facilities for secure storage should be available for property which prisoners keep in their possession (N9).

The Prison Service does not accept responsibility for loss or damage to property either in cell or in storage unless a prisoner can prove the damage was due to the negligence of the Prison Service. "This can be hard to prove and it may be a good idea to try to make sure that only essential things are kept in the prison" (Prisoners' Information Book).

Following a recommendation in the Woodcock Report (1994) to limit the quantity of property in cells, all property in a prisoner's cell (with the exception of certain oversized items) must fit into two standardised boxes. This restriction is known as 'volumetric control' and is designed to ease searching of cells. This restriction has not been without problems, including criticism from the Prison Ombudsman regarding the lack of flexibility of these restrictions: "In my view the fact that the Service does not provide an additional allowance, above usual volumetric control property limits, for educational materials may mean that the Service is not fulfilling this requirement..." (1998: 1). The Director General of the Prison Service rejected the Ombudsman's criticisms on this, but the Ombudsman continues to argue his point: "... I am concerned that, where prisoners are involved in long term courses of study preparing them for a useful life in society after release, their chances of success could be severely undermined by an inability to have ready access to all their course notes" (*ibid.*).

(See also rr 8 Privileges, 27 Beds and bedding, and 41 Search.)

SPECIAL CONTROL, SUPERVISION AND RESTRAINT AND DRUG TESTING

Removal from association

45. (1) *Where it appears desirable, for the maintenance of good order or discipline or in his own interests, that a prisoner should not associate with other prisoners, either generally or for particular purposes, the governor may arrange for the prisoner's removal from association accordingly.*

(2) *A prisoner shall not be removed under this rule for a period of more than 3 days without the authority of a member of the board of visitors or of the Secretary of State. An authority given under this paragraph shall be for a period not exceeding one month, but may be renewed from month to month except that, in the case of a person aged less than 21 years who is detained in prison such an authority shall be for a period not exceeding 14 days, but may be renewed from time to time for a like period.*

(3) *The governor may arrange at his discretion for such a prisoner as aforesaid to resume association with other prisoners, and shall do so if in any case the*

medical officer or a medical practitioner such as is mentioned in rule 20(3) so advises on medical grounds.
(4) This rule shall not apply to a prisoner the subject of a direction given under rule 46(1).

This is perhaps the most controversial of the English Prison Rules. Rule 45 segregation is an administrative action not intended as a punishment but often seen as such. The European Prison Rules have no equivalent provision.

The Prison Act 1952 states only that, "In every prison cells shall be provided for the temporary confinement of refractory or violent prisoners." Punishment cells are not provided for in the Act. Rule 2 requires that "order and discipline shall be maintained with firmness *but with no more restriction than is required for safe custody* and well-ordered community life" (emphasis added). Nothing in r 7 (Classification) requires "a prisoner to be deprived unduly of the society of other persons". No specific authority exists for punishment cells or punitive segregation other than as places to serve cellular confinement in cases of violent or refractory prisoners.

Authorisation and monitoring
Boards of Visitors are expected to take an active role in authorising and reviewing decisions to segregate prisoners under r 45. However, AMBoV, having pressed the Home Office to clarify the issue of legal responsibility, responded, "How can this realistically be our responsibility and I wonder how many occasions has a member actually refused to sign?" (Macfarlane 1983). In fact, Prison Inspectorate reports show that Boards of Visitors have not always assumed responsibility for correcting deficiencies in r 45 procedures. This dual role as 'watchdogs' and as those who must approve r 45 segregation is stated explicitly in CI 26/1990. The conflict of role led Woolf to recommend the abolition of Boards' participation in this decision (1991: para. 12.270), though this recommendation was never implemented.

According to AMBoV, if a member refuses to authorise the use of r 45, "it would be quite wrong" for the governor simply to put the request to another Board member. The governor should request two other members to consider the issue (each having been informed of their colleague's decision and the reasons for it), or the case should be referred to Headquarters. Circular Instruction 6/1993 requires Board members to visit a prisoner personally before authorising continued segregation. Initial authorisation by telephone is only allowed in very exceptional circumstances. The BoV Handbook (1993) states that clear reasons for the segregation must be given and not simply 'in the interests of good order and discipline' or 'because of disruptive behaviour'.

The Annex to AG 32/1995 on Race Relations recommends the ethnic monitoring of the use of segregation.

Regime
Circular Instruction 16/1990 stated that governors and staff should rely on the principle that "the regime for segregated inmates should be as balanced and well integrated as for the rest of the population within the limits of affording them protection and maintaining good order and discipline, and nothing less than that" (para. 19). Prisoners segregated under Rule 45 GOAD (Good Order And Discipline) "...should not be located in punishment cells, unless there is no alternative. They should be allowed to keep their bed and bedding in the cell, unless there is reason to suppose they will

damage or destroy them; and they should not be deprived of any privileges to which they are normally entitled, except those that are incompatible with segregation" (Annex B). Similarly, prisoners segregated by request or for their own protection should not be housed in punishment cells or come into contact with those segregated for good order and discipline. They may share cells and have association with other similarly segregated prisoners, ideally in a section or wing set aside for the purpose.

The Prison Service Headquarters Programmes Group found that prisoners were often held in units for vulnerable prisoners (VPs) unnecessarily (IG 82/1995). The Group also found that sentenced VPs were often held in local prisons longer than appropriate after sentence, not least because some training prisons hesitated to accept prisoners who had been held in segregation at local establishments.

Case law

Following a period of disruption by prisoners at a large number of establishments, a special control unit was established at Wakefield Prison (in accordance with Circular Instruction 35/1974) as a means of containing prisoners who were considered to be troublemakers. Though the unit itself was closed less than a year later, the plaintiff in *Williams v Home Office (No. 2)* (1981) challenged its creation and conditions of use. In 1974, the governor of Wakefield, where the plaintiff was serving a 14 year sentence, requested that Williams be transferred to the control unit. Williams had not been charged with any disciplinary offence under the Prison Rules, but the governor considered him to be a totally subversive and dedicated troublemaker. The control unit committee acting for the Secretary of State under r 45(1) (then r 43) approved the governor's request. Williams brought an action against the Home Office for false imprisonment for the 180 days he spent in the control unit, and a declaration that the Home Office had acted beyond its powers and unlawfully in setting up the unit pursuant to the Circular Instruction. He contended that his detention in the control unit was unlawful because the regime was different from and worse than in the remainder of the prison system and was in breach of the Prison Rules; that the Secretary of State, acting through the control unit committee, had no power to act under r 45(1), since the only person who could do so was the prison governor; that his detention in the unit was in any event unlawful after the first month since there was no review of his case in accordance with r 45(2). He also argued that the unit was punitive in character and contrary not only to the Prison Act 1952 and the Prison Rules, but also to the Bill of Rights 1688, which prohibits 'cruell and unusuall punishments' (which he submitted, was to be interpreted as meaning 'cruel *or* unusual punishments').

The nature of r 45, as opposed to an offence against discipline, was examined in detail. Williams submitted that he was in effect given cellular confinement for 90 days, which was in excess of the maximum of 56 days which could have been imposed for a proved offence under what was then r 51(4)e (now a maximum of 14 days under r 55(e)). He relied on the words of the governor of Hull Prison, who had described the plaintiff as "moving from group to group sowing the seeds of discontent". Williams argued that this was evidence of an incitement to mutiny under what was then r 52(1)(a), for which the maximum penalty was 56 days, and that he was being punished for this offence under the guise of r 45.

Tudor Evans J held that the Secretary of State had power to act under r

45 and that power had been properly exercised by the agency he adopted for that purpose, i.e. the control unit committee. The fact that the control unit committee had not complied with the requirements for review under r 45(2) did not affect the lawfulness of the plaintiff's detention in the unit; the lawfulness of detention could not be affected by its conditions, since they were a matter for the Secretary of State and a prisoner's safeguard against unacceptable conditions lay in his right under the Prison Rules to complain to the prison governor or to the Secretary of State; and that the Bill of Rights only prohibited punishments which were both cruel and unusual, and that on the evidence the regime in the control unit was neither. The principles of natural justice did not require the plaintiff to be given notice and the opportunity to make representations. The judge took into account (which is all he was legally required to do) the standard set for prisons by r 31 of the UN Standard Minimum Rules and Article 3 of the European Convention of Human Rights,[4] in assessing whether the regime at Wakefield Prison's control unit was cruel: "Apart from these standards, the test for what is cruel is objective. I should look at the regime as it was and ask myself whether it was cruel in relation to the sort of person who was in the unit, that is the inveterate troublemaker ... I have no doubt that the regime did not fall below the irreducible minimum, judged by contemporary standards, of public morality ... If this rule were used merely as a device to punish a particular prisoner, it would be highly improper and there would be a breach of the rule, although with what legal effect I have yet to consider." The action was dismissed.

Ten years later the House of Lords in *Hague, Weldon v Home Office* (1991) again addressed the issue of confinement under r 45. Hague was serving a fifteen-year sentence at Parkhurst when he was accused of being a troublemaker and was transferred without notice under what was then Circular Instruction 10/1974 to Wormwood Scrubs, where he was held in segregation for 28 days. Weldon claimed that while he was serving a four-year sentence at Armley, he was beaten by prison officers and locked naked in a stripped cell. The two plaintiffs were claiming damages on the basis that being segregated and detained in intolerable conditions at the two prisons amounted to false imprisonment.

The Court of Appeal decision in *Hague* (1990) established that a decision to place a prisoner on r 45 is subject to judicial review, which subsequently opened all administrative decisions to such review. However, the House of Lords determined in *Hague and Weldon* that prisoners cannot bring an action for damages against the prison authorities or the Home Office for a breach of the Prison Rules or for false imprisonment. Lord Bridge stated that the Rule was not intended to confer a right of action on individual prisoners. The purpose of r 45 was to give the power to segregate prisoners who were liable to disturb the order of the prison and was a purely preventative measure. "Where it was exercised in good faith but not in accordance with the prescribed procedure, it was inconceivable that the legislature intended to confer a cause of action on the prisoner" (*Independent* 4 Sept. 1991). Weldon's placement in a stripped cell and Hague's segregation altered the conditions of their confinement, but did not deprive them of any liberty which they had not already lost when initially confined, so did not constitute the tort of false imprisonment.

---

[4] The European Commission has repeatedly stated that solitary confinement is not in itself inhuman treatment under Article 3 of the Convention.

Lord Ackner stated that prisoners must have a remedy against intolerable conditions. This could include a tort against a prison authority for damages for negligence where, for example, conditions caused the prisoner to suffer injury to health, tort for damages for assault, an action for misfeasance in public office (if malice can be established), and judicial review. However, he agreed that lawful imprisonment could not be rendered unlawful by reason only of the conditions of that imprisonment.

The Court of Appeal in *H v Secretary of State* (1992) determined that a prisoner cannot claim compensation for negligence for damage suffered as a result of segregation under r 45. In this case, the details of the prisoner's previous conviction for sexual offences became known due to a failure by the prison authorities. He was subsequently assaulted by other prisoners and placed under r 45 for his own protection, locked in a single cell for 23 hours a day. The prisoner could not sue over placement on r 45 since the Prison Rules expressly authorise such confinement and could therefore not in itself constitute "intolerable conditions", but was awarded £50 for the assault.

Transfers

Circular Instruction 37/1990 replaced Circular Instruction 10/1974 to incorporate the procedural safeguards introduced by the Court of Appeal in *Hague* (1990). Instruction to Governors 28/1993 has since replaced CI 37/1990 to extend the strategy to all prisoners in Category B training prisons and to sentenced prisoners in local prisons. The courts may review decisions to transfer "disruptive" prisoners without notice. Transfers should be to normal location, and the prisoner should normally return to the prison of origin. "A decision that an inmate should be transferred, and the associated arrangements, must therefore be based on reasoned grounds and must be defensible; and such reasoned grounds must be recorded on the inmate's record by the governor ... On no account must the discretion not to proceed with a disciplinary charge, but to transfer the inmate instead, be exercised with the motive of denying the inmate an opportunity to hear and answer an allegation made against the inmate" (CI 37/1990: 9, 11).

Further, "Inmates must be told of the reasons for their transfer as far as is practicable, and as soon as possible ... an inmate who is segregated at the establishment must be told the reasons as far as is practicable, and as soon as possible ... (and at the latest within 48 hours of the transfer (or segregation)) ... Reasons should be given in writing if the inmate so requests" (CI 37/1990: 13-16). A period of transfer must be "... no longer than is necessary in the interests of good order or discipline and shall in no case exceed six months" (para. 40). Arguably a refusal to give reasons could be open to judicial review, though before IG 28/1993 was issued the courts had held that a prisoner had no legal right to demand reasons (Livingstone and Owen 1999). The prisoner remains at the same local prison during the period of transfer, which under normal circumstances lasts no longer than 28 days.

There is no remission as such under r 45, though r 45(3) confers discretion on the governor to allow a prisoner to resume association. Circular Instruction 26/1990 states that the governor or Head of Custody should "wherever possible" be responsible for exercising the powers under r 45, but that any Governor 5 or above has such authority.

Prison Inspectorate reports have focused on the possibility of excessive numbers of prisoners being segregated under r 45 in a single establishment (with recommendations for reduction of numbers by transfer and the opportunity to come off r 45, or setting up a self-contained unit), the inadequate nature of the regime, and lack of required documentation. Circular Instruction 62/1989 and r 45(2) give governors the power to authorise removal from association for three days (72 hours) without further authority. Circular Instruction 26/1990 states only that "the Medical Officer should, whenever possible, see each inmate segregated under Rule [45] every day. If this is not practicable, the aim should be to see each such inmate at least once a week."

Circular Instruction 26/1990 issued specific directives on the use of r 45 which implemented recommendations of the Prison Department Working Group on the Management of Vulnerable Prisoners in 1989. The Woolf Report recommended and the government accepted the necessity to revise the Rule to make it apply only to prisoners segregated in the interests of good order and discipline and not to those removed from association in their own interests (*Custody, Care and Justice*, para. 5.27). Instead of segregating vulnerable prisoners, "The aim should be ... to ensure that vulnerable prisoners, including those who have been convicted of certain sexual offences, are given the same quality of opportunity as any other prisoner. When a prisoner is victimised, the aim should be to restrict the victimiser and not the victim" (*Custody, Care and Justice*, para. 5.23).

Livingstone and Owen explain that, "The effect of the administrative guidance contained in IG 28/1993 and CI 26/1990 is that prisoners may rely on the doctrine of legitimate expectation in support of a claim to an entitlement to be given reasons for transfer or segregation decision and a right to be heard before segregation is extended beyond three days. It follows that a failure to give reasons for a transfer/segregation decision after twenty-four hours or a failure to provide some kind of hearing to a prisoner before authorising continued segregation beyond three days could leave the prison authorities vulnerable to a successful application for judicial review" (1999: 10.38).

According to PSI 18/1998, cells for young offenders under restricted status must meet the full standards for category A prisoners. Such young offenders may be held in a segregation unit in non-category A cells, but in this case the governor and area manager must agree special watch procedures. Cells for restricted young offenders must be searched once every four weeks.

Both HM Chief Inspector of Prisons and the Committee for the Prevention of Torture rejected the Prison Service's former practice of segregating prisoners who are HIV positive. The Chief Inspector stated that, "An inmate who is medically unfit to be in his cell should be in hospital and not in a segregation unit" (1991: 4.49). The CPT said it: "wishes to emphasise that there is no medical justification for the segregation of an HIV positive prisoner who is well," and that staff at local levels have too much discretion regarding such segregation (1991: para. 167). The Home Office disagreed with their assessment, saying that although HIV positive prisoners who are well may not be on normal location, they are not segregated "in the sense of having no contact with other prisoners". It said managers: "must retain discretion to deal with individual cases in the light of the prisoner's needs and behaviour and of local circumstances" (Home Office response to the CPT 1991: 30).

(See also rr 35-36 Letters and visits.)

Close supervision centres

46. (1) Where it appears desirable, for the maintenance of good order or discipline or to ensure the safety of officers, prisoners or any other person, that a prisoner should not associate with other prisoners, either generally or for particular purposes, the Secretary of State may direct the prisoner's removal from association accordingly and his placement in a close supervision centre of a prison.

(2) A direction given under paragraph (1) shall be for a period not exceeding one month, but may be renewed from time to time for a like period.

(3) The Secretary of State may direct that such a prisoner as aforesaid shall resume association with other prisoners, either within a close supervision centre or elsewhere.

(4) In exercising any discretion under this rule, the Secretary of State shall take account of any relevant medical considerations which are known to him.

Close Supervision Centres (CSCs) were introduced in February 1998 in order to remove from the mainstream those prisoners deemed the most seriously disruptive. There are currently 53 places in five Centres at HMPs Woodhill and Durham, although occupation levels are well below this theoretical maximum. One of the five Centres holds prisoners in segregated conditions, one allows very partial association, and the remaining three allow full association at set times. The three levels are intended to provide a system of progression. CSCs replace the Continuous Assessment Scheme, where especially disruptive prisoners were transferred temporarily and the system of Special Units described in IG 28/1993 (see commentary to r 45).

Unlike the removal of prisoners from association under r 45, the decision to place a prisoner in a Close Supervision Centre requires no independent ratification such as approval from the Board of Visitors, nor is independent authorisation needed to extend the placement beyond the initial month. Allocation does not require the prisoner's consent, though transfer to level three (the least restrictive level of Close Supervision) requires the prisoner's agreement to co-operate with the regime.

Several court cases already appear to be relevant to the placement of prisoners in a Close Supervision Centre. The principles of procedural fairness and natural justice established in *Pierson* (1997) apply readily. In this case, Lord Browne-Wilkinson stated that "Section 35(2) of the Criminal Justice Act 1991, although absolutely general in its terms cannot be construed so as to authorise the exercise of the power, in any manner which would impair the applicant's legal rights or conflict with the basic principles of the law of the UK." Related to this is the Court of Appeal decision in *McAvoy* (1998) regarding the review of categorisation of category A prisoners (see discussion at r 7 Classification of prisoners). In *Ross* (1994), the Court of Appeal heard renewed applications for judicial review of failure of the governor to provide detailed reasons for decisions to segregate a prisoner.

The case of *Mehmet and O'Connor* (1999) is the only one so far directly related to placement in a Close Supervision Centre. This involved the judicial review of a decision for continued segregation without providing reasons or having any formal process of review. The High Court rejected the application on the grounds that the Prison Service was not legally obliged to give reasons for selection for a CSC or for continued detention in one. However, the Prison Service voluntarily agreed to abide by Operating Standards, which were put into place subsequently. The Standards give prisoners the right to know reasons for such decisions, or at least the gist of these reasons, as well as the right to disclosure of the full report where appropriate in the interest of fairness (though this would be in 'exceptional circumstances'). The Standards also make decisions subject to formal assessment and review. Operating Standards are, however, not legally binding.

Use of force

47. (1) *An officer in dealing with a prisoner shall not use force unnecessarily and, when the application of force to a prisoner is necessary, no more force than is necessary shall be used.*
     (2) No officer shall act deliberately in a manner calculated to provoke a prisoner.

This rule is the only authority under which prison officers are entitled to use force (CI 21/1979). "The use of force when it is not necessary, or the use of more force than is necessary to achieve the object, is both a criminal offence and a civil wrong" (Prison Officers' Training Manual). Circular Instruction 58/1988 emphasises that staff should rely on inter-personal skills and persuasion to manage difficult or violent behaviour and resort to force only as a last resort. Circular Instruction 31/1991 reiterated this theme, saying that: "Force must not be used when dealing with an inmate unless this is absolutely necessary and, when the use of force is necessary, no more force shall be used than is absolutely necessary to achieve the required objective" (also Op. Std. B3).

Most officers receive training in control and restraint (C & R) techniques designed "for handling individual prisoners with the least risk of injury to both parties" (*Custody, Care and Justice* 1991: para. 2.7). Such techniques must be regarded as a last resort, should not be continued if the prisoner's behaviour changes and therefore renders the holds unnecessary, and pressure should not be applied to cause pain if this is not absolutely necessary (CI 31/1991 Annex). Only these approved techniques may be used if the removal or restraint of a prisoner is necessary (Op. Std. B4).

The Parliamentary Commissioner for Administration (PCA or Parliamentary Ombudsman, not to be confused with the Prisons Ombudsman) recently criticised the Prison Service for not incorporating improved training guidance on the dangers of control and restraint techniques in the Security Manual, despite the fact that this guidance had first been set out in 1992. The PCA's criticism followed the death of Kenneth Severin, who had a history of serious mental health problems, in HMP Belmarsh in November 1995 during restraint in a struggle with seven prison officers (*The Guardian* 9 March 1999).

In using staves, officers must aim at the arms and legs, as these parts of the body are least likely to suffer serious injury (SO 3E 25: 7). Whenever staves, mini-batons, or side-arm batons are drawn or used, a report must be made to the governor from each member of staff and the senior member of staff present (SO 3E 28: 4), and from the Medical Officer after an examination of the prisoner "at the earliest possible opportunity" (SO 3E 30: 3). European Prison Rule 63.1 requires that officers using force ("no more than is strictly necessary") must report the incident immediately to the director of the institution. The Prison Rules should incorporate this provision and should apply it to any use of force, not only staves.

An officer who uses unnecessary force is liable to action under the Code of Discipline for Prison Officers (CI 55/1990 Annex 1.2).

The Committee for the Prevention of Torture stated that low staff/ prisoner ratios in English prisons may lead to a "significant risk of excessive use of force" (1991: para. 87). An improvement of these ratios increase staff confidence which in turn encourages officers to address problems without rushing and to talk things out instead of resorting to force. "The European Court of Human Rights has moved toward the position that any unjustified use of force in detention amounts to a breach of Article 3 [of the European Convention]" (Livingstone and Owen 1999: 5.69).

The tactical use of water to control prisoners in serious incidents must comply with the same conditions as for the use of force generally. Prisoners must be warned of its impending use and be given time to comply with instructions (IG 4/1993).

(See also commentary to r 11 Requests and complaints.)

Temporary confinement

48.   (1) *The governor may order a refractory or violent prisoner to be confined temporarily in a special cell, but a prisoner shall not be so confined as a punishment, or after he has ceased to be refractory or violent.*

   (2) *A prisoner shall not be confined in a special cell for longer than 24 hours without a direction in writing given by a member of a board of visitors or by an officer of the Secretary of State (not being an officer of a prison). Such a direction shall state the grounds for the confinement and the time during which it may continue.*

Members of Boards of Visitors must authorise removal of association for longer than three days. Despite the change in wording of the Rule, PSI 27/ 1999 clarified that Board members authorise rather than direct this removal.

Three types of cell are used to confine prisoners deemed to be in need of physical restraint and isolation: the stripped cell or 'unfurnished cell' (usually an ordinary cell equipped only with a mattress); the special cell (usually equipped with a double door, soundproofing and furniture which cannot cause injury); and the protected room (with a double door, soundproofing, padded walls, and no furniture). The protected room/ padded cell may only be used on the authority of the medical officer and on medical grounds. According to r 48, special cells may be used for the temporary confinement of refractory or violent prisoners; this does not require medical authorisation.

Rule 48 makes no reference to stripped rooms and protected rooms, even though the unfurnished cell is the most frequently used type of restraint. Prison Statistics state that special cells were used for males 2,715 times and 121 times for females in 1997, roughly proportionate to males and females in the prison population. No statistics are available specifically on the use of unfurnished cells, but protective rooms generally were used 565 times for males and 31 times for females (Home Office 1998b: 124). Use of protective rooms was slightly disproportionate for females, with 5.49 per cent of use being for female prisoners (who made up 4.38 per cent of the prison population in 1997).

The medical officer is to be informed as soon as possible of the removal of a prisoner to a special cell (SO 3E 14). Under Standing Orders, any prisoner confined to 'special accommodation' (which includes stripped cells, special cells, and protected rooms) must be observed every 15 minutes and be visited by the governor and the medical officer twice every 24 hours.

Standing Order 3E defines 'special accommodation' as: "a cell which has been designated as a special cell; or ... an unfurnished cell - that is, a cell in which a prisoner is temporarily confined ... (being either a cell which is specifically designated as one to be used exclusively as an unfurnished cell for temporary confinement ...; or a cell which is designated and usually used for accommodation purposes but from which the usual furniture has been removed) and which is either totally unfurnished or does not contain basic items of furniture such as table and chair and is thus to be considered, for all practical purposes, to be unfurnished ... So far as is practicable, cardboard furniture should be used in preference to none ... Special accommodation may be used for the temporary confinement of a violent or refractory prisoner, but only if the use of such accommodation ... is necessary in order to prevent the prisoner causing self-injury, injuring another prisoner or staff, or damaging property, or creating serious disturbance, and ... has been properly approved in accordance with this order ... No prisoner shall be confined in special accommodation as a punishment, and, as soon as the original justification for the use of special accommodation has ceased, the prisoner must be removed from that accommodation" (SO 3E 2-3).

Standing Order 3E requires that any use of special accommodation or mechanical restraints must be approved by the governor in charge (subject to the exceptions mentioned earlier) and must be documented. Both the Medical Officer and Board of Visitors must receive copies of this documentation. Medical Officers must document the placement of prisoners in protective rooms or restraint jackets for medical purposes, and must notify the Governor and Board of Visitors of such a placement. The Medical Officer must submit a daily list of prisoners so confined to the governor and a weekly list to the Board of Visitors (SO 13 35). Research into suicide and self-harm (Liebling and Krarup 1993) demonstrated that the routine use of unfurnished accommodation for prisoners who self-harm or are potential self-harmers is inappropriate. Rather, "Self-harm is an indicator of poor coping and severe distress and should be treated as such" (AG 21/1993). The Prison Service ended the use of strip cells (seclusion) for those at risk of suicide and self-injury in April 2000.

Standing Order 3E requires that the Board of Visitors must submit written approval for the continued use of special accommodation or mechanical restraints over 24 hours (SO 3E 16).
(See also r 26 Sleeping accommodation.)

Restraints
49. (1) *The governor may order a prisoner to be put under restraint where this is necessary to prevent the prisoner from injuring himself or others, damaging property or creating a disturbance.*
(2) Notice of such an order shall be given without delay to a member of the board of visitors, and to the medical officer or to a medical practitioner such as is mentioned in rule 20(3).
(3) On receipt of the notice, the medical officer, or the medical practitioner referred to in paragraph (2), shall inform the governor whether there are any medical reasons why the prisoner should not be put under restraint. The governor shall give effect to any recommendation which may be made under this paragraph.

(4) A prisoner shall not be kept under restraint longer than necessary, nor shall he be so kept for longer than 24 hours without a direction in writing given by a member of the board of visitors or by an officer of the Secretary of State (not being an officer of a prison). Such a direction shall state the grounds for the restraint and the time during which it may continue.

(5) Particulars of every case of restraint under the foregoing provisions of this rule shall be forthwith recorded.

(6) Except as provided by this rule no prisoner shall be put under restraint otherwise than for safe custody during removal, or on medical grounds by direction of the medical officer or of a medical practitioner such as is mentioned in rule 20(3). No prisoner shall be put under restraint as a punishment.

(7) Any means of restraint shall be of a pattern authorised by the Secretary of State, and shall be used in such manner and under such conditions as the Secretary of State may direct.

The use of restraints is very serious, and the detail in r 49 reflects this. It provides many more administrative directives than r 45 on segregation. In this instance, the Rule provides more detail than European Rules 39 and 40, though they are similar in content.

A body belt is a thick leather belt fastened around the prisoner's waist with handcuffs (iron for men, leather for women) attached to a ring on either side. Its use is prohibited in psychiatric hospitals, and use in prison seems to be confined to a minority of establishments. The use of body belts seems to be decreasing. Body belts were applied 53 times in 1997 (Home Office 1998b: 124), compared to 102 times in 1986, the same amount in 1988 (1991 AMBoV Handbook, 4.4.2 b), and 107 times in 1990 (Prison Statistics 1992: 129). These figures do not reflect the number of prisoners involved or how long the belt was used.

Since "the use of mechanical restraints is particularly undesirable and every effort must be made to avoid recourse to them," governors should consider whether confinement to a stripped cell would not be sufficient (SO 3E 5). Protective clothing may also be used, but only under the prior authority of the governor in charge, or by the most senior officer available if the case is urgent and the governor cannot be contacted (SO 3E 24 and 12). Mechanical restraints require the same standard of authority (SO 3E 12), though a loose canvas restraint jacket may only be used on the instruction of a medical officer and for medical purposes (SO 13 35). Under Standing Orders, any prisoner held in a mechanical restraint or confined to 'special accommodation' (which includes stripped cells, special cells, and protected rooms) must be observed every 15 minutes and be visited by the governor and the medical officer twice every 24 hours.

European Rule 39 does not authorise use of restraints where a prisoner is deemed to be "creating a disturbance", as r 49 does. This definition seems especially vulnerable to abuse. Standing Order 3E does not include "creating a disturbance" as a reason to justify the use of restraints, but only "to prevent a prisoner causing self-injury, injuring another prisoner or staff, or damaging property" (para. 5).

A suggested standard for the use of restraints for the mentally ill states: "A person shall only be subject to physical restraint when and for as long as absolutely necessary to prevent immediate injury to him or herself or others and all such instances shall be recorded (including reason, nature and extent). Unless the person objects he or she is not to be left alone while physically restrained" (Charter Mental Health 2000, 1985). This last requirement would be a useful addition to the Prison Rules.

The Committee for the Prevention of Torture recommended that body belts be stored outside of segregation units, that the issue and use of body belts should always be subject to the express authority of the governor or deputy governor, that prisoners in body belts should be under constant surveillance by appropriately trained staff, and that body belts be removed at the earliest possible opportunity (1991: para. 93). The Home Office accepted all four recommendations, though said that the first two recommendations were not always possible in practice. They accepted the need for safe storage of body belts, but said this was not necessarily possible outside of the segregation unit, and the governor-in-charge is not always available to make decisions in an emergency.

In its 1991 report to the Council of Europe, the Home Office stated: "The only circumstances in which they [restraints] may be used is during the transfer of a prisoner, where the governor, with the concurrence of the medical officer, considers that this is necessary to prevent a prisoner from injuring himself or others, damaging property or creating a disturbance, or by direction of the medical officer. Even then, permission must be granted each day either by a member of the Board of Visitors, or by an official." The Home Office went on to comment: "In the light of recent experience of dangerous offenders and in particular of terrorists it is arguable that the requirement that body restraints should be removed where a prisoner appears in court or before an administrative authority should be modified to allow for their use where this is thought necessary."

Private contractors are now responsible for almost all the escorting of prisoners outside Prison Service Establishments. Prison Service Instruction 35/1997 specifies that governors must give clear instructions to contractors regarding the use of restraints. This includes specific instructions regarding the removal of handcuffs; this decision must not be left to the contracted escort staff.

The Prison Service Security Manual, which is not a public document, contains specific provisions regarding the use of restraints in hospital. According to section 60, several considerations must be taken into account, namely: the medical condition of the prisoner and his or her ability to escape unaided; the prisoner's security category; the nature of the prisoner's offence, risk to the public and staff, or risk of hostage-taking; the motivation to escape, likelihood of assistance, and conduct in custody; and the physical security of the hospital. If staff are in any doubt, they should not remove the restraints. Restraints should be attached to an officer rather than to furniture, etc. Pregnant women must have restraints removed upon arrival in the hospital waiting room except in exceptional circumstances (in which case hospital staff must be informed of this). Female prisoners must not be subject to physical restraints while giving birth, from their arrival at hospital to their departure.
(See also European Prison Rule 38.)

Compulsory testing for controlled drugs
50. (1) *This rule applies where an officer, acting under the powers conferred by section 16A of the Prison Act 1952[11] (power to test prisoners for drugs), requires a prisoner to provide a sample for the purpose of ascertaining whether he has any controlled drug in his body.*

(2) In this rule "sample" means a sample of urine or any other description of sample specified in the authorisation by the governor for the purposes of section 16A of the Prison Act 1952.

(3) When requiring a prisoner to provide a sample, an officer shall, so far as is reasonably practicable, inform the prisoner:

    (a) that he is being required to provide a sample in accordance with section 16A of the Prison Act 1952; and

    (b) that a refusal to provide a sample may lead to disciplinary proceedings being brought against him.

(4) An officer shall require a prisoner to provide a fresh sample, free from any adulteration.

(5) An officer requiring a sample shall make such arrangements and give the prisoner such instructions for its provision as may be reasonably necessary in order to prevent or detect its adulteration or falsification.

(6) A prisoner who is required to provide a sample may be kept apart from other prisoners for a period not exceeding one hour to enable arrangements to be made for the provision of the sample.

(7) A prisoner who is unable to provide a sample of urine when required to do so may be kept apart from other prisoners until he has provided the required sample, save that a prisoner may not be kept apart under this paragraph for a period of more than 5 hours.

(8) A prisoner required to provide a sample of urine shall be afforded such degree of privacy for the purposes of providing the sample as may be compatible with the need to prevent or detect any adulteration or falsification of the sample; in particular a prisoner shall not be required to provide such a sample in the sight of a person of the opposite sex.

Since the introduction of the Prisons (Alcohol Testing) Act 1997, similar provisions are in force regarding testing for alcohol.

According to the Prison Service Order 3610 regarding the smuggling of drugs into prisons, prisoners who are found guilty more than once of smuggling drugs into prison through visits will be liable to frequent drug testing.

The Divisional Court case of *Tremayne* in 1996 rejected the claim that mandatory drug testing contravened Articles 6 or 8 of the European Convention on Human Rights since the provisions did not violate the presumption of innocence or amount to unnecessary interference with privacy.

OFFENCES AGAINST DISCIPLINE

Offences against discipline

51.   A prisoner is guilty of an offence against discipline if he -

    (1) commits any assault;

    (2) detains any person against his will;

    (3) denies access to any part of the prison to any officer or any person (other than a prisoner) who is at the prison for the purpose of working there;

    (4) fights with any person;

    (5) intentionally endangers the health or personal safety of others or, by his conduct, is reckless whether such health or personal safety is endangered;

(6) intentionally obstructs an officer in the execution of his duty, or any person (other than a prisoner) who is at the prison for the purpose of working there, in the performance of his work;

(7) escapes or absconds from prison or from legal custody;

(8) fails to comply with any condition upon which he is temporarily released under rule 9;

(9) administers a controlled drug to himself or fails to prevent the administration of a controlled drug to him by another person (but subject to rule 52);

(10) is intoxicated as a consequence of knowingly consuming any alcoholic beverage;

(11) knowingly consumes any alcoholic beverage other than that provided to him pursuant to a written order under rule 25(1);

(12) has in his possession -

> *(a) any unauthorised article, or*
>
> *(b) a greater quantity of any article than he is authorised to have;*

(13) sells or delivers to any person any unauthorised article;

(14) sells or, without permission, delivers to any person any article which he is allowed to have only for his own use;

(15) takes improperly any article belonging to another person or to a prison;

(16) intentionally or recklessly sets fire to any part of a prison or any other property, whether or not his own;

(17) destroys or damages any part of a prison or any other property, other than his own;

(18) absents himself from any place he is required to be or is present at any place where he is not authorised to be;

(19) is disrespectful to any officer, or any person (other than a prisoner) who is at the prison for the purpose of working there, or any person visiting a prison;

(20) uses threatening, abusive or insulting words or behaviour;

(21) intentionally fails to work properly or, being required to work, refuses to do so;

(22) disobeys any lawful order;

(23) disobeys or fails to comply with any rule or regulation applying to him;

(24) receives any controlled drug, or, without the consent of an officer, any other article, during the course of a visit (not being an interview such as is mentioned in rule 38);

(25) (a) attempts to commit,

> *(b) incites another prisoner to commit, or*
>
> *(c) assists another prisoner to commit or to attempt to commit, any of the foregoing offences.*

Governors handle all but the most serious disciplinary offences, which they must refer to the police for investigation.[5]

The 1899 Prison Rules introduced the first comprehensive disciplinary code for prisons, based on a military model. The system endured relatively unchanged (apart from the abolition of corporal punishment in 1967) until a series of High Court decisions finally refuted the idea that remission lost at

[5] This section quotes from the Prison Service's advice to adjudicators, the Prison Discipline Manual (1995, as revised), cited as the Manual. Adjudicators "are masters of their own procedure" (*Tarrant* (1984)) and may follow the Manual's advice if they choose, but its recommendations are not binding. The Manual contains general guidance as well as model procedures.

disciplinary hearings was a privilege rather than a right. The landmark *St Germain* case in 1979 marked the end of the immunity of the prison disciplinary code from judicial review. The Court of Appeal found that the courts had jurisdiction to ensure compliance by adjudicators with the fundamental principles of natural justice. In some recent cases, the courts have treated the offences created by the disciplinary code as if they were criminal offences: in *Tarrant* (1984), the Divisional Court applied the common law definition of 'mutiny' to what was then r 47(1), and confirmed that the burden of proof at adjudications should be that applied in criminal proceedings, i.e. beyond all reasonable doubt. The Court in *McGrath* (1984) quashed a conviction for 'disobeying any lawful order' (then r 47(19)) when a prisoner had refused to remove his bed from his cell on the basis that Standing Orders had provided no authorisation for the order. However, the Court of Appeal's decision in *King* (1984) (discussed below and in r 11 Requests and complaints) cast doubt on the criminal law analogy.

The Public Order Act 1986 created statutory offences of riot, violent disorder, and affray, all of which may be committed within a prison establishment. However, the series of prison riots in the Spring 1990 caused a reassessment of the case for more specific laws. As a consequence, prison mutiny is now a criminal offence punishable in the courts by a maximum of ten years' imprisonment or a fine or both (Prison Security Act 1992).

r 51(1) (commits any assault; (4) fights with any person)
"Any assault" often includes self-defence, such as with fights between prisoners. A prisoner may be punished for participating in a fight, regardless of who initiated the attack.

r 51(8) (fails to comply with any condition upon which he is temporarily released...)
Justice in Prison recommended the insertion of "knowingly" here (1983: 94).

r 51(9) (administers a controlled drug to himself or fails to prevent the administration of a controlled drug to him by another person)
Prison Service Instruction 20/1998 gives detailed guidance about adjudications following the positive result of a drug test. First, information test certificates count as hearsay evidence. However, they *can* be admitted as evidence where a prisoner disputes the results of a test. PSI 20/1998 says this is because the evidence is of "good quality", and therefore the reliability of the evidence means that its admission is "much less likely to result in unfairness to the accused than is the case with hearsay evidence on other issues".

Second, a prisoner can request that the relevant lab scientist attend as a witness. The decision to do so is at the adjudicator's discretion, but such a request must be considered carefully and on an individual basis, according to the guidance in paras. 5.8-5.21 of the Discipline Manual. Any refusal to grant the attendance of such a witness must be on "proper grounds" (inconvenience is not a 'proper ground') and the reason for refusal must be stated and recorded on the record of hearing for any subsequent appeal.

The Prison Service's drugs strategy, promulgated in 1998, encourages governors to discriminate between more and less harmful drug use in disciplinary decisions.

r 51(12) (has in his possession any unauthorised article, or a greater quantity of any article than he is authorised to have)

A significant difference exists between the prosecution of drug abuse in prisons and the method provided by criminal law. Under the Misuse of Drugs Act 1971 the relevant offence is one of possessing a controlled drug; r 51(12) provides for possession of a controlled article. Thus a charge of possession under the Misuse of Drugs Act would only apply to a measurable quantity of a controlled drug, whereas under r 51(12) a charge may be made out where only traces of the drug, not amounting to a measurable quantity, is found. The charge may be of possession of a pen or razor which has been in contact with, for example, cannabis resin. The suspected substance need not be analysed if there is ''a clear and unambiguous admission of guilt'' and it is not necessary that the prisoner know the precise nature of the drug (Manual, p. 41).

The case law established by McCullough J in *McConkey* (1982) was reviewed by the Court of Appeal in *King* (1984), in which the applicant shared a prison cell with three others. During a routine cell search, officers found a hypodermic needle hidden in a ceiling cavity. The occupants of the cell denied all knowledge of it, but were charged under r 51(12) (then r 47(7)). King's punishment was loss of 14 days' remission. He applied for judicial review of the governor's decision on the grounds that the latter had wrongly construed the Rule by assuming that the charge was proven merely if the applicant had knowledge of the presence of the needle in his cell. King contended that he could only be said to have had the needle in his cell if he had some control over it either by himself or jointly with others.

The Court of Appeal interpreted r 51(12) to require *mens rea* (state of mind or deliberate intent), and held that the governor had misconstrued the subsection because the offence could only be proved if the prisoner had some control over the unauthorised article. The Discipline Manual advises adjudicators in light of this decision that they must be satisfied beyond a reasonable doubt that the prisoner was exercising sole or joint control over an unauthorised article before he or she can be found guilty (pp. 30-31). It also advises governors to try to ensure that the prisoner understands the three elements in the charge, namely presence of an unauthorised article, knowledge of its presence and nature, and that the accused had sole or joint control over the article (p. 30).

r 51(13) (sells or delivers to any person any unauthorised article; and (14) sells or, without permission, delivers to any person any article which he is allowed to have only for his own use)

Justice in Prison (1983) argued that these offences, like r 51(12), require clarification concerning *mens rea*.

r 51(18) (absents himself from any place where he is required to be or is present at any place where he is not authorised to be)

Justice in Prison recommended that the definition of this offence be reworded to clarify that an essential element of the offence is that prisoners know, at the time of committing the offence, the limits which they are under a duty to observe, and also that they have no reasonable excuse for transgressing them. As it stands, the Rule disregards the fact that prisoners might have a reasonable excuse even though they had not been given permission.

r 51(19) (is disrespectful to any officer, or any person (other than a prisoner) who is at the prison for the purpose of working there, or any person visiting a prison; (20) uses threatening, abusive or insulting words or behaviour)

The Discipline Manual specifies that the act or language must have been intended as disrespectful, threatening, or insulting, or that the prisoner was reckless as to whether he or she was being so. The evidence must show how the words or action was disrespectful or abusive. In the case of r 51(20), the target of the abuse does not always need to be named in the charge.

The fact that disrespect to other prisoners is specifically excluded from the Rule seems ironic, given the emphasis in recent years on bullying in prisons and its impact.

r 51(22) (Disobeys any lawful order); (23) (disobeys or fails to comply with any rule or regulation applying to him)

The facts of these offences should be stated clearly. In *McConkey* (1982), the prisoner was charged with an offence against good order and discipline (now abolished, though the principle is the same for other 'catch-all' rules) in that he was 'present at an illegal drug-smoking party' in another prisoner's cell. The Board (which then conducted adjudications for more serious charges) convicted him without it being alleged that he had participated in the smoking of the drug. The court accepted the argument that some element of positive participation had to be proved. Circular Instructions have stressed the need to do away with 'group responsibility'. Similar considerations apply to wilful encouragement or assistance of offences under rr 49(7), (12), (15), (16), (17), (22), and (24).

r 51(24) (Receives any controlled drug or, without the consent of an officer, any other article, during the course of a visit...)

Prison Service Order 3610 states that prisoners who are caught or are believed to be smuggling drugs through visits must have closed or non-contact visits imposed (usually for three months), must be targeted for searches, referred to a drug counsellor, and possibly be subject to a programme of frequent drug testing. Such offences (or suspicion) will also be taken into account for the Incentives and Earned Privileges Scheme, placement on voluntary testing units, categorisation and allocation, and suitability for Home Detention Curfew or other release.

Defences to rule 51(9)

52. It shall be a defence for a prisoner charged with an offence under rule 51(9) to show that:

(a) the controlled drug had been, prior to its administration, lawfully in his possession for his use or was administered to him in the course of a lawful supply of the drug to him by another person;

(b) the controlled drug was administered by or to him in circumstances in which he did not know and had no reason to suspect that such a drug was being administered; or

(c) the controlled drug was administered by or to him under duress or to him without his consent in circumstances where it was not reasonable for him to have resisted.

Justice in Prison (1983) recommended the addition of the following provisions to take account of general defences and the mental element:

"1. (a) A prisoner is not guilty of any of these offences unless he has acted either intentionally or recklessly with respect to each material element of the offence.

(b) Where the act charged is an offence only if it is done in special circumstances, it must be proved that the prisoner, at the time that he did the act, knew that those circumstances existed or was reckless as to their existence.

2. In respect of offences involving the use of force, no offence shall be committed where the prisoner honestly believes that its use is necessary for the purpose of protecting himself or another against unlawful force.

3. No offence shall be committed where the prisoner did the act constituting the offence because he was coerced to do it by the use of, or a threat to use, unlawful force against his person, or the person of another, which a person of reasonable firmness in his situation would have been unable to resist."

Rule 52 takes these considerations into account to some degree, though only regarding the administration of drugs. The same provisions would usefully apply to many other offences against discipline, such as for cases in which prisoners are coerced to bring in drugs or to steal things under duress on behalf of other prisoners.

The Discipline Manual directs that prisoners should not be charged for positive test results obtained through voluntary testing arrangements (e.g. prisoners undergoing treatment programmes for addiction).

A document entitled "Information for Prisoners Who Have Tested Positive for Drugs" should be issued to every prisoner charged with a disciplinary offence following a positive drug test. This leaflet explains how to arrange an independent analysis of the sample if the prisoner so desires.

Disciplinary charges
53. (1) *Where a prisoner is to be charged with an offence against discipline, the charge shall be laid as soon as possible and, save in exceptional circumstances, within 48 hours of the discovery of the offence.*

(2) *Every charge shall be inquired into by the governor.*

(3) *Every charge shall be first inquired into not later, save in exceptional circumstances, than the next day, not being a Sunday or public holiday, after it is laid.*

(4) *A prisoner who is to be charged with an offence against discipline may be kept apart from other prisoners pending the governor's first inquiry.*

Rule 53(1) provides that a charge against discipline shall be *laid* as soon as possible; r 54(1) provides that the prisoner shall be *informed* as soon as possible (not necessarily the same thing), and in any case before the time when the governor inquires into it (emphasis added). Standing Order 3D 7 states that the 48-hour time limit also applies in cases where the police are asked to investigate. European Rule 36.3 states that the prisoner must be informed of the alleged offence, but makes no requirement as to the speed with which this should be done. European Rule 36.2 provides that reports of misconduct shall be presented promptly and decided without delay. The Prison Rules contain no requirement that charges are to be decided without delay, although r 53(3) at least provides that the initial investigation (to be conducted in all cases) will normally occur the day after the charge is laid.

The emphasis on procedural propriety has gradually increased over the last several years. The plaintiff in *Smith* (1984) challenged the decision by a

Board of Visitors (who then conducted adjudications for more serious charges) to substitute a lesser charge. The High Court ruled the Board's decision unlawful on the grounds that the Board itself had no jurisdiction to substitute a lesser charge, and that the prison authorities who were responsible for laying charges could not themselves lay a lesser charge because the fresh charge would not have been laid 'as soon as possible', as required by r 53(1). McCullough J stated: "... the clear intention of the Rules is that a charge should be laid quickly and considered by the governor quickly. I observe that neither [at that time] r 51 nor r 52 requires the Board of Visitors to consider the charge speedily, but this does not detract from the clear intent that the case should reach the governor speedily". A Court of Appeal decision upheld this ruling but indicated that alternative charges could be laid simultaneously. Circular Instruction 18/1986 pointed out that this could cause confusion, and reporting officers are advised to seek advice before deciding on this course of action.

Legal advice to Prison Service Headquarters suggests that charges placed under the wrong Rule do not automatically need to be quashed. If a prisoner were charged under the 1964 Rules where a prison was unaware of the new legislation in place, the punishment is likely to be quashed because the error is more than simply administrative. If, however, a young offender were charged under the 1999 adult rules rather than the YOI rules, the punishment will not automatically be quashed if this was the only error and if the wording of the charge clearly set out the details of what was alleged. The prisoner must not have suffered any unfairness or disadvantage as a result of being charged under the wrong rule number.

r 53(4)

Circular Instruction 27/1984 draws attention to the need for extra care when deciding that a prisoner who is awaiting adjudication for an offence against prison discipline should be segregated under r 53(4) (then r 48(2)). Unlike r 45, a decision to segregate under r 53(4) does not require the authority of the Secretary of State or the Board of Visitors. Rule 53(4) is available only where a governor's first inquiry is pending, and its use is justified only where the reasons for segregation relate to the investigation (e.g. where there is a possibility of collusion, intimidation or suborning of witnesses). When segregation is considered necessary on other grounds, r 45 should be used. Where an offence has been referred to the police for investigation and the governor decides that the prisoner should be segregated, this should also be done under r 45, but such segregation pending police investigation should be used sparingly (SO 3D 10).

Governors are requested to review the grounds for which segregation under r 53(4) is considered to be necessary every seven days. The Circular Instruction tells the governor to "bear in mind:
(i) the prisoner's current health and state of mind, and prison record;
(ii) the risk that the prisoner who has been granted legal representation may withdraw this request merely in order to escape prolonged segregation;
(iii) the fact that a segregated prisoner who has not been granted legal representation might have difficulty in preparing his defence (indeed Webster J in the *Tarrant* judgement cited segregation under r 48(2) [now r 53(4)] as a fact that Boards might consider in granting the prisoner legal representation or assistance).
(iv) in the case of an offender under 16, the legal requirement for full-time education".

The Instruction goes on to warn that a prisoner should not be made to feel that he has in effect been punished with prolonged segregation as a result of requesting legal representation. Accordingly, the governor should consider a temporary transfer for the prisoner, so that he or she can be held on ordinary location. The governor should seek the views of the prisoner's solicitor and discuss the matter with the area manager. It concludes by noting, "Where it has been necessary to keep a prisoner segregated prior to an adjudication the governor ... should bear this in mind (and so inform the prisoner) in making an award, and should record the fact that the award reflects this". Standing Order 3D states that prisoners segregated prior to an adjudication, "should not be located in a segregation unit or any part of the establishment normally used for prisoners undergoing punishment, unless there is no suitable cell available elsewhere. However, where the adjudication room is in the punishment block, a prisoner may be lodged in the punishment block on the morning of the adjudication" (SO 3D 12).

In the circumstances of segregation under r 53(4), the prisoner may lack the opportunity to contact witnesses or make written notes, and may also lack time. According to the Weiler Report on Adjudications (1975): "To ensure that the prisoner has a reasonable time to prepare his defence ... governors have been instructed that there should be at least *two hours* between the service of the charge and the hearing of the charge" (emphasis added). This was called "an absurdly short time limit" (Cohen and Taylor 1978: 33). "Form F1127 should be served on the prisoner at least two hours before the adjudication is due to begin. A written record should be kept of when and by whom form F1127 was issued to the accused in case the form is lost or destroyed. Good practice would be for form F1127, and the form explaining the procedure to be followed (form F1145), to be served the day before the adjudication. In the case of resuming an adjourned hearing the prisoner should also be given at least two hours notice by way of a fresh or renewed form F1127. Exceptionally it may be possible to proceed without the two hours notice for example where a prisoner is well aware that he or she is to face the resumed hearing and is prepared to proceed. In this case it must be recorded in the record of the hearing (form F256) that the prisoner has been offered the chance to delay the resumption of the hearing for a further two hours but has declined" (Manual, para. 2.9).

According to the Prison Discipline Manual, segregation following the initial hearing must be under r 45. "It should not be an automatic measure but be used only where there is a real need, such as the risk of collusion or intimidation relating to the alleged offence which segregation of the accused might prevent" (para. 4.17). The Manual recommends that the need for continued segregation be reviewed at least every seven days and the decisions noted in the prisoner's main record (para. 4.19). If the need for segregation is long term, such as for adjournments for legal representation, "... the governor should consider the need to transfer the prisoner temporarily elsewhere where he or she may be held on ordinary location pending the adjudication" (para. 4.20).

Rights of prisoners charged
54. (1) *Where a prisoner is charged with an offence against discipline, he shall be informed of the charge as soon as possible and, in any case, before the time when it is inquired into by the governor.*

(2) At an inquiry into a charge against a prisoner he shall be given a full opportunity of hearing what is alleged against him and of presenting his own case.

Each charge must contain sufficient explanatory detail to leave the accused no doubt as to the precise nature of the charge against them. If a charge is not one provided for in the Rules, it is not an offence against discipline.

The governor must ask prisoners if they wish to be assisted or legally represented. However, prisoners are not always aware of the full range of possibilities they have for assistance. People tend to assume that if legal representation is refused, then that is the end of the matter. In fact, prisoners may go on to request a 'McKenzie Friend' (a lay adviser or assistant) as an alternative. They may have (at any stage) privileged communications with a solicitor about the adjudication even if legal representation has been refused, and indeed, ask for an adjournment pending receipt of the advice. Thus, the Manual notes that if the governor refuses legal representation the prisoner may nonetheless ask for assistance from an adviser or friend, and the adjudicator "must consider such requests afresh, independently of any decision to refuse legal representation" (para. 3.4). The prisoner should automatically be informed of all options for assistance: natural justice requires that the procedures be proactive, not merely reactive. The Manual therefore instructs that, "At the start of every hearing the adjudicator must ask the prisoner whether he or she wishes to have additional assistance, and if the prisoner expresses interest, must explain about the possibilities of legal assistance or representation or of assistance from a friend or adviser ..." (para. 3.2).

Similarly, prisoners may not be aware (unless specifically informed) that, "An accused who asks before an adjudication takes place to consult a solicitor should be allowed to do so. An adjudicator should adjourn the hearing if, after a charge has been laid, the prisoner who requests it has not had reasonable time to contact a solicitor ... A prisoner who does not know of a solicitor who will act for him or her should be advised to approach the legal aid officer for help in selecting one" (Manual, para. 3.1).

Form 1145 is often the only advance information given to the prisoner about the procedure followed at an adjudication. In contrast to the Manual's advice to adjudicators above, this form tells the prisoner that, "It is for the governor to decide whether or not legal representation can be agreed in your case. If refused, the hearing will continue and you should be ready for this."

In practice, governors now almost never grant requests for legal representation, though some allow a 'McKenzie Friend'. The official response to the visit by the European Committee on the Prevention of Torture in 1994 reported that legal representation had been granted in only four adjudications since 1992 (CPT 1996). The Prison Service Operating Standards state that prisoners should immediately be issued with information on the conduct of disciplinary hearings and offered facilities to prepare their case (Op. Std. D2). This should include Form 1145, as well as access to the Prison Discipline Manual and legal publications if desired. The Prior Committee formally recommended that prison officers assist in preparing prisoners for disciplinary proceedings (1985: para. 10.63). Form 1145 states in its opening paragraph that the Prisoners' Information Book sets out the legal rules about discipline, that the Prison Discipline Manual also gives guidance on procedure, and that prisoners may ask an officer if they want more advice.

While information provided prior to adjudications has improved in recent years, the onus is still on the prisoner to request information: "If the accused, or his or her legal representative, asks before a hearing for a copy of all statements to be submitted in evidence so as to prepare a defence or mitigation these should be supplied at public expense. Arrangements should be made by a member of staff not conducting the hearing who should also provide the names of any witnesses to the incident of which the accused may not know. Copies should also be provided of any statements made or other material discovered in the course of the investigation unless there are compelling grounds for non-disclosure" (Manual, para. 2.20).

The courts examined the discretionary withholding of information in *Raymond* (1985) and declared it desirable, in the interests of justice being seen to be done, that at a hearing a prisoner should be shown a welfare report prepared upon him, even where the applicant had not asked to be shown a copy. (See also *Norley*, below.) The Court of Appeal's decision in *Wilson* (1992) granted prisoners the right to have access to reports against them in order to represent themselves adequately at parole hearings. The Court of Appeal's decision in *Walsh* (1992) also supported this right to information. Though not expressly stated, these decisions imply a similar right for prisoners at disciplinary hearings.

The adjudicator may call any witness whether or not he or she has been named by the reporting officer or the defendant (Halsbury: 1172).

In *Tarrant* (1984), the applicants faced serious charges with heavy penalties before Boards of Visitors (who then conducted adjudications for more serious cases), and their defences had raised issues of law (including the scope of the offence of 'mutiny') which indicated a strong need for legal representation. Following *Fraser v Mudge* (1975), the Court of Appeal held that no prisoner has an automatic right to legal representation or the assistance of a friend or adviser (a McKenzie Friend), but in doing so did not explicitly distinguish between legal representation and assistance. However, the court held that adjudicators had a discretion to grant legal representation and must exercise it in accordance with their duty to ensure that a prisoner has a "full opportunity of presenting his case". The case also established that the burden of proof is on the prosecution, and that the adjudicators must be satisfied 'beyond reasonable doubt' that the prisoner committed the offence with which he is charged. The House of Lords in *Hone v Maze Prison Board of Visitors* (1988) re-emphasised the Court of Appeal's decision in *Fraser v Mudge*, but the Divisional Court's decision in *Tarrant* prevents adjudicators from using these judgements to justify blanket refusals of representation.

The Manual discusses the considerations set out by the Divisional Court in *Tarrant* and the way in which they might affect the adjudicator's decision on whether or not to grant legal representation or assistance (the Tarrant case did not explicitly distinguish between them): (1) the seriousness of the charge and the potential penalty; (2) whether any points of law are likely to arise; (3) the capacity of a particular prisoner to represent his or her own case; (4) procedural difficulties; (5) the need for reasonable speed; and (6) the need for fairness as between prisoners and as between prisoners and prison officers (pp. 8-10 and App. 4). These criteria are not exhaustive, and are not all of the same weight. The need for speed and fairness relates not so much to the decision whether to grant assistance in the individual case, so much as the granting and organising of assistance in cases generally. "For example, it would be a grave error for [an adjudicator] to decide, on the basis of [one of the first four criteria] that assistance should be granted, and then to refuse assistance in order to speed things up" (Macfarlane 1983: 5).

Representation may also be appropriate for prisoners who plead guilty to a simple case but may need help with mitigation (Fitzgerald 1984; Prior Report 1985: 10.26). Young prisoners and those with mental health problems might appear to be particularly disadvantaged by the denial of legal representation. The Manual urges the adjudicator that, where he or she refuses an application for legal assistance or representation, the record of the hearing demonstrates that it was properly considered (Manual, para. 3.11; also Op. Std. D6 and commentary).

Requests from legal representatives or advisers for facilities go through the governor for security and disciplinary considerations. Where an adjudicator receives such requests, he or she may recommend that they be granted, but "Where the governor considering the request for facilities cannot provide them and the adjudicator believes that this prejudices a fair hearing, there may be no alternative but to dismiss the charge" (Manual, para. 3.17).

Although the Prison Service has provided detailed written procedural guidelines (the Prison Discipline Manual) for the assistance of adjudicators hearing disciplinary charges, no equivalent detailed written advice has been directed to prisoners themselves.

The prisoner charged should be allowed to sit at a table and be provided with writing material at all adjudications. Those who have difficulty hearing or understanding English should receive assistance from the adjudicator, staff, or if necessary an interpreter so they can participate fully in the proceedings. A prisoner who applies to consult a solicitor before or after an adjudication should be allowed to do so, although a hearing will not necessarily be adjourned for this reason (SO 3D 20, 22, and 23). Disciplinary procedures should follow the rules of natural justice (Op. Std. D3).

Rule 54(2) and European Rule 36.3 are similar in that neither make reference to lay or legal representation of prisoners at adjudications. Rule 54(2) should be revised to reflect recent case law decisions providing for representation in limited circumstances.

In *Smith* (1984) (see r 53 above) the High Court held that the practice of proceeding with an alternative charge if the original one fails is inconsistent with r 54(1). The guidance in the Disciplinary Manual has incorporated this ruling.

In *Norley* (1984), Webster J said that there is no duty imposed by s. 47(2) of the Prison Act (requiring the Secretary of State to ensure that a person who is charged with an offence under the rules shall be given a proper opportunity of presenting his case) and r 54(2) to consider the exercise of the undoubted discretion to allow legal representation unless the adjudicator is asked to do so. The court accepted that there might be exceptional and unusual cases in which such a duty would arise, such as where the prisoner was incapable of understanding the possibility that legal representation might be granted, or was not capable of making the application. However, the judge commended the guidance issued by the Home Office that the adjudicator should ask a prisoner if he wished to seek legal representation. Governors must now ask prisoners if they want assistance or legal representation during the adjudication, but the Prison Rules should also be amended to this end.

The Hull Prison *St. Germain* cases (1979) were referred back to the Divisional Court for consideration on the merits. The court said that s. 47(2) of the Prison Act and r 54(2) were declaratory of one of the basic rules of natural justice, namely that every party to a dispute has a right to a fair hearing. "He must know what evidence has been given and what statements have been made affecting him; and then he must be given a fair opportunity to correct or contradict them". The Courts of Appeal in *Wilson* (1992) and *Walsh* (1992) confirmed this right. Referring back to Megaw LJ in the Court of Appeal, the Divisional Court said that a mere breach of procedural rules would not justify or require interference by the courts; for there would have to be "some failure to act fairly - fairly, having regard to all the circumstances and such unfairness could reasonably be regarded as having caused a substantial, as distinct from a trivial or merely technical injustice, which was capable of remedy".

Governor's punishments
55. (1) If he finds a prisoner guilty of an offence against discipline the governor may, subject to paragraph (2) and to rule 57, impose one or more of the following punishments:
>   (a) caution;
>   (b) forfeiture for a period not exceeding 42 days of any of the privileges under rule 8;
>   (c) exclusion from associated work for a period not exceeding 21 days;
>   (d) stoppage of or deduction from earnings for a period not exceeding 84 days and of an amount not exceeding 42 days earnings;
>   (e) cellular confinement for a period not exceeding 14 days;
>   (f) in the case of a short-term or long-term prisoner, an award of additional days not exceeding 42 days;
>   (g) in the case of a prisoner otherwise entitled to them, forfeiture for any period of the right, under rule 43(1), to have the articles there mentioned.

(2) An award of a caution shall not be combined with any other punishment for the same charge.
(3) If a prisoner is found guilty of more than one charge arising out of an incident, punishments under this rule may be ordered to run consecutively but, in the case of an award of additional days, the total period added shall not exceed 42 days and, in the case of an award of cellular confinement, the total period shall not exceed 14 days.
(4) In imposing a punishment under this rule, the governor shall take into account any guidelines that the Secretary of State may from time to time issue as to the level of punishment that should normally be imposed for a particular offence against discipline.

Forfeiture of remission to be treated as an award of additional days
56. (1) In this rule, "existing prisoner" and "existing licensee" have the meanings assigned to them by paragraph 8(1) of Schedule 12 to the Criminal Justice Act 1991[12].
(2) In relation to any existing prisoner or existing licensee who has forfeited any remission of his sentence, the provisions of Part II of the Criminal Justice Act 1991 shall apply as if he had been awarded such number of additional days as equals the numbers of days of remission which he has forfeited.

Offences committed by young persons
57. (1) In the case of an offence against discipline committed by an inmate who was under the age of 21 when the offence was committed (other than an offender in relation to whom the Secretary of State has given a direction under

section 13(1) of the Criminal Justice Act 1982[13] that he shall be treated as if he had been sentenced to imprisonment) rule 55 shall have effect, but -

> *(a) the maximum period of forfeiture of privileges under rule 8 shall be 21 days;*
> *(b) the maximum period of stoppage of or deduction from earnings shall be 42 days and the maximum amount shall be 21 days;*
> *(c) the maximum period of cellular confinement shall be 7 days.*

(2) In the case of an inmate who has been sentenced to a term of youth custody or detention in a young offender institution, and by virtue of a direction of the Secretary of State under section 13 of the Criminal Justice Act 1982, is treated as if he had been sentenced to imprisonment for that term, any punishment imposed on him for an offence against discipline before the said direction was given shall, if it has not been exhausted or remitted, continue to have effect as if made pursuant to rule 55.

Governors in English and Welsh prisons have more disciplinary powers than their counterparts elsewhere in the UK (e.g. the maximum number of days which may be added in Scotland is 14 days instead of the 42 days in England for a single offence).

The Prison Rules contain no equivalent to European Prison Rule 37, which prohibits as a punishment for disciplinary offences: "corporal punishment, punishment by placing in a dark cell and all cruel, inhuman or degrading punishment". Article 3 of the European Convention on Human Rights states that "no-one shall be subjected to torture or to inhuman or degrading treatment or punishment".

The Prison Rules also have no equivalent to European Rules 36.1 and 36.4. In the case of European Rule 36.1 (that no prisoner is to be punished except in accordance with the law or regulations, and never twice for the same act), this is a serious omission. The Prior Report recommended that it should not be possible for a person to be proceeded against in the disciplinary system or in the courts for an alleged offence of which he has already in substance been convicted or acquitted in the other system (1985: 5.16).

Under r 55(d) governors may deduct as little or as much of a prisoner's earnings as they see fit within the specified limits (CI 3/1992: 4). 'One day's pay' equals one-seventh of a prisoner's weekly pay, regardless of the number of days per week a prisoner works.

Prisoners serving a punishment in cellular confinement must be observed by an officer at least once an hour and visited daily by the chaplain and by the medical officer (SO 3D 48(b)).

After the Criminal Justice Act 1991, 'additional days' replaced 'loss of remission' under r 55(f). Like loss of remission, it postpones the date of release (for the prisoners eligible for automatic conditional release) without the possibility of extending the original sentence. For longer term prisoners, the added days extend the parole eligibility date and two-thirds point (for those on discretionary conditional release), and the expiry date of any licence.

The most serious cases go to the police for investigation and subsequently to the outside courts if necessary. If the Crown Prosecution Service decides not to proceed with a case, the governor may decide whether to proceed with a disciplinary charge. If the CPS chooses to prosecute, the governor may not proceed with a disciplinary charge and must inform the prisoner as such (SO 3D 7(a and b)). Governors should also have a record of the referral and the outcome of each case so that they may be monitored locally and centrally (CI 3/1992: 15). Annex A of Circular Instruction 3/1992 offers guidelines to governors regarding the types of cases which are appropriate to refer to the police for outside investigation, though the guidelines are not mandatory. The governor may refer certain escapes to the outside courts (CI 3/1992 Annex A 2), though failure to return from release on temporary licence should be handled internally.

Governors must prove cases "beyond a reasonable doubt", and since *Leech* (1988) their decisions are subject to judicial review.

Justice in Prison (1983) recommended that if all privileges are to be forfeited as a punishment under r 55(1)(b), then the adjudication should list each of the forfeited privileges individually, and recommended that the Rules be amended to make this compulsory. This punishment should only be given in addition to cellular confinement in exceptional circumstances, and for no more than seven days. "To deprive a prisoner in solitary confinement of possessions like letters, photographs, books and a radio for a period longer than seven days is, in our view, inhumane".

The current maximum period for forfeiture of privileges is 42 days, though "Educational notebooks, attendance at educational classes and correspondence courses should not normally be forfeited unless specifically included in the award. General notebooks, drawing books, radios and permission to purchase postage stamps should also not normally be forfeited" (SO 3D 39). Time spent in hospital and days on which a prisoner attends court both count as part of the punishment period (SO 3D 63 and 64). While disciplinary offences frequently have consequences for a prisoner's regime level under the Incentives and Earned Privileges Scheme, the Incentives Scheme is *not* part of the prison disciplinary system.

The Secretary of State issues guidance to governors regarding appropriate levels of punishments for certain breaches of discipline. For example, Prison Service Order 3610 gives specific ranges of punishments for prisoners caught smuggling drugs into prisons through visits, which governors "must have regard to" when they decide a punishment.

AG 32/1995 on Race Relations recommends the ethnic monitoring of all adjudications and punishments.

Cellular confinement

58. *When it is proposed to impose a punishment of cellular confinement, the medical officer, or a medical practitioner such as is mentioned in rule 20(3), shall inform the governor whether there are any medical reasons why the prisoner should not be so dealt with. The governor shall give effect to any recommendation which may be made under this rule.*

European Prison Rule 38.1 requires prior medical certification not just for cellular confinement but also for: "any other punishment which might have an adverse effect on the health of the prisoner," thus covering, for example, a combined punishment under r 55(b) and (c) amounting to cellular confinement. European Rule 38.3 requires the medical officer to make daily visits to a prisoner undergoing such punishment and advise if he thinks the termination or alteration of the punishment is necessary on the grounds of physical or mental health. European Rule 38 is therefore more extensive than r 58.

According to the Discipline Manual, "No cellular confinement will be imposed unless the medical officer has indicated that the prisoner is fit to undergo the punishment. This duty may not be delegated to other health care staff ... The medical officer will visit daily to assess the physical, emotional and mental well-being of the prisoner and will note on the prisoner's medical record whether or not he or she remains fit to undergo the punishment. This duty may not be delegated to other health care staff. If the prisoner is unfit the medical officer will advise the governor and the punishment must be terminated" (paras. 7.20 and 7.24). As mentioned previously, this guidance directly contradicts that given by the Committee for the Prevention of Torture, which stated that the dual role of discipline and health care compromises the doctor/patient relationship.

According to the BoV Handbook (1993), prisoners undergoing a punishment of cellular confinement may be refused a visit.

Governors should not normally place a pregnant woman in segregation as a disciplinary measure. However, a pregnant prisoner may be located in a segregation unit during the day provided that there is a bell and that she is observed at regular intervals (CI 2/1988; also Discipline Manual, para. 7.13).

The adjudication record (F256) notes the medical officer's certification of the prisoner's fitness for adjudication, whether the prisoner is fit for cellular confinement, and whether there are other medical factors potentially in the prisoner's favour which it would be just to draw to attention. The certification should be limited specifically to the punishment of cellular confinement.

(See also rr 20-21 Medical attendance and r 79 Members [of Boards of Visitors] visiting prisons.)

Prospective award of additional days

59. (1) *Subject to paragraph (2), where an offence against discipline is committed by a prisoner who is detained only on remand, additional days may be awarded notwithstanding that the prisoner has not (or had not at the time of the offence) been sentenced.*

(2) *An award of additional days under paragraph (1) shall have effect only if the prisoner in question subsequently becomes a short-term or long-term prisoner whose sentence is reduced, under section 67 of the Criminal Justice Act 1967[14], by a period which includes the time when the offence against discipline was committed.*

The Criminal Justice Act 1991 abolished the system of remission in October 1992. Prisoners may no longer forfeit remission in response to indiscipline, but instead have extra days added. The limit for 'extra days' is 42 days for a single offence, and the total amount added cannot exceed the release date of the original sentence. See the commentary to r 55 Governor's punishments for further details.

Suspended punishments

60. (1) *Subject to any directions given by the Secretary of State, the power to impose a disciplinary punishment (other than a caution) shall include power to direct that the punishment is not to take effect unless, during a period specified in the direction (not being more than six months from the date of the direction), the prisoner commits another offence against discipline and a direction is given under paragraph (2).*

(2) *Where a prisoner commits an offence against discipline during the period*

> specified in a direction given under paragraph (1) the person dealing with that
> offence may -
>> (a) direct that the suspended punishment shall take effect;
>> (b) reduce the period or amount of the suspended punishment and direct
>>   that it shall take effect as so reduced;
>> (c) vary the original direction by substituting for the period specified a
>>   period expiring not later than six months from the date of variation; or
>> (d) give no direction with respect to the suspended punishment.

According to *Justice in Prison*, "The percentage of subsequently activated
sentences is low. This suggests to us that the small number of suspended
cases might reasonably be increased. The adjudicating bodies ought,
therefore, to be encouraged to make greater use of this power" (1983: 107).
This sentiment applies equally today.

Remission and mitigation of punishments and quashing of findings of guilt
61. *(1) The Secretary of State may quash any finding of guilt and may remit any
    punishment or mitigate it either by reducing it or by substituting another
    award which is, in his opinion, less severe.*
    *(2) Subject to any directions given by the Secretary of State, the governor may
    remit or mitigate any punishment imposed by a governor or the board of
    visitors.*

Circular Instruction 23/1991 states that prisoners who want to complain
about a decision regarding the restoration of remission (now removal of
days added) may do so through normal grievance procedures, but that such
complaints will automatically go to the area managers since governors will
have already given written reasons for their decisions. "The review
conducted by the area manager's Office will largely concentrate on
procedural matters and consistency of awards, although any complaint
raised by the inmate will be thoroughly investigated" (CI 23/1991: 20).
Further appeal is to the Prisons Ombudsman who will make a
recommendation to the Director General.

r 61(2)
Governors have the power to remit or mitigate disciplinary punishments
only in limited circumstances, i.e. where there is an application for the
removal of added days (SO 3D 72 and CI 3/1992: 11). Added days are the
most common penalty.
    Circular Instruction 23/1991 instructs governors not to take into account
the gravity of the original disciplinary offence when considering applications for removal of added days, though: "they will need to consider,
particularly in the case of the most serious offences, whether it is
appropriate for a significant change of attitude on the prisoner's part to
be rewarded by restoration of a part of the remission forfeited [as it was
then] rather than the whole amount." Removal of added days: "should be
used to reward prisoners who take a constructive approach towards their
imprisonment. Prisoners who genuinely seek or make the most of the
opportunities for work, education, PE, and other regime activities, and
those who respect trust placed on them (for instance in the granting of
home leave or temporary release) should benefit from these arrangements."
It should also "acknowledge a genuine change of attitude on the prisoner's
part, whether or not this is made apparent in the prisoner's participation in

regime or other activities. Simply keeping out of trouble may not always be an indication of such a change of heart, but for some prisoners will constitute a significant achievement that deserves recognition."

Removal of added days should not be allowed to undermine the status of added days as the most serious punishment available (CI 23/1991: 14). The criminal offence for which a prisoner is serving a sentence is not relevant to the addition of days or their removal (CI 23/1991: 11).

In *Campbell and Fell v UK* (1984) one of the prisoners, Fr. Fell, asked the Parkhurst Board to restore some or all of the remission he had forfeited following a mutiny charge at Albany four years before. He was told that remission would not be restored because he was in litigation against the deputy governor and a member of staff. Webster J called this a 'material irregularity', but added that a decision under r 61(2) (then r 56(2)) would not normally be a matter for judicial review. He did not quash the finding, but said the case must be re-heard before a different panel.

The minimum qualifying period for removal of added days is now six months for adult prisoners (four months for those in Young Offender Institutions), and there is no limit on the amount which can be removed. Governors may announce their decision immediately to the prisoner, though in any event the prisoner must receive written confirmation of the decision within seven days of the application being considered, regardless of whether the decision had already been conveyed orally (CI 23/1991: 16).

The Circular also introduced standard documentation for such applications and decisions, including "a clear right to make oral representations, and a commitment to reasoned replies," as well as "a new statement of the 'principles' for [removal of added days], which shifts the emphasis to rewarding a constructive approach to imprisonment in the first instance, whilst acknowledging the achievement that staying out of trouble represents for many inmates."

Prisoners who wish to support their application orally before the governor must be allowed to do so. Governors may also request the prisoner's presence, but cannot enforce attendance if the prisoner does not wish to be present (CI 23/1991: 12). Adult prisoners will be eligible for further consideration of removal of added days six months after the first date of eligibility (in other words, twelve months after the commission of the offence), providing no further days have been added (for young offenders, this period is four months) (CI 23/1991: 19).

PART III

OFFICERS OF PRISONS

General duty of officers
62. (1) It shall be the duty of every officer to conform to these Rules and the rules and regulations of the prison, to assist and support the governor in their maintenance and to obey his lawful instructions.
(2) An officer shall inform the governor promptly of any abuse or impropriety which comes to his knowledge.

Gratuities forbidden
63. No officer shall receive any unauthorised fee, gratuity or other consideration in connection with his office.

Search of officers
64. An officer shall submit himself to be searched in the prison if the governor so directs. Any such search shall be conducted in as seemly a manner as is consistent with discovering anything concealed.

Transactions with prisoners
65. (1) No officer shall take part in any business or pecuniary transaction with or on behalf of a prisoner without the leave of the Secretary of State.
(2) No officer shall without authority bring in or take out, or attempt to bring in or take out, or knowingly allow to be brought in or taken out, to or for a prisoner, or deposit in any place with intent that it shall come into the possession of a prisoner, any article whatsoever.

Contact with former prisoners
66. No officer shall, without the knowledge of the governor, communicate with any person whom he knows to be a former prisoner or a relative or friend of a prisoner or former prisoner.

Communications to the press
67. (1) No officer shall make, directly or indirectly, any unauthorised communication to a representative of the press or any other person concerning matters which have become known to him in the course of his duty.
(2) No officer shall, without authority, publish any matter or make any public pronouncement relating to the administration of any institution to which the Prison Act 1952 applies or to any of its inmates.

All prison employees are required to sign an abbreviated version of s. 2 of the Official Secrets Act: "My attention had been drawn to the provisions of the Official Secrets Act set out on the back of this document and I am fully aware of the serious consequences which may follow any breach of those provisions". However, since the revision of the Act in 1989, disclosure of information relating to prisons is only an offence if it facilitates the commission of a crime.

It is also an offence for anyone to receive information obtained by

someone working within the prison system, if they knew or had reasonable grounds to know it was 'official', and also to attempt to obtain such information (Cohen and Taylor 1978: 6-8).
(See commentary to r 79.)

Code of discipline
68. *The Secretary of State may approve a code of discipline to have effect in relation to officers, or such classes of officers as it may specify, setting out the offences against discipline, the awards which may be made in respect of them and the procedure for dealing with charges.*

Rule 1(v) of the Code of Discipline for Prison Officers states that it is a disciplinary offence for any officer knowingly to make: "any false, misleading or inaccurate statement either orally or in any official document or book". The Police and Criminal Evidence Act 1984 required that racially discriminatory behaviour was added to the police discipline code. Although the Race Relations Manual sets out guidance for staff as well as a Race Relations Policy, no equivalent provision exists in the Code of Discipline for Prison Officers.

Emergencies
69. *Where any constable or member of the armed forces of the Crown is employed by reason of any emergency to assist the governor of a prison by performing duties ordinarily performed by an officer of a prison, any reference in Part II of these Rules to such an officer (other than a governor) shall be construed as including a reference to a constable or a member of the armed forces of the Crown so employed.*

PART IV

PERSONS HAVING ACCESS TO A PRISON

Prohibited articles

70. No person shall, without authority, convey into or throw into or deposit in a prison, or convey or throw out of a prison, or convey to a prisoner, or deposit in any place with intent that it shall come into the possession of a prisoner, any money, clothing, food, drink, tobacco, letter, paper, book, tool, controlled drug, firearm, explosive, weapon or other article whatever. Anything so conveyed, thrown or deposited may be confiscated by the governor.

Control of persons and vehicles

71. (1) Any person or vehicle entering or leaving a prison may be stopped, examined and searched. Any such search of a person shall be carried out in as seemly a manner as is consistent with discovering anything concealed.

(2) The governor may direct the removal from a prison of any person who does not leave on being required to do so.

Viewing of prisons

72. (1) No outside person shall be permitted to view a prison unless authorised by statute or the Secretary of State.

(2) No person viewing the prison shall be permitted to take a photograph, make a sketch or communicate with a prisoner unless authorised by statute or the Secretary of State.

Visitors

73. (1) Without prejudice to any other powers to prohibit or restrict entry to prisons, and to his powers under rules 34 and 35, the Secretary of State may, with a view to securing discipline and good order or the prevention of crime or in the interests of any persons, impose prohibitions on visits by a person to a prison or to a prisoner in a prison for such periods of time as he considers necessary.

(2) Paragraph (1) shall not apply in relation to any visit to a prison or prisoner by a member of the board of visitors of the prison, or justice of the peace, or to prevent any visit by a legal adviser for the purposes of an interview under rule 38 or visit allowed by the board of visitors under rule 35(6).

The European Prison Rules have no equivalent to rr 70-72. (With reference to r 72, see commentary to r 62.)

Restrictions on visitors are set out in Prison Service Order 3610 and are designed primarily to restrict the entry of drugs into prisons. According to the Order, governors must ensure that both prisoners and visitors are made aware of the arrangements.

The Order states that social visitors caught smuggling drugs into prisons through visits will normally be banned from the prison under r 73 for at least three months. If a ban is not imposed, visits from that visitor must be held in closed or non-contact conditions for at least six months. If a ban on visits lasts longer than three months, the governor must review the ban at three-month intervals. Following the end of the ban, the visitor must visit in closed or non-contact conditions for (usually) a further three months. The governor must also target the visitor for searching. Governors must give the reason for any ban to both the visitor and the prisoner in writing. A system must also be in place for appeals against bans.

Visits from journalists in a professional capacity are generally not allowed. If, however, the governor agrees to allow such a visit, the journalist must sign a statement that no material from an interview may be used for professional purposes without the consent of the governor (SO 5A 37A). However, following the House of Lords decision in the case of *Simms* and *O'Brien* in 1999 (which overturned the Court of Appeal in *Simms* (1998)), visits by journalists investigating alleged wrongful convictions - but for no other reason - should be allowed to go ahead. Whether this restriction on freedom of expression can stand up in court following the start of the Human Rights Act is questionable. Prisoners are free to communicate with journalists via letters.

PART V

BOARDS OF VISITORS

Disqualification for membership

74. *Any person, directly or indirectly interested in any contract for the supply of goods and services to a prison, shall not be a member of the board of visitors for that prison and any member who becomes so interested in such a contract shall vacate office as a member.*

Board of visitors

75. *(1) A member of the board of visitors for a prison appointed by the Secretary of State under section 6(2) of the Prison Act 1952[15] shall subject to paragraphs (3) and (4) hold office for three years, or such lesser period as the Secretary of State may appoint.*

   (2) A member -

     (a) appointed for the first time to the board of visitors for a particular prison; or

     (b) reappointed to the board following a gap of a year or more in his membership of it,

   shall, during the period of 12 months following the date on which he is so appointed or (as the case may be) reappointed, undertake such training as may reasonably be required by the Secretary of State.

   (3) The Secretary of State may terminate the appointment of a member if he is satisfied that -

     (a) he has failed satisfactorily to perform his duties;

     (b) he has failed to undertake training he has been required to undertake under paragraph (2), by the end of the period specified in that paragraph;

     (c) he is by reason of physical or mental illness, or for any other reason, incapable of carrying out his duties;

     (d) he has been convicted of such a criminal offence, or his conduct has been such, that it is not in the Secretary of State's opinion fitting that he should remain a member; or

     (e) there is, or appears to be or could appear to be, any conflict of interest between the member performing his duties as a member and any interest of that member, whether personal, financial or otherwise.

   (4) Where the Secretary of State:

     (a) has reason to suspect that a member of the board of visitors for a prison may have so conducted himself that his appointment may be liable to be terminated under paragraph (3)(a) or (d); and

     (b) is of the opinion that the suspected conduct is of such a serious nature that the member cannot be permitted to continue to perform his functions as a member of the board pending the completion of the Secretary of State's investigations into the matter and any decision as to whether the member's appointment should be terminated, he may suspend the member from office for such period or periods as he may reasonably require in order to complete his investigations and determine whether or not the appointment of the member should be

so terminated; and a member so suspended shall not, during the period of his suspension, be regarded as being a member of the board, other than for the purposes of this paragraph and paragraphs (1) and (3).
(5) A board shall have a chairman and a vice chairman who shall be members of the board.
(6) The Secretary of State shall -
  (a) upon the constitution of a board for the first time, appoint a chairman and a vice chairman to hold office for a period not exceeding twelve months;
  (b) thereafter appoint, before the date of the first meeting of the board in any year of office of the board, a chairman and vice chairman for that year, having first consulted the board; and
  (c) promptly fill, after first having consulted the board, any casual vacancy in the office of chairman or vice chairman.
(7) The Secretary of State may terminate the appointment of a member as chairman or vice chairman of the board if he is satisfied that the member has -
  (a) failed satisfactorily to perform his functions as chairman (or as the case may be) vice chairman;
  (b) has grossly misconducted himself while performing those functions.

According to the BoV Handbook, people over the age of 60 are unlikely to be appointed for the first time, nor are members re-appointed after they reach 70. In addition to not being involved in contracts for goods and services to a prison, members of the BoV may not also be prison visitors or voluntary associates.

Appointment should not be based on political views, though candidates are asked about this in order to ensure a proportionate balance of membership. Board membership is reviewed every three years; re-appointment is not automatic.

Familiarity with rules and regulations is important for Board members: "One of my initial impressions was that the Prison Service is always concerned to ensure that prisoners comply with the Prison Rules, but there does not seem to be a similar commitment on the part of the Service to comply with the Rules itself. In my view it is vitally important for the new Board members to know and understand the Rules so that they can see if they are followed by their establishment" (Byron 1985). As part of the changes to the Prison Rules, the 1999 version recognises this need through the requirement for training in r 75(2).

Proceedings of boards
76. *(1) The board of visitors for a prison shall meet at the prison once a month or, if they resolve for reasons specified in the resolution that less frequent meetings are sufficient, not fewer than eight times in twelve months.*
(2) The board may fix a quorum of not fewer than three members for proceedings.
(3) The board shall keep minutes of their proceedings.
(4) The proceedings of the board shall not be invalidated by any vacancy in the membership or any defect in the appointment of a member.

Referring to r 76's provision for exceptions to monthly meetings, AMBoV stated: "It is doubtful whether any Board could have a proper reason for meeting less than once a month". The AMBoV Handbook comments that, "Board meetings should be held at least once a month with papers distributed well in advance" (1991 AMBoV Handbook, 1.3.3c). However it also states that "Boards in adult prisons should meet at least eight times a year or monthly in the case of Young Offender Institutions" (1991: 1.3.3).

Perhaps more surprising is the statement in the BoV Handbook (1993) that the head governor of the establishment should also attend the Board's monthly meetings "unless unavoidably detained". While this guidance can be exercised responsibly, using the governor as a source of information about current issues in an establishment, it may also compromise the independence of a Board, or at least the appearance of independence.

One of the main concerns in the Chief Inspector of Prisons' Annual Report (1999) was of inconsistency between prisons of the same type. Boards of Visitors now hold meetings amongst the Chairmen of particular types of prisons.

General duties of boards
77. *(1) The board of visitors for a prison shall satisfy themselves as to the state of the prison premises, the administration of the prison and the treatment of the prisoners.*
(2) The board shall inquire into and report upon any matter into which the Secretary of State asks them to inquire.
(3) The board shall direct the attention of the governor to any matter which calls for his attention, and shall report to the Secretary of State any matter which they consider it expedient to report.
(4) The board shall inform the Secretary of State immediately of any abuse which comes to their knowledge.
(5) Before exercising any power under these Rules the board and any member of the board shall consult the governor in relation to any matter which may affect discipline.

A source of confusion exists in the similarity of title between 'Board of Visitor' and 'prison visitor'. The latter is a volunteer who befriends individual prisoners, whereas the duties of Boards are set out in the Prison Rules by authority of s. 6 of the 1952 Prison Act (see r 35 Personal letters and visits).

HM Chief Inspector of Prisons has commented that "[The Inspectorate] do not always find that Boards are given facilities to match their interest in the life of the establishments they serve. Though many Boards have members assigned to particular areas of the establishment's work, which in some cases results in observer membership of the relevant management committee, others feel themselves to be denied or do not seek detailed information on current issues. It is our experience that a Board's contribution can be correlated with the degree to which it is given access to information" (1991: 1.41).

r 77(1)
Despite the provision in r 77(1), the extent to which Boards can monitor the administration of a prison in practice is questionable. Administrative decisions such as non-disciplinary segregation or transfer are highly discretionary and notoriously difficult to challenge. Board members have a direct role in approving the administrative segregation of prisoners under r 45, but this directly opposes their role as independent 'watchdogs' over a prison (see commentary to r 45 Removal from association). The Raison Committee on the local monitoring of prisons suggested that the definition

of the Board's role be changed to say that Boards should satisfy themselves that: "within the necessary framework of security and order, prisoners are justly treated in decent conditions and provided with opportunities to lead a law-abiding and useful life in custody and after release" (1995: 27). The Committee argued that this should include monitoring, but not determining, the use of segregation.

In order to establish criteria by which Boards may 'satisfy' themselves that all is in order, the AMBoV Handbook advises Board members to refer frequently to the Rules, Standing Orders and Circular Instructions, the European Prison Rules and conditions found in other institutions. Visits should be conducted never less than fortnightly; r 79(1) specifies that visits (unlike members' other duties) shall be done by rota. "It is a Board's duty to ensure that visits are made at all times and prisoners' and staff welfare will best be served if that duty is carried out without fear or favour".

r 77(4)

AMBoV interprets the duties of Boards under this section very widely: "Boards should not interpret 'abuse' only as individual dereliction of duty: if a prison was persistently in breach of the Prison Rules, Standing Orders or Circular Instructions (for example, inadequate accommodation, lack of exercise or deficient supplies of materials) then, whatever the reason for the breach (overcrowding or shortage of staff, for example), it constitutes an abuse of the standards which Parliament and the Secretary of State have authorised. Nor should Boards restrict their publicity of any abuses or deficiencies which come to their attention to the internal channels of the Prison Department" (1984 AMBoV Handbook, para. 3C (19)). The revised edition of the Handbook (most recently 1998) lists specific issues which the Board members should consider during their visits.

(See also r 22(2) Notification of illness or death, r 35(6) Personal letters and visits, and r 43(1) Prisoners' property).

Particular duties

78. (1) The board of visitors for a prison and any member of the board shall hear any complaint or request which a prisoner wishes to make to them or him.

(2) The board shall arrange for the food of the prisoners to be inspected by a member of the board at frequent intervals.

(3) The board shall inquire into any report made to them, whether or not by a member of the board, that a prisoner's health, mental or physical, is likely to be injuriously affected by any conditions of his imprisonment.

AMBoV recommends that, apart from their statutory duties, Boards should publicise the right to make applications to them through "clearly worded notices prominently displayed on the wings, in the library, in the punishment and segregation areas. The information provided should try to give some indication of both the extent and the limits of the boards' powers." The Handbook also encourages members to be open to informal approaches and suggests for them to wear distinctive name badges stating 'Board of Visitors' (1991 AMBoV Handbook, 4.2.3 c and d). Members should not assume prior knowledge of their role by people in prisons: "Boards would probably be surprised to discover the ignorance or misconceptions of their role held by prisoners and sometimes staff" (1991 AMBoV Handbook, 1.3.2 h).

In carrying out their duties, Board members are bound by the Official

Secrets Act 1989. Other confidential information must also not be disclosed, even if the Act does not specifically protect the information. This would include information such as prisoners' personal affairs or the handling of management problems. Boards must have specific written information from the individual involved in order to have access to a prisoner's confidential medical records or staff's personal files.

According to the BoV Handbook, members should inform prisoners personally of the outcome of their application to a Board member.

r 78(2) and (3)
According to the 1984 AMBoV Handbook, members of Boards have an obligation to satisfy themselves about the quality of the food and prisoners' physical and mental health every time they carry out an inspection visit: "... a Board which neglected or turned a blind eye to matters relating to staff facilities and welfare would be neglecting its statutory duty". The 1998 AMBoV Handbook sets out specific questions for members to use as guidelines on their visits, as does their 1993 BoV Handbook. Boards must devise an incident procedure in agreement with the governor in accordance with Circular Instruction 38/1981 (para 1.3.3).

The BoV Handbook (1993) states that Board members should not accept invitations to act as a McKenzie Friend for adjudications.

Members visiting prisons
79. *(1) The members of the board of visitors for a prison shall visit the prison frequently, and the board shall arrange a rota whereby at least one of its members visits the prison between meetings of the board.*
(2) A member of the board shall have access at any time to every part of the prison and to every prisoner, and he may interview any prisoner out of the sight and hearing of officers.
(3) A member of the board shall have access to the records of the prison.

Addressing a meeting of Southwest Boards of Visitors nearly 20 years ago, the then Prison Department Director of Operational Policy said: "Can we be certain that some members have visited the prison at unusual hours to see what's going on? Has the rota become so fixed that Board members do not like to visit when it's someone else's turn? I know the problems, but it would be good to see more unscheduled visits taking place" (Faulkner 1982: 20). The same comments apply today.

AMBoV states: "Denial of access to records should be regarded as a serious matter ... Boards should adopt a critical approach to information and statistics provided by the Service ... Even where a critical approach is adopted the board should not rely entirely on information and data provided by the Service itself" (1991 AMBoV Handbook, 1.3.4 f and g).
(See also r 11 Requests and complaints and r 45 Removal from association.)

Annual report
80. *(1) The board of visitors for a prison shall, in accordance with paragraphs (2) and (3) below, from time to time make a report to the Secretary of State concerning the state of the prison and its administration, including in it any advice and suggestions they consider appropriate.*
(2) The board shall comply with any directions given to them from time to time by the Secretary of State as to the following matters:
    (a) the period to be covered by a report under paragraph (1);

(b) *the frequency with which such a report is to be made; and*

(c) *the length of time from the end of the period covered by such a report within which it is to be made;*

either in respect of a particular report or generally; providing that no directions may be issued under this paragraph if they would have the effect of requiring a board to make or deliver a report less frequently than once in every 12 months.

(3) Subject to any directions given to them under paragraph (2), the board shall, under paragraph (1), make an annual report to the Secretary of State as soon as reasonably possible after 31st December each year, which shall cover the period of 12 months ending on that date or, in the case of a board constituted for the first time during that period, such part of that period during which the board has been in existence.

Boards are required to report annually to the Secretary of State, but they are not currently required to publish this report. The AMBoV Handbook states: "Increasingly boards are publishing their reports and sending them to local newspapers, radio and television. A long report could be accompanied by a summary of significant comments which can be used as a press release. Members may discuss any matter publicly except information which might help an escape or possibly breach security; confidential information, particularly about an investigation; personal details about a prisoner or member of staff. They are bound by the Official Secrets Act. However no prosecution has ever been brought against a board member and it is unlikely to happen unless a flagrant breach of security were to be involved. The report could also be sent to the local courts, local organisations which might be sources for recruiting new members, MPs, select committees, the Inspectorate, penal reform groups etc." (1991: para. 1.3.2 g).

For many years, it has been the policy of successive Prison Ministers that Boards of Visitors should be encouraged to publish their annual reports. AMBoV considers that Board members have a social duty to make themselves accountable to the community and report on conditions in their prison. It recommends that reports should be published and distributed internally on staff and prisoner notice boards and in the prison library (1991 AMBoV Handbook, 1.3.2 h). The Committee for the Prevention of Torture suggested that the Government consider requiring Boards to publish their annual reports (though their comments on certain issues could remain confidential) (1991: para. 200). The Raison Committee believed that Boards' annual reports should be published "as a matter of course" (1995: 28).

PART VI

SUPPLEMENTAL

Delegation by governor
81.   *The governor of a prison may, with the leave of the Secretary of State, delegate any of his powers and duties under these Rules to another officer of that prison.*

The Prior Committee recommended that governors have the discretion to delegate any adjudication to an officer not below the rank of governor IV or, as at present, to the deputy governor if of lower rank (1985: 11.67).

Contracted out prisons
82.   *(1) Where the Secretary of State has entered into a contract for the running of a prison under section 84 of the Criminal Justice Act 1991[16] ("the 1991 Act") these Rules shall have effect in relation to that prison with the following modifications -*
   (a) references to an officer in the Rules shall include references to a prisoner custody officer certified as such under section 89(1) of the 1991 Act and performing custodial duties;
   (b) references to a governor in the Rules shall include references to a director approved by the Secretary of State for the purposes of section 85(1)(a) of the 1991 Act except -
      (i) in rules 45, 48, 49, 53, 54, 55, 61 and 81 where references to a governor shall include references to a controller appointed by the Secretary of State under section 85(1)(b) of the 1991 Act, and
      (ii) in rules 62(1), 66 and 77 where references to a governor shall include references to the director and the controller;
   (c) rule 68 shall not apply in relation to a prisoner custody officer certified as such under section 89(1) of the 1991 Act and performing custodial duties.
   (2) Where a director exercises the powers set out in section 85(3) (b) of the 1991 Act (removal from association, temporary confinement and restraints) in cases of urgency, he shall notify the controller of that fact forthwith.

Contracted out parts of prisons
83.   *Where the Secretary of State has entered into a contract for the running of part of a prison under section 84(1) of the Criminal Justice Act 1991, that part and the remaining part shall each be treated for the purposes of Parts II to IV and Part VI of these Rules as if they were separate prisons.*

Contracted out functions at directly managed prisons
84.   *(1) Where the Secretary of State has entered into a contract under section 88A(1) of the Criminal Justice Act 1991 ("the 1991 Act") for any functions at a directly managed prison to be performed by prisoner custody officers who are authorised to perform custodial duties under section 89(1) of the 1991 Act, references to an officer in these Rules shall, subject to paragraph (2), include references to a prisoner custody officer who is so authorised and who is*

performing contracted out functions for the purposes of, or for purposes connected with, the prison.
(2) Paragraph (1) shall not apply to references to an officer in rule 68.
(3) In this rule, "directly managed prison" has the meaning assigned to it by section 88A(5) of the 1991 Act.

In sum, these Rules give directors of private prisons the same powers as governors, with a few notable exceptions: except "in cases of urgency", the director must refer to a Controller (the Crown Servant appointed by the Secretary of State to oversee the running of a particular private prison) for disciplinary adjudications and punishments, removal from association, confinement in a special cell, and for applying restraints.

Revocations and savings
85. *(1) Subject to paragraphs (2) and (3) below, the Rules specified in the Schedule to these Rules are hereby revoked.*
(2) Without prejudice to the Interpretation Act 1978[17], where a prisoner committed an offence against discipline contrary to rule 47 of the Prison Rules 1964[18] prior to the coming into force of these Rules, those rules shall continue to have effect to permit the prisoner to be charged with such an offence, disciplinary proceedings in relation to such an offence to be continued, and the governor to impose punishment for such an offence.
(3) Without prejudice to the Interpretation Act 1978, any award of additional days or other punishment or suspended punishment for an offence against discipline awarded or imposed under any provision of the rules revoked by this rule, or those rules as saved by paragraph (2), or treated by any such provision as having been awarded or imposed under the rules revoked by this rule, shall have effect as if awarded or imposed under the corresponding provision of these Rules.

ANNEX A

The European Prison Rules 1987

REVISED EUROPEAN VERSION OF THE STANDARD MINIMUM RULES FOR THE TREATMENT OF PRISONERS

Preamble

The purposes of these rules are:

a. to establish a range of minimum standards for all those aspects of prison administration that are essential to human conditions and positive treatment in modern and progressive systems;

b. to serve as a stimulus to prison administrations to develop policies and management style and practice based on good contemporary principles of purpose and equity;

c. to encourage in prison staffs professional attitudes that reflect the important social and moral qualities of their work and to create conditions in which they can optimise their own performance to the benefit of society in general, the prisoners in their care and their own vocational satisfaction;

d   to provide realistic basic criteria against which prison administrations and those responsible for inspecting the conditions and management of prisons can make valid judgements of performance and measure progress towards higher standards.

It is emphasised that the rules do not constitute a model system and that, in practice, many European prison services are already operating well above many of the standards set out in the rules and that others are striving, and will continue to strive, to do so. Wherever there are difficulties or practical problems to be overcome in the application of the rules, the Council of Europe has the machinery and the expertise available to assist with advice and the fruits of the experience of the various prison administrations within its sphere.

In these rules, renewed emphasis has been placed on the precepts of human dignity, the commitment of prison administrations to humane and positive treatment, the importance of staff roles and effective modern management approaches. They are set out to provide ready reference, encouragement and guidance to those who are working at all levels of prison administration. The explanatory memorandum that accompanies the rules is intended to ensure the understanding, acceptance and flexibility that are necessary to achieve the highest realistic level of implementation beyond the basic standards.

PART I

THE BASIC PRINCIPLES

1. The deprivation of liberty shall be effected in material and moral conditions which ensure respect for human dignity and are in conformity with these rules.

2. The rules shall be applied impartially. There shall be no discrimination on grounds of race, colour, sex, language, religion, political or other opinion, national or social origin, birth, economic or other status. The religious beliefs and moral precepts of the group to which a prisoner belongs shall be respected.

3. The purposes of the treatment of persons in custody shall be such as to sustain their health and self-respect and, so far as the length of sentence permits, to develop their sense of responsibility and encourage those attitudes and skills that will assist them to return to society with the best chance of leading law-abiding and self-supporting lives after their release.

4. There shall be regular inspections of penal institutions and services by qualified and experienced inspectors appointed by a competent authority. Their task shall be, in particular, to monitor whether and to what extent these institutions are administered in accordance with existing laws and regulations, the objectives of the prison services and the requirements of these rules.

5. The protection of the individual rights of prisoners with special regard to the legality of the execution of detention measures shall be secured by means of a control carried out, according to national rules, by a judicial authority or other duly constituted body authorised to visit the prisoners and not belonging to the prison administration.

6. (1) These rules shall be made readily available to staff in the national languages;
(2) They shall also be available to prisoners in the same languages and in other languages so far as is reasonable and practicable.

PART II

THE MANAGEMENT OF PRISON SYSTEMS

Reception and registration

7. (1) No person shall be received in an institution without a valid commitment order.
(2) The essential details of the commitment and reception shall immediately be recorded.

8. In every place where persons are imprisoned, a complete and secure record of the following information shall be kept concerning each prisoner received:

(a) information concerning the identity of the prisoner;

(b) the reasons for commitment and the authority therefore;

(c) the day and hour of admission and release.

9. Reception arrangements shall conform with the basic principles of the rules and shall assist prisoners to resolve their urgent personal problems.

10. (1) As soon as possible after reception, full reports and relevant information about the personal situation and training programme of each prisoner with a sentence of suitable length in preparation for ultimate release shall be drawn up and submitted to the director for information or approval as appropriate.

(2) Such reports shall always include reports by a medical officer and the personnel in direct charge of the prisoner concerned.

(3) The reports and information concerning prisoners shall be maintained with due regard to confidentiality on an individual basis, regularly kept up to date and only accessible to authorised persons.

The allocation and classification of prisoners

11. (1) In allocating prisoners to different institutions or regimes, due account shall be taken of their judicial and legal situation (untried or convicted prisoner, first offender or habitual offender, short sentence or long sentence), of the special requirements of their treatment, of their medical needs, their sex and age.

(2) Males and females shall in principle be detained separately, although they may participate together in organised activities as part of an established treatment programme.

(3) In principle, untried prisoners shall be detained separately from convicted prisoners unless they consent to being accommodated or involved together in organised activities beneficial to them.

(4) Young prisoners shall be detained under conditions which as far as possible protect them from harmful influences and which take account of the needs peculiar to their age.

12. The purposes of classification or reclassification of prisoners shall be:

(a) to separate from others those prisoners who, by reasons of their criminal records or their personality, are likely to benefit from that or who may exercise a bad influence; and

(b) to assist in allocating prisoners to facilitate their treatment and social resettlement taking into account the management and security requirements.

13. So far as possible separate institutions or separate sections of an institution shall be used to facilitate the management of different treatment regimes or the allocation of specific categories of prisoners.

Accommodation

14. (1) Prisoners shall normally be lodged during the night in individual cells except in cases where it is considered that there are advantages in sharing accommodation with other prisoners.
(2) Where accommodation is shared it shall be occupied by prisoners suitable to associate with others in those conditions. There shall be supervision by night, in keeping with the nature of the institution.

15. The accommodation provided for prisoners, and in particular all sleeping accommodation, shall meet the requirements of health and hygiene, due regard being paid to climatic conditions and especially the cubic content of air, a reasonable amount of space, lighting, heating and ventilation.

16. In all places where prisoners are required to live or work:
(a) the windows shall be large enough to enable the prisoners, *inter alia*, to read or work by natural light in normal conditions. They shall be so constructed that they can allow the entrance of fresh air except where there is an adequate air conditioning system. Moreover, the windows shall, with due regard to security requirements, present in their size, location and construction as normal an appearance as possible;
(b) artificial light shall satisfy recognised technical standards.

17. The sanitary installations and arrangements for access shall be adequate to enable every prisoner to comply with the needs of nature when necessary and in clean and decent conditions.

18. Adequate bathing and showering installations shall be provided so that every prisoner may be enabled and required to have a bath or shower, at a temperature suitable to the climate, as frequently as necessary for general hygiene according to season and geographical region, but at least once a week. Wherever possible there should be free access at all reasonable times.

19. All parts of an institution shall be properly maintained and kept clean at all times.

Personal hygiene

20. Prisoners shall be required to keep their persons clean, and to this end they shall be provided with water and with such toilet articles as are necessary for health and cleanliness.

21. For reasons of health and in order that prisoners may maintain a good appearance and preserve their self-respect, facilities shall be provided for the proper care of the hair and beard, and men shall be enabled to shave regularly.

Clothing and bedding

22. (1) Prisoners who are not allowed to wear their own clothing shall be provided with an outfit of clothing suitable for the climate and

adequate to keep them in good health. Such clothing shall in no manner be degrading or humiliating.

(2) All clothing shall be clean and kept in proper condition. Under-clothing shall be changed and washed as often as necessary for the maintenance of hygiene.

(3) Whenever prisoners obtain permission to go outside the institution, they shall be allowed to wear their own clothing or other inconspicuous clothing.

23. On the admission of prisoners to an institution, adequate arrangements shall be made to ensure that their personal clothing is kept in good condition and fit for use.

24. Every prisoner shall be provided with a separate bed and separate and appropriate bedding which shall be kept in good order and changed often enough to ensure its cleanliness.

Food

25. (1) In accordance with the standards laid down by the health authorities, the administration shall provide the prisoners at the normal times with food which is suitably prepared and presented, and which satisfies in quality and quantity the standards of dietetics and modern hygiene and takes into account their age, health, the nature of their work, and so far as possible, religious or cultural requirements.

(2) Drinking water shall be available to every prisoner.

Medical services

26. (1) At every institution there shall be available the services of at least one qualified general practitioner. The medical services should be organised in close relation with the general health administration of the community or nation. They shall include a psychiatric service for the diagnosis and, in proper cases, the treatment of states of mental abnormality.

(2) Sick prisoners who require specialist treatment shall be transferred to specialised institutions or to civil hospitals. Where hospital facilities are provided in an institution, their equipment, furnishings and pharmaceutical supplies shall be suitable for the medical care and treatment of sick prisoners, and there shall be a staff of suitably trained officers.

(3) The services of a qualified dental officer shall be available to every prisoner.

27. Prisoners may not be submitted to any experiments which may result in physical or moral injury.

28. (1) Arrangements shall be made wherever practicable for children to be born in a hospital outside the institution. However, unless special arrangements are made, there shall in penal institutions be the necessary staff and accommodation for the confinement and postnatal care of pregnant women. If a child is born in prison, this fact shall not be mentioned in the birth certificate.

(2) Where infants are allowed to remain in the institution with their mothers, special provision shall be made for a nursery staffed by qualified persons, where the infants shall be placed when they are not in the care of their mothers.

29. The medical officer shall see and examine every prisoner as soon as possible after admission and thereafter as necessary, with a view particularly to the discovery of physical or mental illness and the taking of all measures necessary for medical treatment; the segregation of prisoners suspected of infectious or contagious conditions; the noting of physical or mental defects which might impede resettlement after release; and the determination of the fitness of every prisoner to work.

30. (1) The medical officer shall have the care of the physical and mental health of the prisoners and shall see, under the conditions and with a frequency consistent with hospital standards, all sick prisoners, all who report illness or injury and any prisoner to whom attention is specially directed.
(2) The medical officer shall report to the director whenever it is considered that a prisoner's physical or mental health has been or will be adversely affected by continued imprisonment or by any condition of imprisonment.

31. (1) The medical officer or a competent authority shall regularly inspect and advise the director upon:
(a) the quantity, quality, preparation and serving of food and water;
(b) the hygiene and cleanliness of the institution and prisoners;
(c) the sanitation, heating, lighting and ventilation of the institution;
(d) the suitability and cleanliness of the prisoners' clothing and bedding.
(2) The director shall consider the reports and advice that the medical officer submits according to Rules 30, paragraph 3, and 31, paragraph 1, and, when in concurrence with the recommendations made, shall take immediate steps to give effect to those recommendations; if they are not within the director's competence or if the director does not concur with them, the director shall immediately submit a personal report and the advice of the medical officer to higher authority.

32. The medical services of the institution shall seek to detect and shall treat any physical or mental illness or defects which may impede a prisoner's resettlement after release. All necessary medical, surgical and psychiatric services including those available in the community shall be provided to the prisoner to that end.

Discipline and punishment

33. Discipline and order shall be maintained in the interests of safe custody, ordered community life and the treatment objectives of the institution.

34. (1) No prisoner shall be employed, in the service of the institution, in any disciplinary capacity.
(2) This rule shall not, however, impede the proper functioning of arrangements under which specified social, educational or sports

activities or responsibilities are entrusted under supervision to prisoners who are formed into groups for the purposes of their participation in regime programmes.

35. The following shall be provided for and determined by the law or by the regulation of the competent authority:
    (a) conduct constituting a disciplinary offence;
    (b) the types and duration of punishment which may be imposed;
    (c) the authority competent to impose such punishment;
    (d) access to, and the authority of, the appellate process.

36. (1) No prisoner shall be punished except in accordance with the terms of such law or regulation, and never twice for the same act.
    (2) Reports of misconduct shall be presented promptly to the competent authority who shall decide on them without undue delay.
    (3) No prisoner shall be punished unless informed of the alleged offence and given a proper opportunity of presenting a defence.
    (4) Where necessary and practicable prisoners shall be allowed to make their defence through an interpreter.

37. Collective punishments, corporal punishment, punishment by placing in a dark cell, and all cruel, inhuman or degrading punishment shall be completely prohibited as punishments for disciplinary offences.

38. (1) Punishment by disciplinary confinement and any other punishment which might have an adverse effect on the physical or mental health of the prisoner shall only be imposed if the medical officer, after examination, certifies in writing that the prisoner is fit to sustain it.
    (2) In no case may such punishment be contrary to, or depart from, the principles stated in Rule 37.
    (3) The medical officer shall visit daily prisoners undergoing such punishment and shall advise the director if the termination or alteration of the punishment is considered necessary on grounds of physical or mental health.

Instruments of restraint

39. The use of chains and irons shall be prohibited. Handcuffs, restraint-jackets and other body restraints shall never be applied as a punishment. They shall not be used except in the following circumstances:
    (a) if necessary, as a precaution against escape during a transfer, provided that they shall be removed when the prisoner appears before a judicial or administrative authority unless that authority decides otherwise;
    (b) on medical grounds by direction and under the supervision of the medical officer;
    (c) by order of the director, if other methods of control fail, in order to protect a prisoner from self-injury, injury to others or to prevent serious damage to property; in such instances the director shall at once consult the medical officer and report to the higher administrative authority.

40. The patterns and manner of use of the instruments of restraint authorised in the preceding paragraph shall be decided by law or

regulation. Such instruments must not be applied for any longer time than is strictly necessary.

Information to and complaints by prisoners

41. (1) Every prisoner shall on admission be provided with written information about the regulations governing the treatment of prisoners of the relevant category, the disciplinary requirements of the institution, the authorised methods of seeking information and making complaints, and all such other matters as are necessary to understand the rights and obligations of prisoners and to adapt to the life of the institution.
(2) If a prisoner cannot understand the written information provided, this information shall be explained orally.

42. (1) Every prisoner shall have the opportunity every day of making requests or complaints to the director of the institution or the officer authorised to act in that capacity.
(2) A prisoner shall have the opportunity to take to, or to make requests or complaints to, an inspector of prisons or to any other duly constituted authority entitled to visit the prison without the director or other members of the staff being present. However, appeals against formal decisions may be restricted to the authorised procedures.
(3) Every prisoner shall be allowed to make a request or complaint, under confidential cover, to the central prison administration, the judicial authority or other proper authorities.
(4) Every request or complaint addressed or referred to a prison authority shall be promptly dealt with and replied to by this authority without undue delay.

43. (1) Prisoners shall be allowed to communicate with their families and, subject to the needs of treatment, security and good order, persons or representatives of outside organisations and to receive visits from these persons as often as possible.
(2) To encourage contact with the outside world there shall be a system of prison leave consistent with the treatment objectives in Part IV of these rules.

44. (1) Prisoners who are foreign nationals should be informed, without delay, of their right to request contact and be allowed reasonable facilities to communicate with the diplomatic or consular representative of the state to which they belong. The prison administration should co-operate fully with such representatives in the interests of foreign nationals in prison who may have special needs.
(2) Prisoners who are nationals of states without diplomatic or consular representation in the country and refugees or stateless persons shall be allowed similar facilities to communicate with the diplomatic representative of the state which take charge of their interests or national or international authority whose task it is to serve the interests of such persons.

45. Prisoners shall be allowed to keep themselves informed regularly of the news by reading newspapers, periodicals and other publications, by radio

or television transmissions, by lectures or by any similar means as authorised or controlled by the administration. Special arrangements should be made to meet the needs of foreign nationals with linguistic difficulties.

Religious and moral assistance

46. So far as practicable, every prisoner shall be allowed to satisfy the needs of his religious, spiritual and moral life by attending the services or meetings provided in the institution and having in his possession any necessary books or literature.

47. (1) If the institution contains a sufficient number of prisoners of the same religion, a qualified representative of that religion shall be appointed and approved. If the number of prisoners justifies it and conditions permit, the arrangement should be on a full-time basis.
(2) A qualified representative appointed or approved under paragraph I shall be allowed to hold regular services and activities and to pay pastoral visits in private to prisoners of his religion at proper times.
(3) Access to a qualified representative of any religion shall not be refused to any prisoner. If any prisoner should object to a visit of any religious representative, the prisoner shall be allowed to refuse it.

Retention of prisoners' property

48. (1) All money, valuables, and other effects belonging to prisoners which under the regulations of the institution they are not allowed to retain shall on admission to the institution be placed in safe custody. An inventory thereof shall be signed by the prisoner. Steps shall be taken to keep them in good condition. If it has been found necessary to destroy any article, this shall be recorded and the prisoner informed.
(2) On the release of the prisoner, all such articles and money shall be returned except insofar as there have been authorised withdrawals of money or the authorised sending of any such property out of the institution, or it has been found necessary on hygienic grounds to destroy any article. The prisoner shall sign a receipt for the articles and money returned.
(3) As far as practicable, any money or effects received for a prisoner from outside shall be treated in the same way unless they are intended for and permitted for use during imprisonment.
(4) If a prisoner brings in any medicines, the medical officer shall decide what use shall be made of them.

Notification of death, illness, transfer, etc

49. (1) Upon the death or serious illness of or serious injury to a prisoner, or removal to an institution for the treatment of mental illness or abnormalities, the director shall at once inform the spouse, if the prisoner is married, or the nearest relative and shall in any event inform any other person previously designated by the prisoner.
(2) A prisoner shall be informed at once of the death or serious illness of any near relative. In these cases and wherever circumstances allow,

the prisoner should be authorised to visit this sick relative or see the deceased either under escort or alone.

(3) All prisoners shall have the right to inform at once their families of imprisonment or transfer to another institution.

Removal of prisoners

50. (1) When prisoners are being removed to or from an institution, they shall be exposed to public view as little as possible, and proper safeguards shall be adopted to protect them from insult, curiosity and publicity in any form.

(2) The transport of prisoners in conveyances with inadequate ventilation or light, or in any way which would subject them to unnecessary physical hardship or indignity shall be prohibited.

(3) The transport of prisoners shall be carried out at the expense of the administration and in accordance with duly authorised regulations.

PART III

PERSONNEL

51. In view of the fundamental importance of the prison staff to the proper management of the institutions and the pursuit of their organisational and treatment objectives, prison administrations shall give high priority to the fulfilment of the rules concerning personnel.

52. Prison staff shall be continually encouraged through training, consultative procedures and a positive management style to aspire to humane standards, higher efficiency and a committed approach to their duties.

53. The prison administration shall regard it as an important task continually to inform public opinion of the roles of the prison system and the work of the staff, so as to encourage public understanding of the importance of their contribution to society.

54. (1) The prison administration shall provide for the careful selection on recruitment or in subsequent appointments of all personnel. Special emphasis shall be given to their integrity, humanity, professional capacity and personal suitability for the work.

(2) Personnel shall normally be appointed on a permanent basis as professional prison staff and have civil service status with security of tenure subject only to good conduct, efficiency, good physical and mental health and an adequate standard of education. Salaries shall be adequate to attract and retain suitable men and women; employment benefits and conditions of service shall be favourable in view of the exacting nature of the work.

(3) Whenever it is necessary to employ part-time staff, these criteria should apply to them as far as that it is appropriate.

55. (1) On recruitment or after an appropriate period of practical experience, the personnel shall be given a course of training in their general
and specific duties and be required to pass theoretical and practical
tests unless their professional qualifications make that unnecessary.

(2) During their career, all personnel shall maintain and improve their
knowledge and professional capacity by attending courses of in-service
training to be organised by the administration at suitable intervals.

(3) Arrangements should be made for wider experience and training
for personnel whose professional capacity would be improved by this.

(4) The training of all personnel should include instruction in the
requirements and application of the European Prison Rules and the
European Convention on Human Rights.

56. All members of the personnel shall be expected at all times to conduct
themselves and perform their duties so as to influence the prisoners for
good by their example and to command their respect.

57. (1) So far as possible the personnel shall include a sufficient number of
specialists such as psychiatrists, psychologists, social workers,
teachers, trade, physical education and sports instructors.

(2) These and other specialist staff shall normally be employed on a
permanent basis. This shall not preclude part-time or voluntary
workers when that is appropriate and beneficial to the level of support
and training they can provide.

58. (1) The prison administration shall ensure that every institution is at all
times in the full charge of the director, the deputy director or other
authorised official.

(2) The director of an institution should be adequately qualified for that
post by character, administrative ability, suitable professional training
and experience.

(3) The director shall be appointed on a full-time basis and be available
or accessible as required by the prison administration in its management instructions.

(4) When two or more institutions are under the authority of one
director, each shall be visited at frequent intervals. A responsible
official shall be in charge of each of these institutions.

59. The administration shall introduce forms of organisation and management systems to facilitate communication between the different categories
of staff in an institution with a view to ensuring co-operation between the
various services, in particular, with respect to the treatment and re-
socialisation of prisoners.

60. (1) The director, deputy, and the majority of the other personnel of the
institution shall be able to speak the language of the greatest number of
prisoners, or a language understood by the greatest number of them.

(2) Whenever necessary and practicable the services of an interpreter
shall be used.

61. (1) Arrangements shall be made to ensure at all times that a qualified
and approved medical practitioner is able to attend without delay in
cases of urgency.

(2) In institutions not staffed by one or more full-time medical officers, a part-time medical officer or authorised staff of a health service shall visit regularly.

62. The appointment of staff in institutions or parts of institutions housing prisoners of the opposite sex is to be encouraged.

63. (1) Staff of the institutions shall not use force against prisoners except in self-defence or in cases of attempted escape or active or passive physical resistance to an order based on law or regulations. Staff who have recourse to force must use no more than is strictly necessary and must report the incident immediately to the director of the institution.
(2) Staff shall as appropriate be given special technical training to enable them to restrain aggressive prisoners.
(3) Except in special circumstances staff performing duties which bring them into direct contact with prisoners should not be armed. Furthermore, staff should in no circumstances be provided with arms unless they have been fully trained in their use.

PART IV

TREATMENT OBJECTIVES AND REGIME

64. Imprisonment is by the deprivation of liberty a punishment in itself. The conditions of imprisonment and the prison and the prison regimes shall not, therefore, except as incidental to justifiable segregation or the maintenance of discipline, aggravate the suffering inherent in this.

65. Every effort shall be made to ensure that the regimes of the institutions are designed and managed so as:
(a) to ensure that the conditions of life are compatible with human dignity and acceptable standards in the community;
(b) to minimise the detrimental effects of imprisonment and the differences between prison life and life at liberty which tend to diminish the self-respect or sense of personal responsibility of prisoners;
(c) to sustain and strengthen those links with relatives and the outside community that will promote the best interests of prisoners and their families;
(d) to provide opportunities for prisoners to develop skills and aptitudes that will improve their prospects of successful resettlement after release.

66. To these ends all the remedial, educational, moral, spiritual and other resources that are appropriate should be made available and utilised in accordance with the individual treatment needs of prisoners. Thus the regimes should include:
(a) spiritual support and guidance and opportunities for relevant work, vocational guidance and training, education, physical education, the

development of social skills, counselling, group and recreational activities;

(b) arrangements to ensure that these activities are organised, so far as possible, to increase contacts with and opportunities within the outside community so as to enhance the prospects for social resettlement after release;

(c) procedures for establishing and reviewing individual treatment and training programmes for prisoners after full consultations among the relevant staff and with individual prisoners who should be involved in these as far as practicable;

(d) communications systems and a management style that will encourage appropriate and positive relationships between staff and prisoners that will improve the prospects for effective and supportive regimes and treatment programmes.

67. (1) Since the fulfilment of these objectives requires individualisation of treatment and, for this purpose, a flexible system of allocation, prisoners should be placed in separate institutions or units where each can receive the appropriate treatment and training.

(2) The type, size, organisation and capacity of these institutions or units should be determined essentially by the nature of the treatment to be provided.

(3) It is necessary to ensure that prisoners are located with due regard to security and control but such measures should be the minimum compatible with safety and comprehend the special needs of the prisoner. Every effort should be made to place prisoners in institutions that are open in character or provide ample opportunities for contacts with the outside community. In the case of foreign nationals, links with people of their own nationality in the outside community are to be regarded as especially important.

68. As soon as possible after admission and after a study of the personality of each prisoner with a sentence of a suitable length, a programme of treatment in a suitable institution shall be prepared in the light of the knowledge obtained about individual needs, capacities and dispositions, especially proximity to relatives.

69. (1) Within the regimes, prisoners shall be given the opportunity to participate in activities of the institution likely to develop their sense of responsibility, self-reliance and to stimulate interest in their own treatment.

(2) Efforts should be made to develop methods of encouraging co-operation with and the participation of the prisoners in their treatment. To this end prisoners shall be encouraged to assume, within the limits specified in Rule 34, responsibilities in certain sectors of the institution's activity.

70. (1) The preparation of prisoners for release should begin as soon as possible after reception in a penal institution. Thus, the treatment of prisoners should emphasise not their exclusion from the community but their continuing part in it. Community agencies and social workers should, therefore, be enlisted wherever possible to assist the staff of the institution in the task of social rehabilitation of the prisoners

particularly maintaining and improving the relationships with their families, with other persons and with the social agencies. Steps should be taken to safeguard, to the maximum extent compatible with the law and the sentence, the rights and other social benefits of prisoners.

(2) Treatment programmes should include provision for prison leave which should also be granted to the greatest extent possible on medical, educational, occupational, family and other social grounds.

(3) Foreign nationals should not be excluded from arrangements for prison leave solely on account of their nationality. Furthermore, every effort should be made to enable them to participate in regime activities together so as to alleviate their feelings of isolation.

Work

71. (1) Prison work should be seen as a positive element in treatment, training and institutional management.

(2) Prisoners under sentence may be required to work, subject to their physical and mental fitness as determined by the medical officer.

(3) Sufficient work of a useful nature, or if appropriate other purposeful activities shall be provided to keep prisoners actively employed for a normal working day.

(4) So far as possible the work provided shall be such as will maintain or increase the prisoner's ability to earn a normal living after release.

(5) Vocational training in useful trades shall be provided for prisoners able to profit thereby and especially for young prisoners.

(6) Within the limits compatible with proper vocational selection and with the requirements of institutional administration and discipline, the prisoners shall be able to choose the type of employment in which they wish to participate.

72. (1) The organisation and methods of work in the institutions shall resemble as closely as possible those of similar work in the community so as to prepare prisoners for the conditions of normal occupational life. It should thus be relevant to contemporary working standards and techniques and organised to function within modern management systems and production processes.

(2) Although the pursuit of financial profit from industries in the institutions can be valuable in raising standards and improving the quality and relevance of training, the interests of the prisoners and of their treatment must not be subordinated to that purpose.

73. Work for prisoners shall be assured by the prison administration:

(a) either on its own premises, workshops and farms; or

(b) in co-operation with private contractors inside or outside the institution in which case the full normal wages for such shall be paid by the persons to whom the labour is supplied, account being taken of the output of the prisoners.

74. (1) Safety and health precautions for prisoners shall be similar to those that apply to workers outside.

(2) Provision shall be made to indemnify prisoners against industrial injury, including occupational disease, on terms not less favourable than those extended by law to workers outside.

75. (1) The maximum daily and weekly working hours of the prisoners shall be fixed in conformity with local rules or custom in regard to the employment of free workmen.
(2) Prisoners should have at least one rest day a week and sufficient time for education and other activities required as part of their treatment and training for social resettlement.

76. (1) There shall be a system of equitable remuneration of the work of prisoners.
(2) Under the system prisoners shall be allowed to spend at least a part of their earnings on approved articles for their own use and to allocate a part of their earnings to their family or for other approved purposes.
(3) The system may also provide that a part of the earnings be set aside by the administration so as to constitute a savings fund to be handed over to the prisoner on release.

Education

77. A comprehensive education programme shall be arranged in every institution to provide opportunities for all prisoners to pursue at least some of their individual needs and aspirations. Such programmes should have as their objectives the improvement of the prospects for successful social resettlement, the morale and attitudes of prisoners and their self-respect.

78. Education should be regarded as a regime activity that attracts the same status and basic remuneration within the regime as work, provided that it takes place in normal working hours and is part of an authorised individual treatment programme.

79. Special attention should be given by prison administrations to the education of young prisoners, those of foreign origin or with particular cultural or ethnic needs.

80. Specific programmes of remedial education should be arranged for prisoners with special problems such as illiteracy or innumeracy.

81. So far as practicable, the education of prisoners shall:
    (a) be integrated with the educational system of the country so that after their release they many continue their education without difficulty;
    (b) take place in outside educational institutions.

82. Every institution shall have a library for the use of all categories of prisoners, adequately stocked with a wide range of both recreational and instructional books, and prisoners shall be encouraged to make full use of it. Wherever possible the prison library should be organised in co-operation with community library services.

Physical education, exercise, sport and recreation

83. The prison regime shall recognise the importance to physical and mental health of properly organised activities to ensure physical fitness, adequate exercise and recreational opportunities.

84. Thus a properly organised programme of physical education, sport and other recreational activity should be arranged within the framework and objectives of the treatment and training regime. To this end space, installations and equipment should be provided.

85. Prison administrations should ensure that prisoners who participate in these programmes are physically fit to do so. Special arrangements should be made, under medical direction, for remedial physical education and therapy for those prisoners who need it.

86. Every prisoner who is not employed in outdoor work, or located in an open institution, shall be allowed, if the weather permits, at least one hour of walking of suitable exercise in the open air daily, as far as possible, sheltered from inclement weather.

Pre-release preparation

87. All prisoners should have the benefit of arrangements designed to assist them in returning to society, family life and employment after release. Procedures and special courses should be devised to this end.

88. In the case of those prisoners with longer sentences, steps should be taken to ensure a gradual return to life in society. This aim may be achieved, in particular, by a pre-release regime organised in the same institution or in another appropriate institution, or by conditional release under some kind of supervision combined with effective social support.

89. (1) Prison administrations should work closely with the social services and agencies that assist released prisoners to re-establish themselves in society, in particular with regard to family life and employment.
(2) Steps must be taken to ensure that on release prisoners are provided, as necessary, with appropriate documents and identification papers and assisted in finding suitable homes and work to go to. They should also be provided with immediate means of subsistence, be suitably and adequately clothed having regard to the climate and season, and have sufficient means to reach their destination.
(3) The approved representatives of the social agencies or services should be afforded all necessary access to the institution and to prisoners with a view to making a full contribution to the preparation for release and after-care programme of the prisoner.

PART V

ADDITIONAL RULES FOR SPECIAL CATEGORIES

90. Prison administrations should be guided by the provisions of the rules as a whole so far as they can appropriately and in practice be applied for the benefit of those special categories of prisoners for which additional rules are provided hereafter.

Untried prisoners

91. Without prejudice to legal rules for the protection of individual liberty or prescribing the procedure to be observed in respect of untried prisoners, these prisoners, who are presumed to be innocent until they are found guilty, shall be afforded the benefits that may derive from Rule 90 and treated without restrictions other than those necessary for the penal procedure and the security of the institution.

92. (1) Untried prisoners should be allowed to inform their families of their detention immediately and given all reasonable facilities for communication with family and friends and persons with whom it is in their legitimate interest to enter into contact.
(2) They shall also be allowed to receive visits from them under humane conditions subject only to such restrictions and supervision as are necessary in the administration of justice and of the security and good order of the institution.
(3) If an untried prisoner does not wish to inform any of these persons, the prison administration should not do so on its own initiative unless there are good, overriding reasons as, for instance, the age, state of mind or any other incapacity of the prisoner.

93. Untried prisoners shall be entitled, as soon as imprisoned, to choose a legal representative, or shall be allowed to apply for free legal aid where such aid is available and to receive visits from that legal adviser with a view to their defence and to prepare and hand to the legal adviser, and to receive, confidential instructions. On request they shall be given the free assistance of an interpreter for all essential contacts with the administration and for their defence. Interviews between prisoners and their legal advisers may be within sight but not within hearing, either direct or indirect, of the police or institution staff. The allocation of untried prisoners shall be in conformity with the provisions of Rule 11, paragraph 3.

94. Except when there are circumstances that make it undesirable, untried prisoners shall be given the opportunity of having separate rooms.

95. (1) Untried prisoners shall be given the opportunity of wearing their own clothing if it is clean and suitable.
(2) Prisoners who do not avail themselves of this opportunity, shall be supplied with suitable dress.
(3) If they have no suitable clothing of their own, untried prisoners shall be provided with civilian clothing in good condition in which to appear in court or on authorised outings.

96. Untried prisoners shall, whenever possible, be offered the opportunity to work but shall not be required to work. Those who choose to work shall be paid as other prisoners. If educational or trade training is available, untried prisoners shall be encouraged to avail themselves of these opportunities.

97. Untried prisoners shall be allowed to procure at their own expense or at the expense of a third party such books, newspapers, writing materials and

other means of occupation as are compatible with the interests of the administration of justice and the security and good order of the institution.

98. Untried prisoners shall be given the opportunity of being visited and treated by their own doctor or dentist if there is reasonable ground for the application. Reasons should be given if the application is refused. Such costs as are incurred shall not be the responsibility of the prison administration.

Civil Prisoners

99. In countries where the law permits imprisonment by order of a court under any non-criminal process, persons so imprisoned shall not be subjected to any greater restriction or severity than is necessary to ensure safe custody and good order. Their treatment shall not be less favourable than that of untried prisoners, with the reservation, however, that they may be required to work.

Insane and mentally abnormal prisoners

100. (1) Persons who are found to be insane should not be detained in prisons and arrangements shall be made to remove them to appropriate establishments for the mentally ill as soon as possible.

(2) Specialised institutions or sections under medical management should be available for the observation and treatment of prisoners suffering gravely from other mental disease or abnormality.

(3) The medical or psychiatric service of the penal institutions shall provide for the psychiatric treatment of all prisoners who are in need of such treatment.

(4) Action should be taken, by arrangement with the appropriate community agencies, to ensure where necessary the continuation of psychiatric treatment after release and the provision of social psychiatric after-care.

ANNEX B

HM Prison Service Race Relations Policy Statement

1. The Prison Department is committed absolutely to a policy of racial equality and to the elimination of discrimination in all aspects of the work of the Prison Service. It is opposed also to any display of racial prejudice, either by work or conduct, by any member of this service in his dealings with any other person.

2. All prisoners should be treated with humanity and respect. All prisoners should be treated impartially and without discrimination on the grounds of colour, race or religion. Insulting, abusive or derogatory language towards prisoners will not be tolerated.

3. Race relations concern every member of the Prison Service. It is the responsibility of every member of staff to ensure that the Department's policy is carried out in relation to other members of staff as well as prisoners.

4. Members of minority religious groups have the same right to practice their faith as those of the majority faith. Wherever feasible in prison circumstances arrangements are made to give them the same practical opportunity to do so.

5. All inmates should have equal access to the facilities provided in the establishment including jobs. The distribution of inmates throughout the establishment and its facilities should as far as is practicable and sensible be broadly responsive to the ethnic mix of the establishment.

6. No particular racial group should be allowed to dominate any activity in the establishment to the unfair exclusion of others.

REFERENCES

Cases

Anderson v Home Office, The Times 8 October 1965.
Anderson (1984) *R v Secretary of State ex parte Anderson* (1984) 1 All ER 920.
Arbon v Anderson (1943) KB 252.
Ashdown (1973) *R v Ashdown, The Times* 2 November 1973.
Barrow (1991) *R v Leicester City Justices, ex parte Barrow and another* (1991) 2 WLR 974.
Bayliss and Barton v Home Secretary and Governor of HMP Frankland (1993) *Legal Action* Feb. 1993, 16.
Becker v Home Office (1972) 2 All ER 676.
Bounds v Smith (1977) 430 U.S. 817.
Bowen (1998) *R v Secretary of State, ex p Bowen* (1998) Unreported, 26 January 1998.
Bradley (1991) *R v Parole Board, ex p Bradley* (1991) 1 WLR 134.
Brooks v Home Office (1999) *The Times* 17 Feb. 1999.
D'Arcy v Prison Commissioners (1956) Criminal Law Review 56.
Doody, Pierson, Smart and Pegg (1992) Judgement 6 May 1992.
Doody (1994) *R v Home Secretary, ex p Doody* (1994) 1 AC 531.
Duggan (1994) *R v Home Secretary, ex p Duggan* (1994) 3 All ER 277.
Egerton v Home Office (1978) *Criminal Law Review* 494.
Ferguson v Home Office (1977) *The Times* 8 October 1977.
Flood (1998) *R v Home Secretary, ex p Flood* (1998) 2 All ER 313.
Fraser v Mudge (1975) 3 All ER 78.
Freeman v Home Office (No.2) (1984) QB 524.
Georghiades (1992) *R v Parole Board ex parte Georghiades, Independent* 22 May 1992 and 27 May 1992.
Guilfoyle v Home Office (1981) QB 309.
Gunnell (1985) *R v Chairman of the Parole Board, ex p Gunnell* (1985) Crim LR 105.
H v Home Office, Independent 6 May 1992.
Hague (1990) 3 All ER 687.
Hague and Weldon (1992) *R v Deputy Governor of Parkhurst Prison ex parte Hague, and Weldon v Home Office* (1992) 1 AC 58 (CA); also (1991) 3 All ER 733; (1991) 3 WLR 340 (HL).
Hepworth (1997) *R v Secretary of State for the Home Department, ex p Hepworth* (1997) Unreported, 25 March 1997.
Hickling (1986) *R v Secretary of State for the Home Department ex parte Hickling and JH (a minor)* (1986) 1 FLR 543.
Hone v Maze (1988) *R v Board of Visitors of Her Majesty's Prison The Maze ex parte Hone* (1988) AC 379.
King (1984) *R v Deputy Governor of Camp Hill Prison ex parte King (Court of Appeal)* (1984) 3 All ER 897.
Kirkham v Chief Constable of the Greater Manchester Police (1990) 2 QB 283.
Knight v Home Office (1990) 3 All ER 237.
Leech v Deputy Governor of Parkhurst Prison (1988) AC 533.
Leech (No. 2) (1994) *R v Home Secretary, ex p Leech (No. 2)* (1994) QB 198.
McAvoy (1984) *R v Secretary of State ex parte McAvoy* (1984) 3 All ER 417.
McAvoy (1998) *R v Home Secretary, ex p McAvoy* (1998) 1 WLR 790.
McConkey (1982) *R v Board of Visitors of High Point Prison ex parte McConkey, The Times* 23 September 1982.
McGrath (1984) *R v Board of Visitors of Swansea Prison ex parte McGrath, The Times* November 1984.
McKiernan (1985) *R v Board of Visitors of The Maze Prison ex parte McKiernan*, 5 June 1985 (unreported).
Main (1998) *R v Secretary of State, ex p Main* (1998) 2 All ER 491.
Mehmet and O'Connor (1999)
Middleweek v Chief Constable of the Merseyside Police, (Note) (1990) 3 All ER 283.

Mohammed Zulfikar (1995) *R v Secretary of State, ex p Mohammed Zulfikar* (1995) Unreported, 21 July 1995.

Nahar (1983) *R v Commissioner of Police in the Metropolis ex parte Nahar and others, The Times* 28 May 1983.

Norley (1984) *R v Board of Visitors of Blundeston ex parte Norley* 4 July 1984 (unreported).

O'Dhuibhir (1997) *R v Home Secretary, ex p O'Dhuibhir* (1997) COD 315.

Olotu v Home Office and Crown Prosecution Service (1997) 1 WLR 328.

Payne v Home Office, 2 May 1977 (unreported).

Peries (1997) *R v Home Secretary, ex p Peries* (1997) *The Times*, 30 July 1997.

Pierson (1997) *R v Home Secretary, ex p Pierson* (1997) 3 WLR 492.

Purcell (1998) *R v Home Secretary, ex p Purcell* (1998) *The Times*, 5 March 1998.

Racz v Home Office (1992) 6 June 1992 and *The Guardian* 20 October 1992.

Raymond v Honey (1982) 1 All ER 756.

Raymond (1985) *R v Board of Visitors of Wandsworth Prison ex parte Raymond, The Times* 17 June 1985 (QBD).

Ross (1994) *R v Home Secretary, ex p Ross* (1994) *The Times*, 9 June 1994.

St Germain (No.1) (1979) *R v Board of Visitors of Hull Prison ex parte St Germain (No.1)* (1979) 1 All ER 701 (Court of Appeal).

St Germain (No.2) (1979) *R v Board of Visitors of Hull Prison ex parte St Germain (No.2)* (1979) 3 All ER 545.

Simms (1998) *R v Secretary of State for the Home Department, ex p Simms* (1998) 2 All ER 491.

Smith (1984) *R v Board of Visitors of Dartmoor Prison ex parte Smith, The Times* 12 July 1984.

Tarrant (1984) *R v Secretary of State ex parte Tarrant and another* (1984) 1 All ER 799 and (1984) 2 WLR 613.

Tremayne (1996) *R v Secretary of State for the Home Department, ex p Tremayne* (1996) Unreported, 2 May 1996.

Umoh v Home Office (No.2) (1987) 1 All ER 1211.

Walsh (1992) 6 May 1992.

Weldon v Home Office (1990) 3 All ER 672.

Williams v Home Office (No.2) (1981) 1 All ER 1211.

Wilson (1992) Unreported.

Wynne (1992) *R v Secretary of State for the Home Department ex parte Wynne* (1992) 2 All ER 619.

Council of Europe

(26 November 1991) *Report to the United Kingdom Government on the visit to the United Kingdom carried out by the European Committee for the Prevention of Torture and Inhuman or Degrading Treatment or Punishment (CPT)*. CPT/Inf. (91) 15.

(26 November 1991) *Response of the United Kingdom to the Report of the European Committee for the Prevention of Torture and Inhuman or Degrading Treatment or Punishment (CPT) on its Visit to the United Kingdom*. CPT/Inf. (91) 16.

(1993) Committee for the Prevention of Torture and Inhuman or Degrading Treatment or Punishment, *Third General Report*. CPT/Inf(93)12.

(1996) Committee for the Prevention of Torture and Inhuman or Degrading Treatment or Punishment, Government Response from the UK regarding the visit of the CPT in 1994. CPT/Inf(96) 12, 27.

(1998) *Human Rights Information Bulletin* 42 H/Inf. (98) 2.

Bamber v UK (1997) App. No. 33742/96, 11 September 1997.

Boyle and Rice (1988). Judgement 27 April 1988.

Brady v UK (1981) 3 EHHR 297.

Campbell and Fell v UK Report 12 May 1982. Judgement 28 June 1984.

Campbell v UK (1992) *Guardian* 2 April 1992.

Campbell v UK (1993) 15 EHHR 137.

Golder v UK Report 1 June 1973.

Kavanagh v UK (1992), App. 19085/91, Commission decision 9 Dec. 1992.

McCallum (1990). Judgement of 30 August 1990. (1991) 13 ECHR 597.

McFeely v UK (1981) 3 EHHR 161.

McVeigh, O'Neill, Evans v UK Report 18 March 1981.

Pfeifer and Plankl v Austria (1992) 14 EHHR 692.

Reed v UK 5 EHHR 114.

Silver v UK. Judgement 25 March 1983. Resolution of Committee of Ministers 24 March 1982.

Tejendrasingh v UK Reports 12 October 1983 and 13 May 1985.

Thynne, Wilson and Gunnell v UK (1991). Judgement of 25 October 1990. 13 EHRR 666.

TV v Finland (1994) 18 EHHR CD 179.

8025/78 v UK 115 D & R 242.

Books and Articles

AIDS Advisory Committee (1995) *The Review of HIV and AIDS in Prison*. London: AIDS Advisory Committee.

AMBoV (1984) "Resolutions debated at AMBoV annual meeting, November 1983". *AMBoV Quarterly* 12, 3.

AMBoV (1984 and 1991) Association of Members of Boards of Visitors Handbook.

AMBoV (1998) "Practical Guide to Monitoring Prisons".

AMBoV Quarterly, July 1983.

Ashman, P. (1992) "Prisons, Special Hospitals, Accountability and Public Law - European Requirements". Paper given at Public Law Workshop, London: 12 June 1992.

Board of Visitors Handbook (1993) London: Board of Visitors.

Byron, P. (January 1985) Letters to the Editor, *AMBoV Quarterly*, 2.

Casale, S. (1984) *Minimum Standards for Prison Establishments*. London: NACRO.

Casale, S. and Plotnikoff, J. (1989) *Minimum Standards in Prisons: A Programme of Change*. London: NACRO.

Casale, S. and Plotnikoff, J. (1990) *Regimes for Remand Prisoners*. London: Prison Reform Trust.

Charter Mental Health 2000 (1985) Declaration on the Rights of Mentally Ill People: The Promotion of Mental Health.

Cohen, S. and Taylor, L. (1978) *Prison Secrets*. RAP/NCCL.

Committee on the Administration of Justice (1998) *A Guide to Prisoners' Rights and Prison Law in Northern Ireland*. Belfast: Shanway Distributors.

Deloitte, Haskins, and Sells (1989) Practicality of Private Sector Involvement in the Remand System. London: Home Office.

Education, Science and Arts Committee (March 1991), Second Report: *Prison Education*. House of
 Commons Paper 311-II.

Faulkner, D. (October 1982) Text of address to SW Region BoV. *Prison Service Journal*, 18.

Fawcett, J. (1985) Applications of the European Convention on Human Rights. In M. Maguire *et al* (ed) *Accountability and Prisons - Opening up a Closed World*. Tavistock.

Fitzgerald, E. (April 1984) Legal representation before Boards of Visitors: the aftermath of Tarrant. *AMBoV Quarterly*, 1.

Fitxgerald, E. (21 January 1992) The Rights of Lifers and the Implications of the Walsh Decision. London: Doughty Street Chambers.

Flynn, N. and Price, D. (1995) *Education in Prisons: A National Survey*. London: Prison Reform Trust.

Goodman, A. (1986/7) *Probation Intervention with Prisoners During and After Their Sentence (Through-Care and After-Care)*. Inner London Probation Service.

Governors' Branch of the Society of Court and Public Servants (1983) *Prison Standards*.

Guardian: (10 August 1985) Mother parted from baby wins prison review.
   (21 August 1985) Separation of mother and baby in goal ruled lawful.
   (6 March 1991) Call to speed up jail psychiatric reports.
   (13 May 1992) re: *Doody et al.*

(20 October 1992) The tort of misfeasance.

(25 July 1996) re: exemplary damages from Clerkenwell Magistrates' Court.

(9 March 1999) Prison Service 'at fault' over death of black inmate.

Gunn, J., Maden T., and Swinton, M. (1990) *Mentally Disordered Prisoners* (revised May 1991). London: Home Office.

Haines, K. (1990) *After-care Services for Released Prisoners: A Review of the Literature.* Cambridge Institute of Criminology.

Halsbury's *Laws of England: Prisons* (1982) 4th edn. Butterworth.

HM Chief Inspector of Prisons (1990) *Report of a Review by Her Majesty's Chief Inspector of Prisons for England and Wales of Suicide and Self-Harm in Prison Service Establishments in England and Wales.* Cm 1383.

(1992) HMCIP Report: HMP Canterbury.

(1994) HMCIP: Annual Report 1993-94.

(1995) HMCIP Report: HMP Holloway.

(1995) *Prison Discipline Manual,* as amended.

(1996) HMCIP Discussion Paper: *Patient or Prisoner? A new strategy for health care in prisons.*

(1997) HMCIP Report: HMYOI Glen Parva.

(1997a) HM Chief Inspector of Prisons *Thematic Review: Young Offenders.*

(1997b) HM Chief Inspector of Prisons *Women in Prison: A Thematic Review.*

(1998) HMCIP Report: HMP Dartmoor.

(1999) HMCIP Annual Report, 1997 - 1998.

(1999) *Suicide is Everyone's Concern.* HMCIP thematic review.

HM Chief Inspector of Prisons for Scotland (1984) Report, Cmnd 9636.

(December 1991) Report of the HM Chief Inspector of Prisons January 1990-1991.

HM Chief Inspectors of Prisons and Social Work Services for Scotland (1998) *Women Offenders - A Safer Way: A Review of Community Disposals and the Use of Custody for Women Offenders in Scotland.* Edinburgh: The Scottish Office.

Home Office (undated) Code of Discipline for Prison Officers.

(undated) *Prison Service Security Manual,* as amended.

(1975) *Manual on the Conduct of Adjudications in Prison Department Establishments* (Weiler Report).

(1977) *Prisons and the Prisoner.*

(1980) Prison Department Report.

(1982-83) First Report of the Education, Science and Arts Committee, *Prison Education* HC 45.

Governmental Reply to the First Report of the Education, Science and Arts Committee, Cmnd 9126.

(1984) Police and Criminal Evidence Act (PACE) *Codes of Practice.*

(May 1984) *Suicides in Prison.* HM Chief Inspector of Prisons.

(July 1984) Current Recommended Standards for the Design of New Prison establishments (unpublished).

(July 1991) Citizen's Charter cm 1599 HMSO.

(September 1991) *Custody, Care and Justice,* cm 1647 HMSO.

(December 1991) Criminal Justice Act 1991 Detailed Guides, 'Early Release'.

House of Commons Home Affairs Committee (1987), State and Use of Prisons. HC Paper 35.

House of Commons Home Affairs Committee (1997), *The Management of the Prison Service (Public and Private),* vol. I, Second Report. HC 57.

Independent: (7 August 1991) Unrepresented litigants are entitled to an assistant.

(4 Sept. 1991) Prisoners cannot claim false imprisonment.

(12 June 1992) Prisons chief points towards liberal reform.

Irish News (19 June 1992) "Maghaberry: What really happened?"

JUSTICE (1983) *Justice in Prison.*

Kaufmann, P. (1998) "Prisoners' Rights and the European Convention of Human Rights". Course paper, Liberty course on the Human Rights Act, May 1998.

Learmont Report (1995), *Review of Prison Service Security in England and Wales and the Escape from Parkhurst Prison on Tuesday 3rd January 1995.* Cm 3020.

Leech, M. (1999) *The Prisons Handbook*, 3rd edition. Winchester: Waterside Press.

Liebling, A. (1992) *Suicides in Prison*. London: Routledge.

Liebling, A. and Krarup, H. (1993) *Suicide Attempts in Male Prisons*. London: Home Office.

Liebling, A. and Price, D., with the advice of Anthony Bottoms (1999) *An Exploration of Staff-Prisoner Relationships at HMP Whitemoor*. Prison Service Research Report No. 6. Institute of Criminology, University of Cambridge.

Livingstone, S. and Owen, T. (1999) *Prison Law* (2nd edition). Oxford: Oxford University Press.

Loucks, N. (1995) *Anything Goes: The Use of the 'Catch-All' Disciplinary Rule in Prison Service Establishments*. London: Prison Reform Trust.

Loucks, N. (1998) *HMP Cornton Vale: Drugs and Alcohol, Violence and Bullying, Suicide and Self-Injury, and Backgrounds of Abuse*. Scottish Prison Service Occasional Paper, Report No. 1/1998. Edinburgh: SPS.

May Committee (1979) Report of the Committee of Inquiry into the UK Prison Services (May Report) Cmnd 7673.

McGurk, B. and Fludger, N. (1987) "Prison Sanitation facilities and Related Factors Influencing Prisoners' Preference for Cell Sharing". In B. McGurk *et al.*, eds., *Applying Psychology to Imprisonment: Theory and Practice*. London: HMSO.

Marin, B. (1983) *Inside Justice - A Comparative Analysis of Practices and Procedures for the Determination of Offences against Discipline in Prisons of Britain and the US*. Associated University Presses.

Morgan, R. (1980) "How resources are used in the prison system." In R. King and R. Morgan, eds., *The Future of the Prison System*. Aldershot: Gower.

Morgan, R. (1992) "Prisons Accountability Revisited." Paper given at Public Law Workshop, London: 12 June 1992.

National Association for the Care and Resettlement of Offenders (NACRO) (January 1985) Prison standards - briefing paper. London: NACRO.

National Association of Probation Officers (NAPO) (May 1985) *Criminal Justice - An Alternative Strategy*. London: National Association of Probation Officers.

Neale, K. (1985) "The Prison Rules in Europe". *Prison Information Bulletin*. Council of Europe.

Observer: (2 Dec. 1990) One prisoner in five mentally ill - official.

Owen, T. (1991), "Prisoners' rights." *New Law Journal*, vol. 140, p. 1328.

Peddie, B. (1999) "Prison Rules". Legal Services Agency Seminar, *Prisons and the Law*, Glasgow, 15 March 1999.

Prison Reform Trust (1984) *Working Their Time - A Report on Prison Industries*.

(1985) *Prison Medicine - Ideas on Health Care in Penal Establishments*.

(1992) *Prison Report* 19:4.

(1999) *Prisoners' Information Book*.

Prison Service (1984 unpublished) Prison Service Training College Adjudications Training Package, and Training Manual: Initial Training System for New Entrant Prison Officers.

(1985) *Report of the Committee on the Prison Disciplinary System* (Prior Report) Cmnd 9641.

(1988) *Directory and Guide on Religious Practice in HM Prison Service*.

(1989) Prison Design Briefing System.

(1990) Tender Documents for the Operating Contract of Wolds Remand Prison, schedule 2 and 3.

(July 1990) *Report on an Efficiency Scrutiny of the Prison Medical Service, Vol. I*.

(April 1991) Race Relations Manual. HM Prison Service.

(February 1992) Prison Statistics: England and Wales 1990, Cm 1800.

(1994) *Prison Service Operating Standards*.

(1994) Working Party of Three Royal Medical Colleges on the Education and Training of Doctors in the Health Care Service for Prisoners.

(Oct. 1997) *Prison Service Review*.

(1998a) *Prisons-Probation Review: Final Report*.

(1998b) *Prison Statistics, England and Wales 1997*. Cm 4017.

(1997-8) HM Prison Service Annual Report and Accounts 1996-97, HC 274.

(Feb. 1999a) *Quinquennial Review of the Prison Service: Evaluation of Performance 1992-93 to 1997- 98.*

(Feb. 1999b) *Quinquennial Review of the Prison Service: Prior Options Report.*

(1999) *Performance Standards Programme.*

(1999) Prison Service Headquarters, Statistics on Prison Population by Category. Personal communication.

Prisons Ombudsman (1998) Annual Report 1997. Cm 3984

Quinn, P. (1995) "Reflexivity Run Riot: The Survival of the Prison Catch-All". *Howard Journal* 34: 354.

Raison Committee (1995) *Committee on Local Monitoring of Prison Establishments* (Chairman: Sir Timothy Raison). London: Prison Reform Trust.

Singleton, N., Meltzer, H., and Gatward, R., with J. Coid and D. Deasy (1998) *Psychiatric Morbidity among Prisoners: A survey carried out in 1997 by the Social Survey Division of ONS on behalf of the Department of Health.* Office for National Statistics. London: HMSO.

Stern, V. (1989), *Bricks of Shame: Britain's Prisons.* London: Penguin.

United Nations Special Rapporteur on the Independence of Judges and Lawyers (1996) *Annual Report.* E/CN 4/1996/37.

Vagg, J. and Dünkel, F. (1994) "Conclusions". In F. Dünkel and J. Vagg, eds. *Untersuchungshaft und Untersuchungshaftvollzug /Waiting for Trial: International Perspectives on the Use of Pre-Trial Detention and the Rights and Living Conditions of Prisoners Waiting for Trial.*

Woodcock Enquiry (1994), *The Escape from Whitemoor Prison on Friday 9th September 1994.* Report of the Enquiry into the Escape of Six Prisoners from the Special Security Unit at Whitemoor Prison, Cambridgeshire, on Friday 9th September 1994. Cm 2741.

Woolf Report (1991) Prison Disturbances April 1990, Cm 1456 HMSO.

INDEX

Prison Rules: A Working Guide

The Millennium edition, fully revised and updated

Nancy Loucks

This book is the most up-to-date and comprehensive guide to the rules and regulations by which our prisons are run. Totally re-written to take account of the 1999 Prison Rules and all recent developments in the courts, **Prison Rules: A Working Guide** is an invaluable reference work for prison staff, probation officers, lawyers, members of Boards of Visitors, students of penal policy, and prisoners themselves.

Each Prison Rule is cited in full with the relevant Prison Service Orders and Prison Service Instructions. A commentary following each rule, drawing upon a wide variety of sources, outlines the practical implications for prison management, staff, and prisoners alike.

Prison Rules: A Working Guide quotes extensively from case-law on prisoners' rights and entitlements. It also draws upon reports from HM Chief Inspector of Prisons and successive official reports and inquiries.

Nancy Loucks studied criminology at Pomona College, Claremont, California, and at Wolfson College, Cambridge. She is currently based in Scotland where she works as an independent researcher in criminology and prison policy. She is an Honorary Fellow of the Department of Social Work, University of Edinburgh.

Prison Reform Trust
15 Northburgh Street
London EC1V 0JR

The Prison Reform Trust gratefully acknowledges the support of the Robert Gavron Charitable Trust in helping to meet the costs of this publication,

£12.95

Registered charity no: 1035525. Company limited by guarantee no: 2906362. Registered in England.

Printed in Great Britain by
Whitstable Litho Printers Ltd., Whitstable, Kent.